I0812767

IMAGES
of America

MILLTOWN

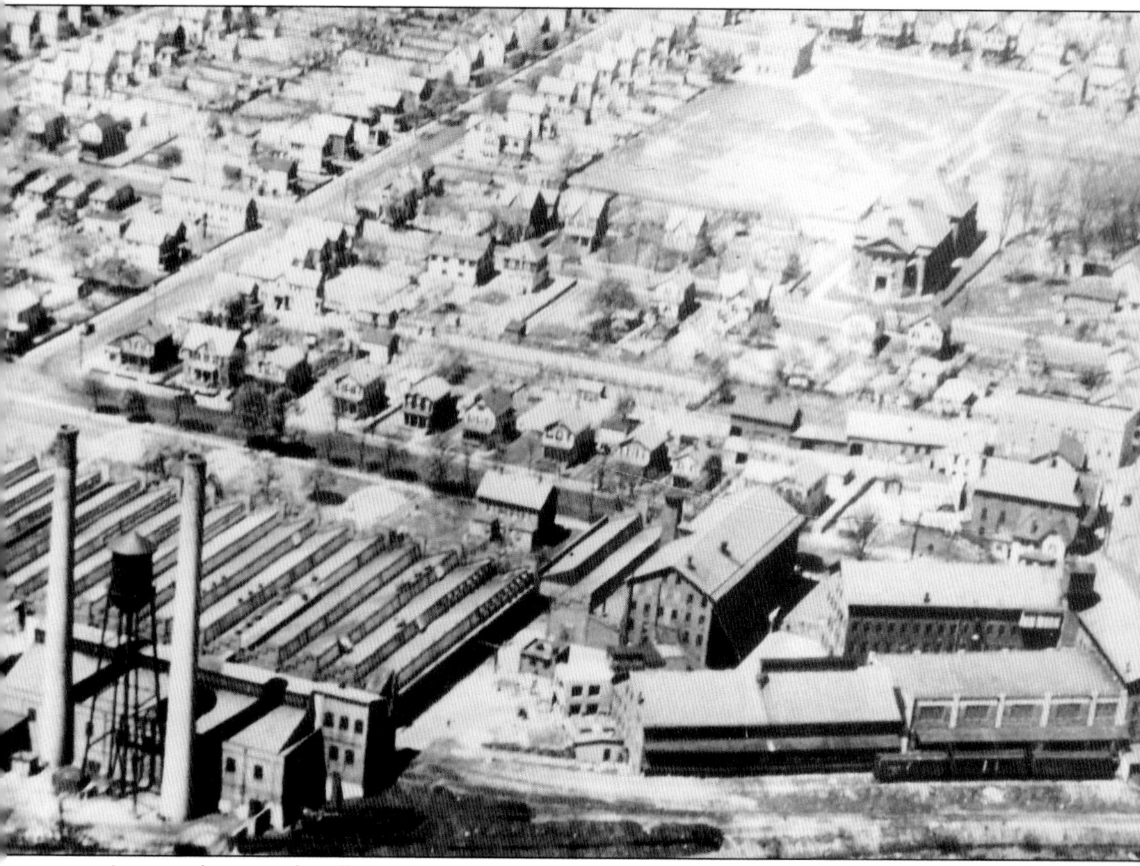

An aerial view of Mill Pond and the Michelin complex, c. 1940s. (Courtesy of Milltown Historical Society.)

IMAGES of America

MILLTOWN

Milltown Centennial Committee

ARCADIA PUBLISHING

ISBN 978-0-7385-4517-2

Published by Arcadia Publishing
Charleston, South Carolina

Printed in the Unites States of America

Library of Congress Catalog Card Number: 2006921686

For all general information contact Arcadia Publishing at:
Telephone 843-853-2070
Fax 843-853-0044
E-mail sales@arcadiapublishing.com
For customer service and orders:
Toll-Free 1-888-313-2665

Visit us on the Internet at www.arcadiapublishing.com

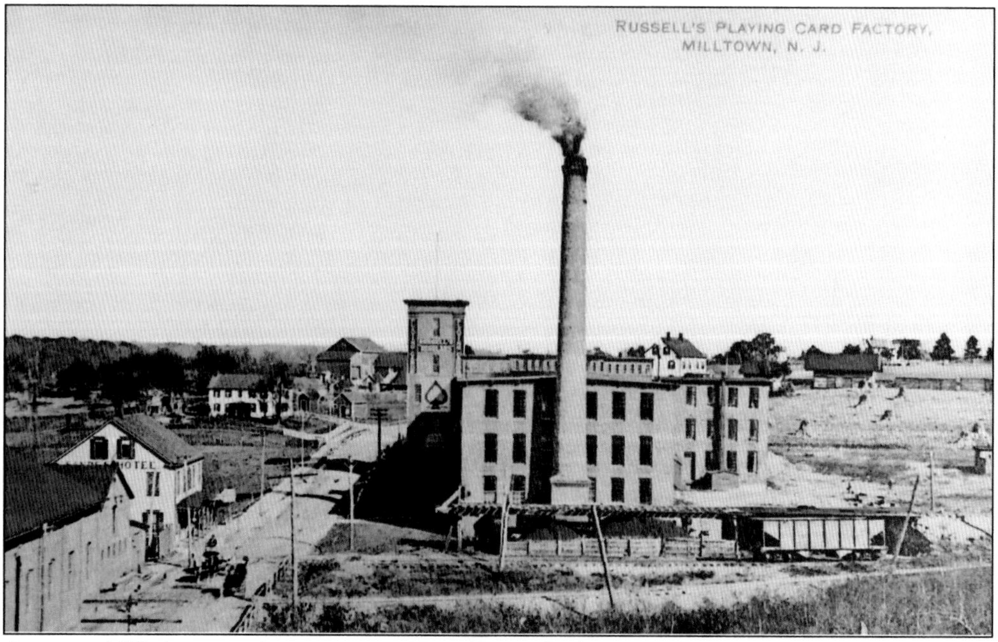

A view of Washington Avenue, *c.* 1905–1907, with the Russell Playing Card factory on the right. On the left is the trolley car barn, next to Sayre's Hotel. Further to the left is Conrad Kuhlthau's farm, and Kuhlthau Brothers' Coal and Feed. On the right is the Raritan River Railroad Station and the Funk farm. (Courtesy of Rita Carina.)

Contents

Acknowledgments 6

Introduction 7

1. All Aboard 9
2. Batter Up! 21
3. School Days 33
4. No Place Like Home 45
5. The French Connection 61
6. Fireworks! 75
7. Taking Care of Business 87
8. Honor and Glory 99
9. To Protect and Serve 111
10. North Side, South Side, All Around the Town 125

Acknowledgments

Throughout this book, we credit the owner or first contributor of each photograph, postcard, or document. The Committee would also like to give special thanks to the following individuals and organizations who helped make our work easier:

Rita Carina—Rita's vast collection of Milltown memorabilia could fill its own museum. Her detailed notes describing each of her photographs were invaluable.

Charlie Nenninger—Days before retiring, Charlie made available the entire collection of historic Milltown photographs that had been gracing the walls of his barber shop for thirty-seven years.

Ken Selover Sr.—Because of his long-term involvement with the town, most especially the Milltown Rescue Squad, Ken Selover Sr. provided many rare and unusual shots.

The Schwendeman family—One of the town's oldest families, the Schwendemans first came to Milltown in 1859. They permitted the Committee to duplicate their entire family photograph album.

The Lown family—Although old postcards of Milltown are plentiful, it was the handwritten information on the back of those contributed by the Lown family that made identification and dating of the photographs possible.

The Milltown Historical Society—First formed in 1968, the Milltown Historical Society is dedicated to preserving Milltown's history. The Society generously allowed the Book Committee to meet at the museum, and freely loaned photographs for this book.

The Eureka Fire Museum—The history of firefighting in Milltown is preserved at the Eureka Fire Museum, which provided many of the photographs in the "To Protect and Serve" section of this book.

David Freese, Photo Plaza—Thanks to Dave for his donations of film and rush-processing for the duplication of many of these photographs.

The Milltown Centennial Book Committee
Jim Corbett, Chairman
Noreen Manfredi, Editor
Brian E. Harto, Photograph Editor
David Bruce Schwendeman
Paulette Crabiel Wahler
Joan Herbert Whitman

Introduction

In 1971, a small, friendly New Jersey town celebrated a significant event. As seventy-five years had passed since the town's official incorporation on May 7, 1896, local residents thought it appropriate to celebrate Milltown's official 75th birthday. The results were a year of commemorative events and the writing of an enduring book of historical information, *The Story of Milltown*, by H. Rodney Luery. Residents, schoolchildren, and historians have come to depend on this book as the definitive source of information on how this small town (1.6 square miles in size) came to be. Until now, however, there has not been available a description of how much Milltown has changed over the years since its incorporation.

On May 7, 1996, the borough of Milltown will reach another milestone—its 100th anniversary. As the centennial approaches, the residents of Milltown are again gathering to plan celebrations and document the colorful history of the borough. There is a growing sense here that, despite monumental local and global changes, and the suburban sprawl of surrounding towns, Milltown has maintained old-fashioned values and a unique small-town charm. For families, like mine, who have adopted Milltown, as well as the numerous families who have been here for generations, community pride transcends the varied backgrounds and interests of the town's current residents.

Described over the years as tranquil, family-oriented, and resembling something right out of a Norman Rockwell painting, Milltown has still grown and changed along with the rest of Middlesex County. Today, some of the historic architecture is gone, and all the farms have been replaced by tree-shaded homes with flower-filled yards. As I write this, the picturesque Main Street Bridge, long a home for fishermen, sweethearts, and photographers, is being replaced. Ford Avenue, once the industrial hub for Bergen's Mill, Meyer's Rubber Company, and the Michelin Tire Company, is in need of renovation. The clay pit that once provided the raw material for local brickwork is now home to the East Millage Village Shopping Center. Milltown's grandest Victorian mansion, French School, and trolley barn are only memories.

Yet, another industrial site on Washington Avenue, formerly the Russell Playing Card Factory, was saved from the wrecking ball and converted to "The Mill" condominiums, without disturbing its period facade. Many fine old homes still grace borough streets, and a log cabin surrounded by scenic grounds peacefully coexists in a neighborhood of custom homes. Two of the town's older farmhouses have become the home of the Milltown Historic Society and are used as a museum. They stand right next to Milltown's historic Main Street firehouse which was once used as a school, and the Eureka Fire Museum.

To commemorate Milltown's Centennial, and to try and define Milltown's elusive appeal, the members of the Centennial Committee have gathered the photographic history in this book. From the days when the town was known as Bergen's Mill, through the arrival of industry, the sacrifices of residents during war, and the hardships brought on by economic reversals, Milltown has persevered. Time-honored traditions, such as the Fourth of July parade, school graduations, and summers at "the old swimmin' hole," endure, even as the town embraces new ideas and activities, one hundred years later.

Many Milltown families opened up their dusty photograph albums, and allowed committee members to pore over their baby pictures, wedding photographs, and graduation snapshots. Organizations dug deep into their archives and rooted through piles of storage boxes, searching for just the right picture. Long hours were contributed by committee members who sorted, duplicated, and captioned these photographs. The result is a visual history that reflects Milltown through one hundred years of pride and vitality.

Since today's events are tomorrow's history, the photographic story of Milltown is an ever-changing composite. It is the fond hope of the Centennial Committee that Milltown memories help to ensure continuing devotion to preservation of the history of "the Greatest Little Town in the Land."

Noreen Manfredi and the Milltown Centennial Book Committee
June 1995

References

Artwork of Middlesex County. W.H. Parish Publishing Company: 1896.
Deibert, Frederick W. *Rails Up the Raritan*. N.p.: 1983.
DiClerico, James M. and Pavele, Barry J. *The Jersey Game*. N.p.: 1991.
Karasik, Gary. *New Brunswick and Middlesex County*. N.p.: 1986.
Luery, Rodney. *The Story of Milltown*. N.p.: 1971.
"Milltown Fire Department Sixtieth Anniversary Program." Milltown Fire Department: 1971.
"Milltown Rescue Squad Fiftieth Anniversary Program." Milltown Rescue Squad: 1987.
"St. Paul's United Church of Christ." St. Paul's United Church of Christ: 1972.

One

All Aboard

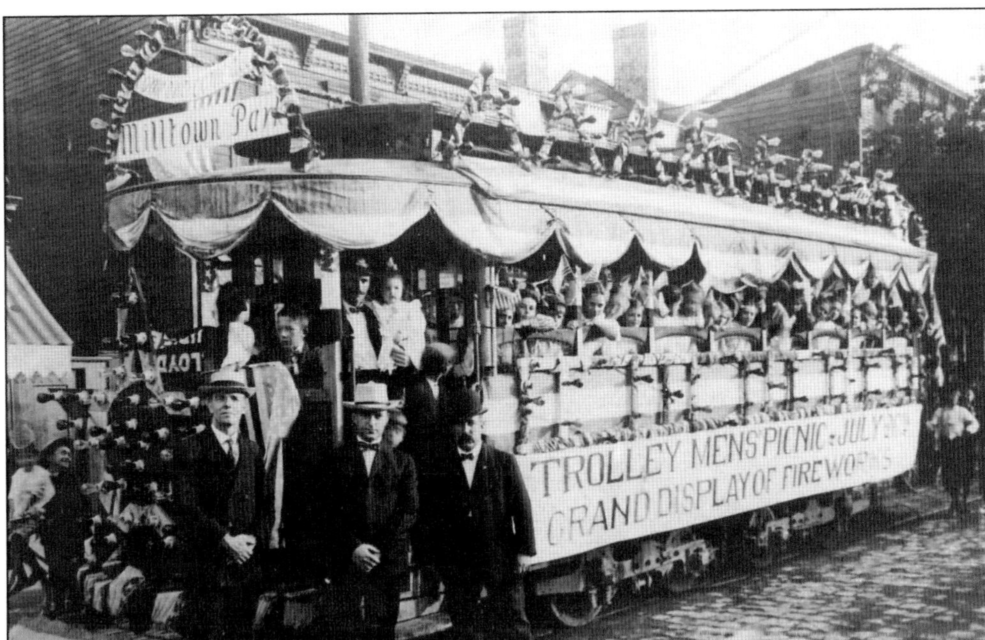

The sign on this trolley says "Come One, Come All, Milltown Park—Trolley Men's Picnic on July 26th—Grand Display of Fireworks." This is a *c.* 1915 photograph. (Courtesy of Charles Schork.)

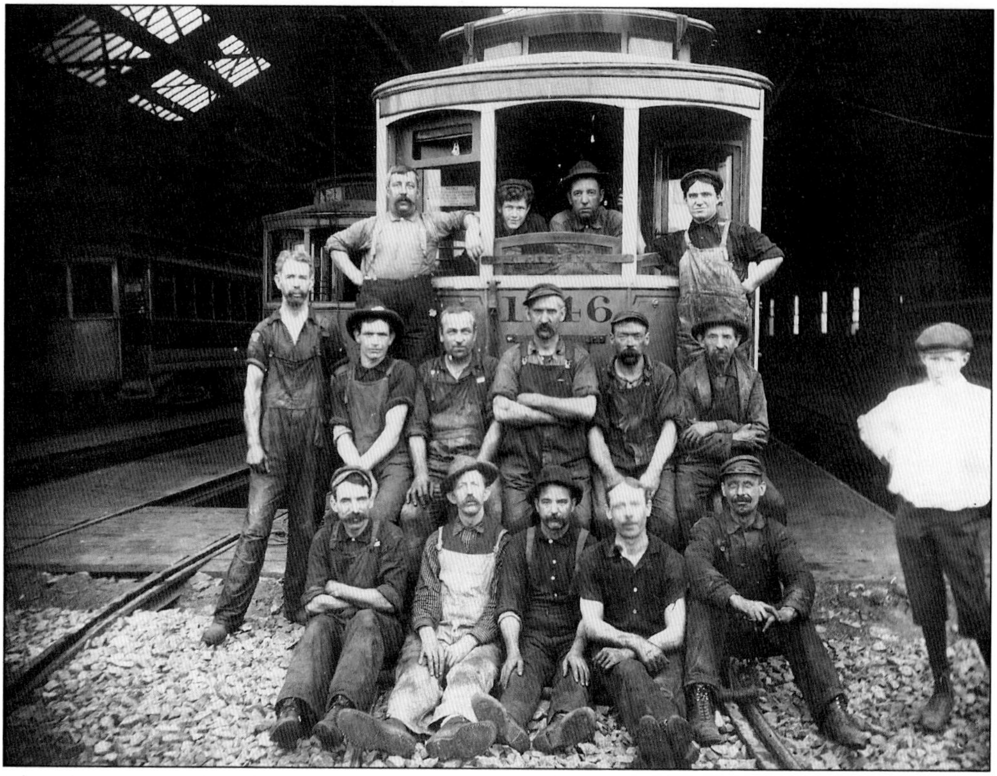

This photograph of employees of the Middlesex and Somerset Traction Company was taken in the car barn. (Courtesy of Milltown Historical Society.)

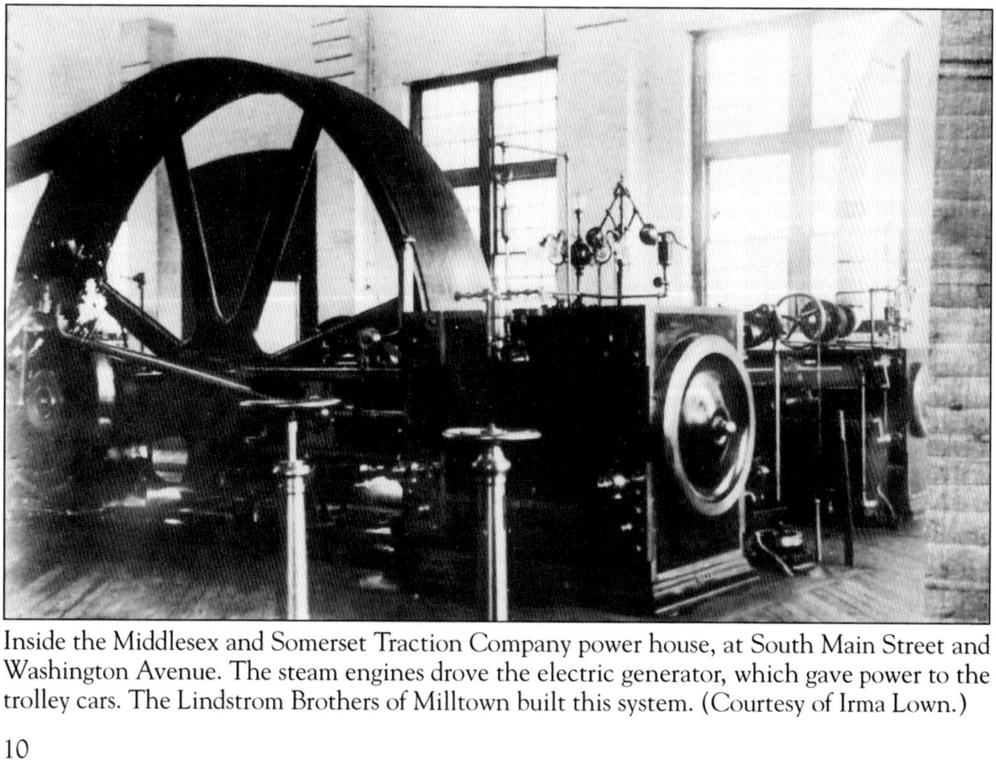

Inside the Middlesex and Somerset Traction Company power house, at South Main Street and Washington Avenue. The steam engines drove the electric generator, which gave power to the trolley cars. The Lindstrom Brothers of Milltown built this system. (Courtesy of Irma Lown.)

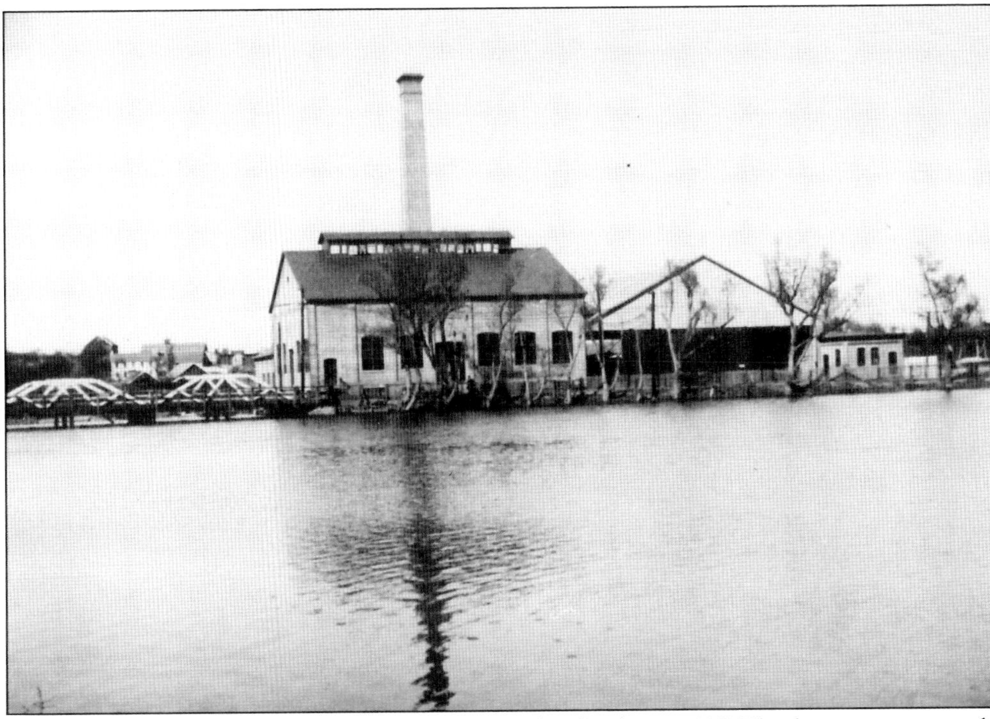

The Brunswick Traction Company power house and trolley barn, 1895. This location is currently the Hess gas station, at Washington and Main. (Courtesy of Mark Steeber.)

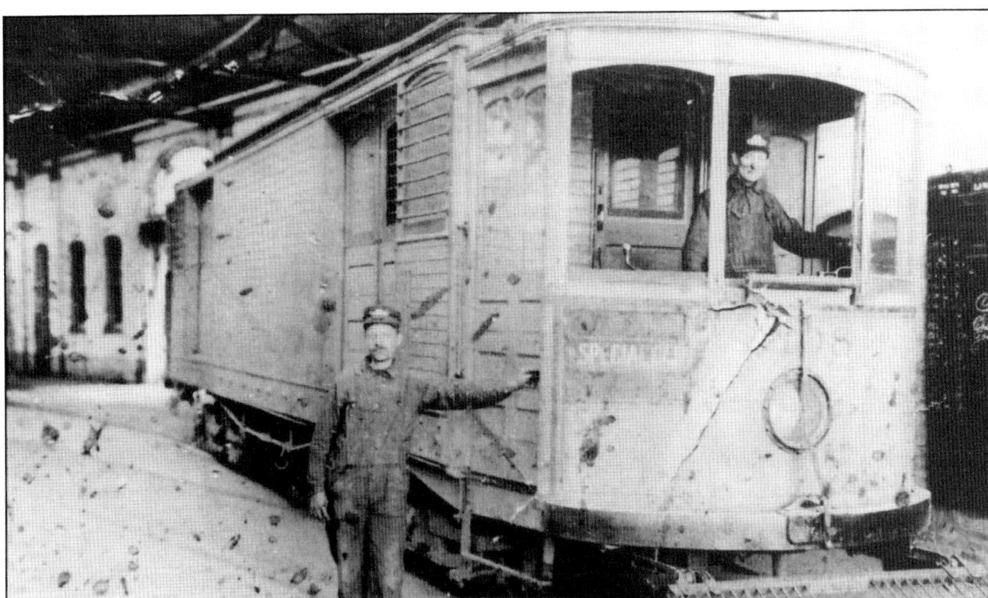

A trolley inside the car barn. Mr. Oehl is standing next to the trolley. (Courtesy of Norm and Rita Carina.)

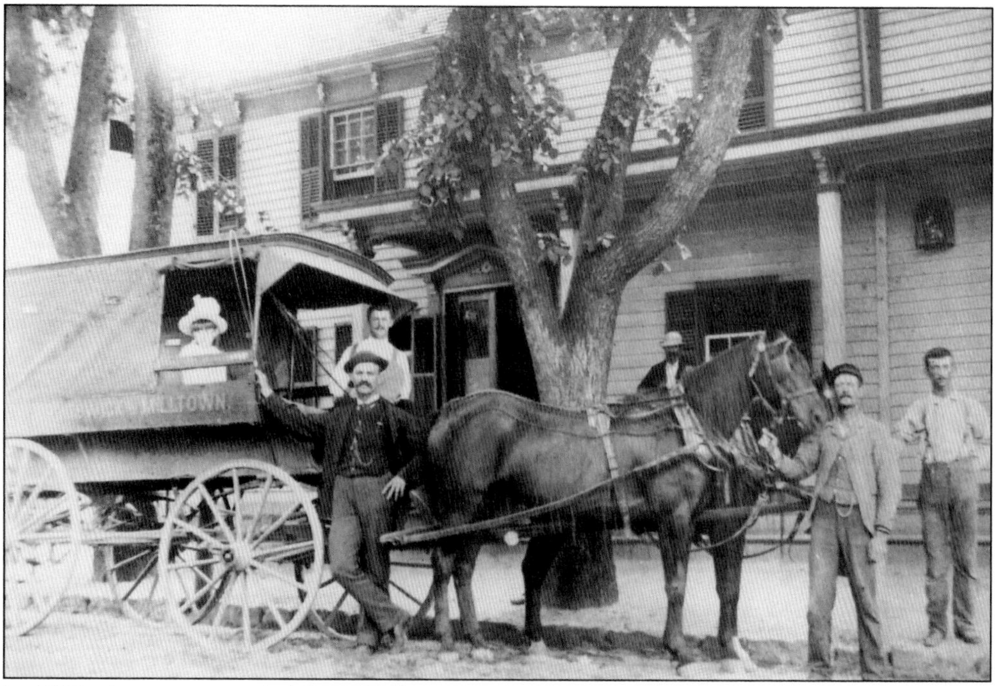

In 1899, this stage traveled from Milltown to New Brunswick. Here, it has stopped in front of Kohlhepp's Union Hotel, now the Milltown Tavern. Charles Hodapp, the owner of the stage coach, is leaning against it. Prescott Crawford is the driver, and Hodapp's daughter is the passenger. (Courtesy of Rita Carina.)

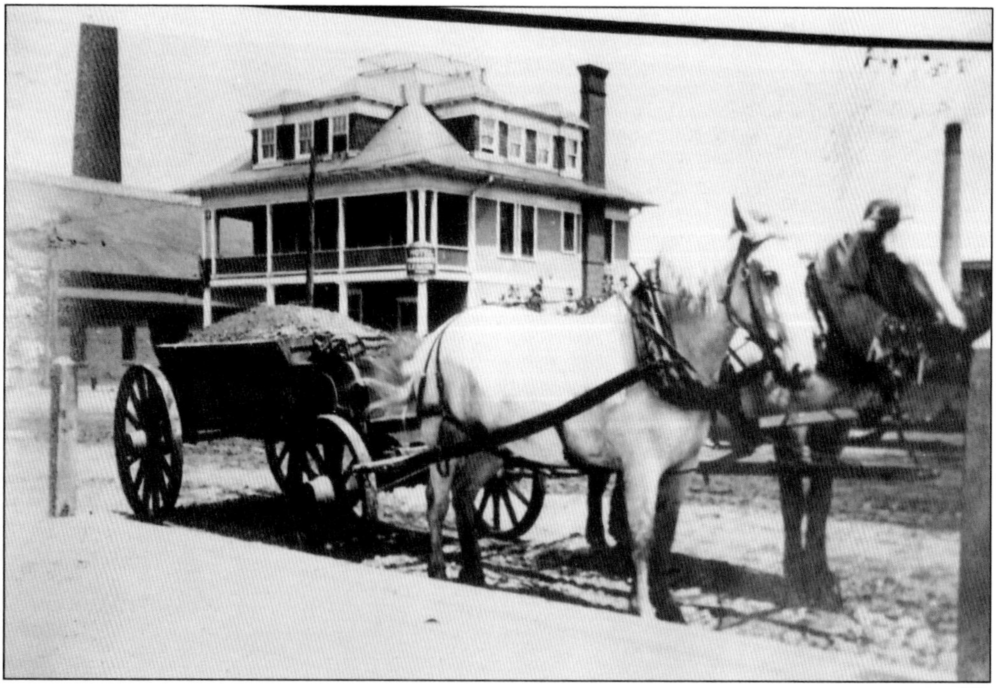

This 1915 coal delivery is bound for the Union Hotel. Sayre's Hotel Marguerite, now the Golden Lion Inn, can be seen across the street. (Courtesy of Hazel Jacobsen Denhard.)

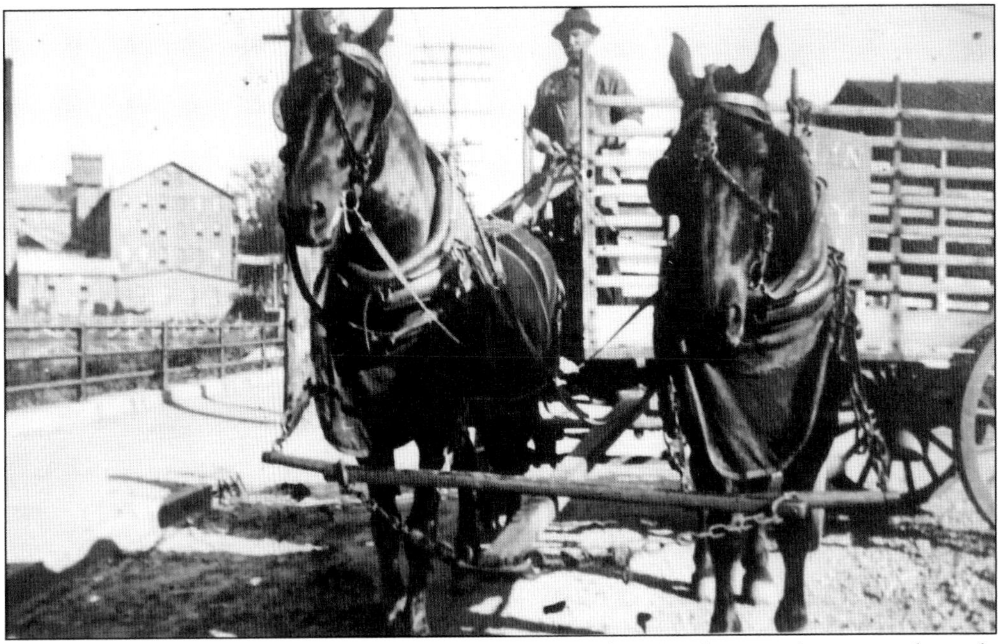

George Detzler steers his wagon onto South Main Street from Washington Avenue in the early 1900s. Mr. Detzler owned a tavern on Washington Avenue. (Courtesy of Hazel Jacobsen Denhard.)

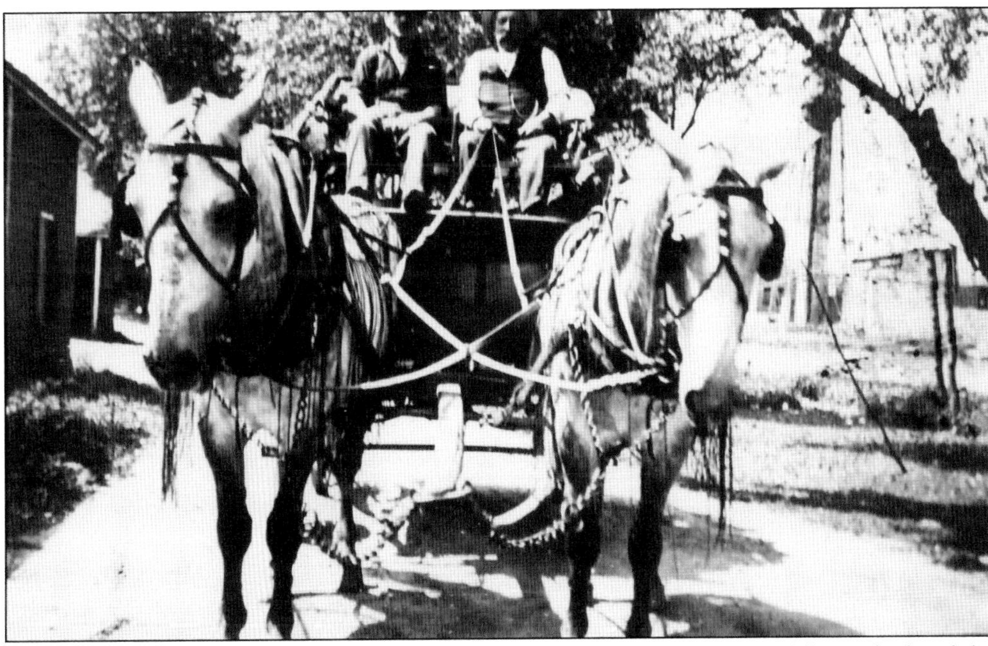

Kohlhepp's Union Hotel became Denhard's Union Hotel when Conrad Kohlhepp died and the establishment was taken over by his son-in-law, Ferdinand Denhard. Here, the hotel receives a delivery of Krueger's beer from Newark, c. 1910. (Courtesy of Hazel Jacobsen Denhard.)

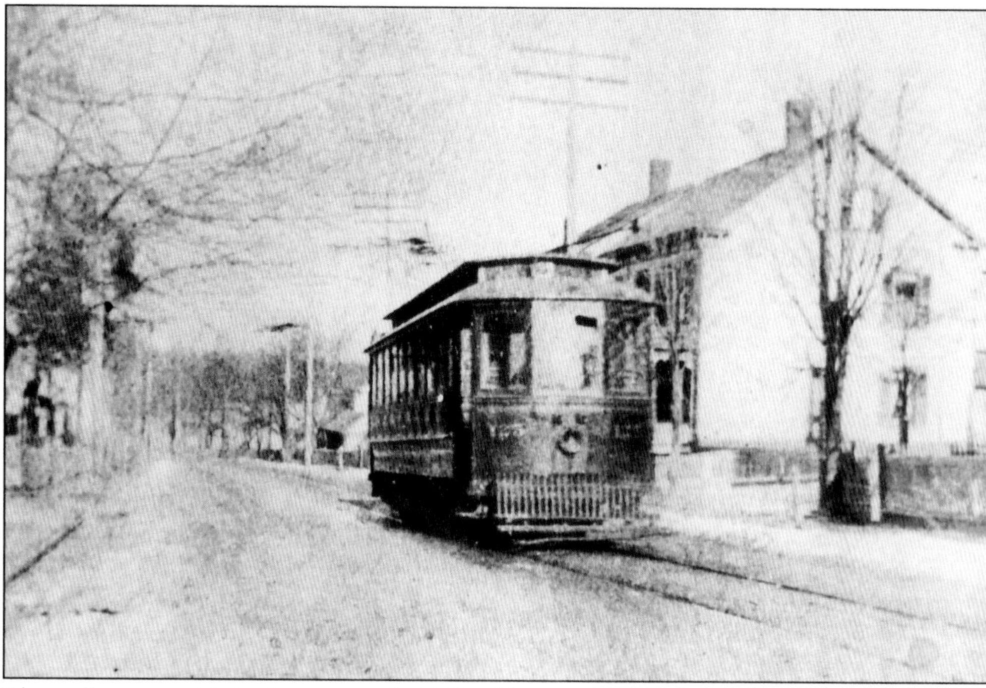

The trolley car on Main Street, *c.* early 1900s. (Courtesy of Irma Lown.)

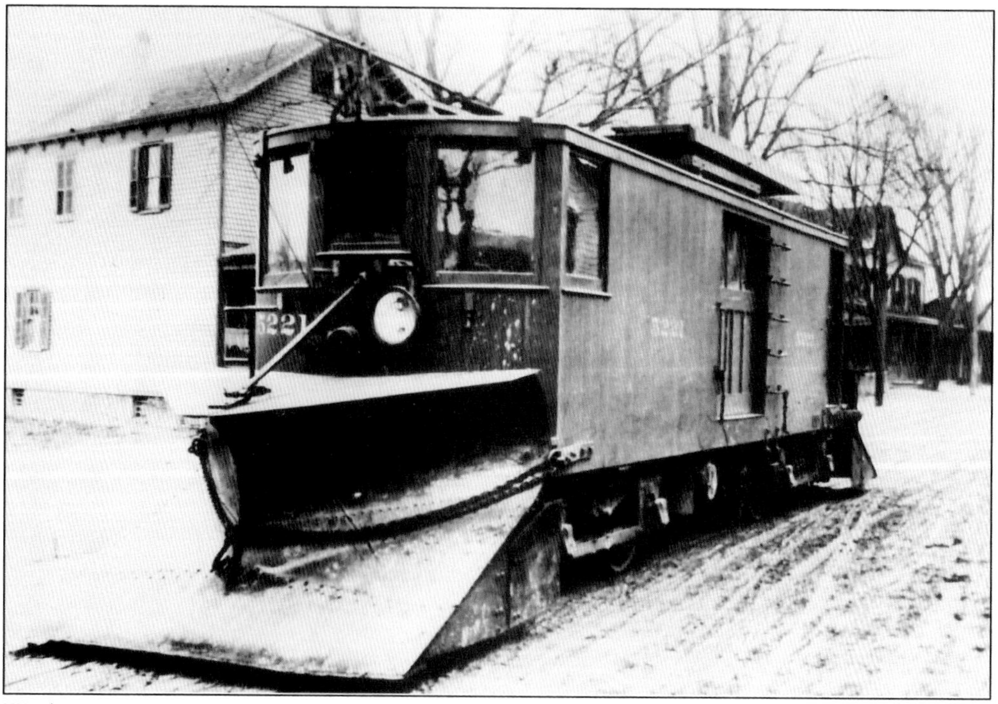

Work car #5221 was built by Russell in 1912. It is shown here in 1914 on South Main Street. This car was still in operation in 1992, acting as a repair car for New Jersey Transit. (Courtesy of William E. Christian Jr.)

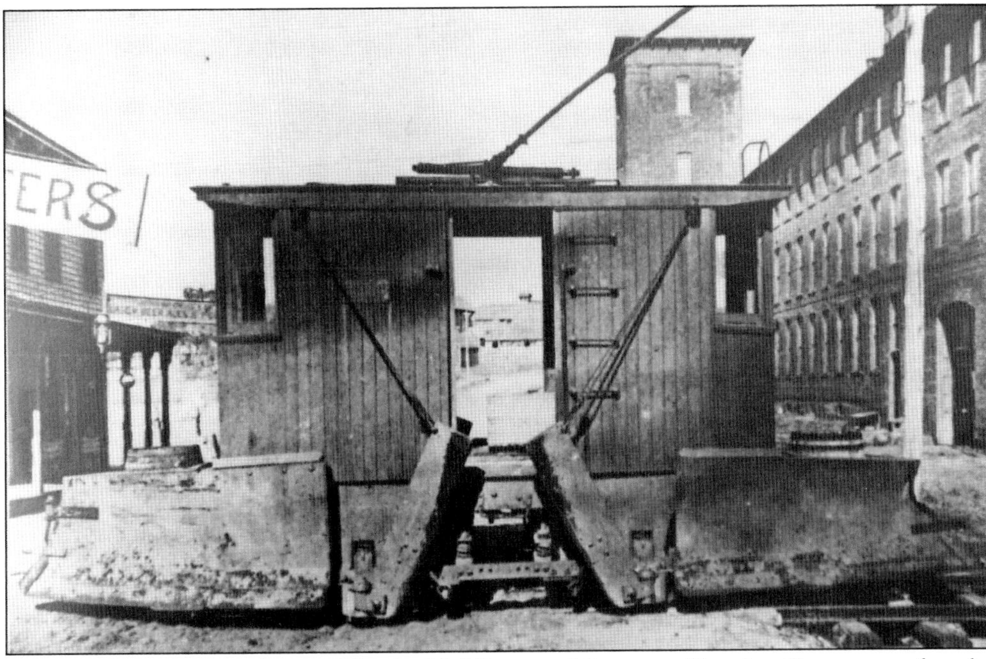

A single truck plow, used in 1907 by the Middlesex and Somerset Traction Company to free the tracks of snow and debris. This picture was taken on Washington Avenue. (Courtesy of Special Collections and Archives, Rutgers University Libraries.)

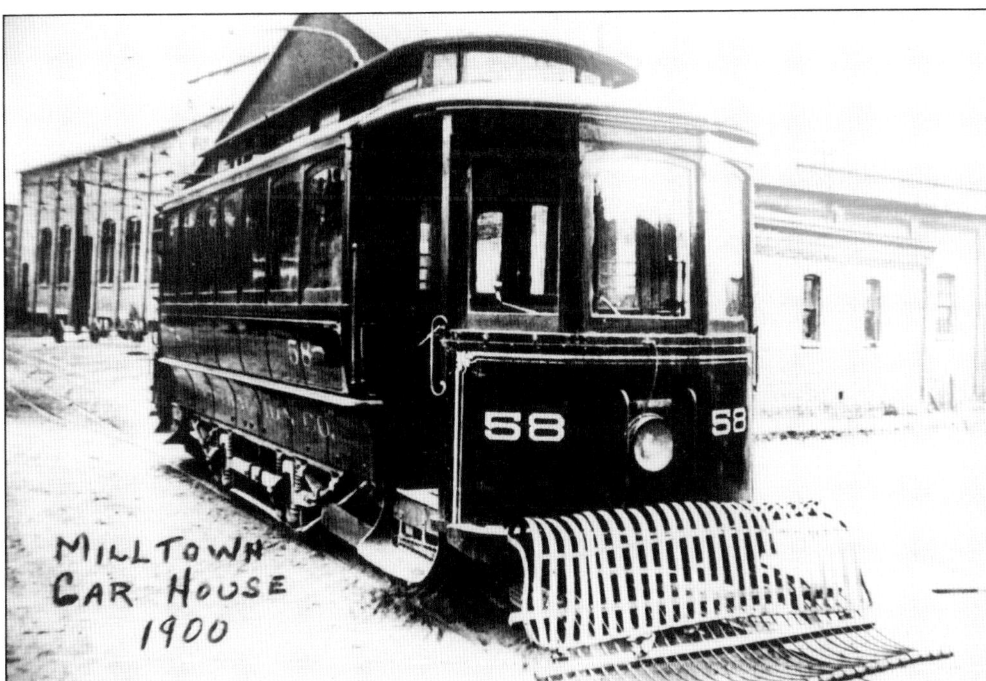

Trolley #58, at the car barn at South Main Street and Washington Avenue. (Courtesy of Charlie Nenninger.)

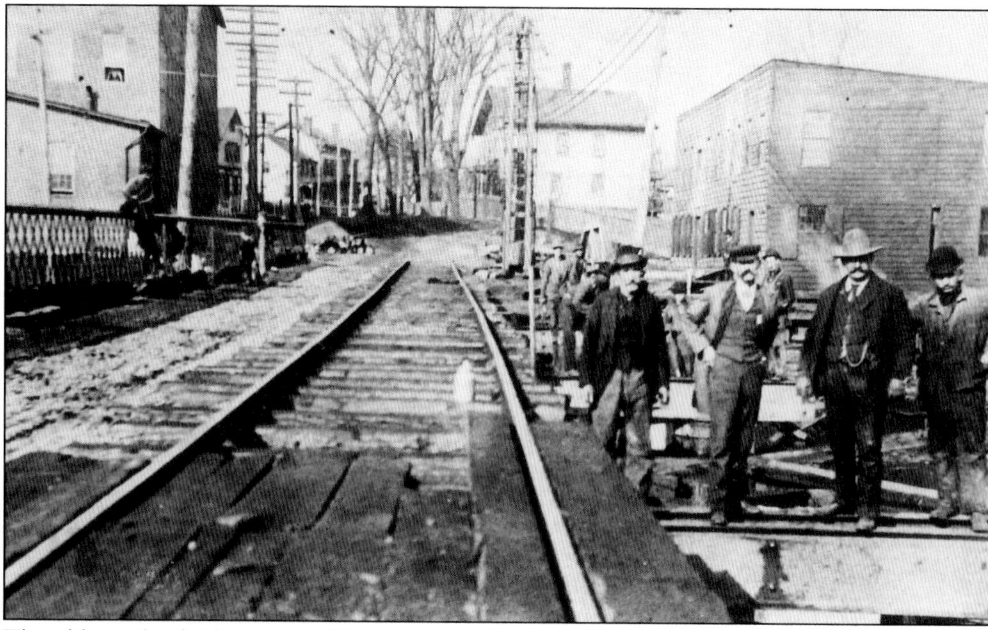

The old wooden bridge gets its "Queen trusses" removed by the Turner Construction Company of Newark in 1905. The company is still in business today. The man with the flat cap and vest is Inspector John Van Liew Booream. On the right is the Rinky Dink factory, and, further back, Charles Hodapp's confectionery. (Courtesy of Irma Lown.)

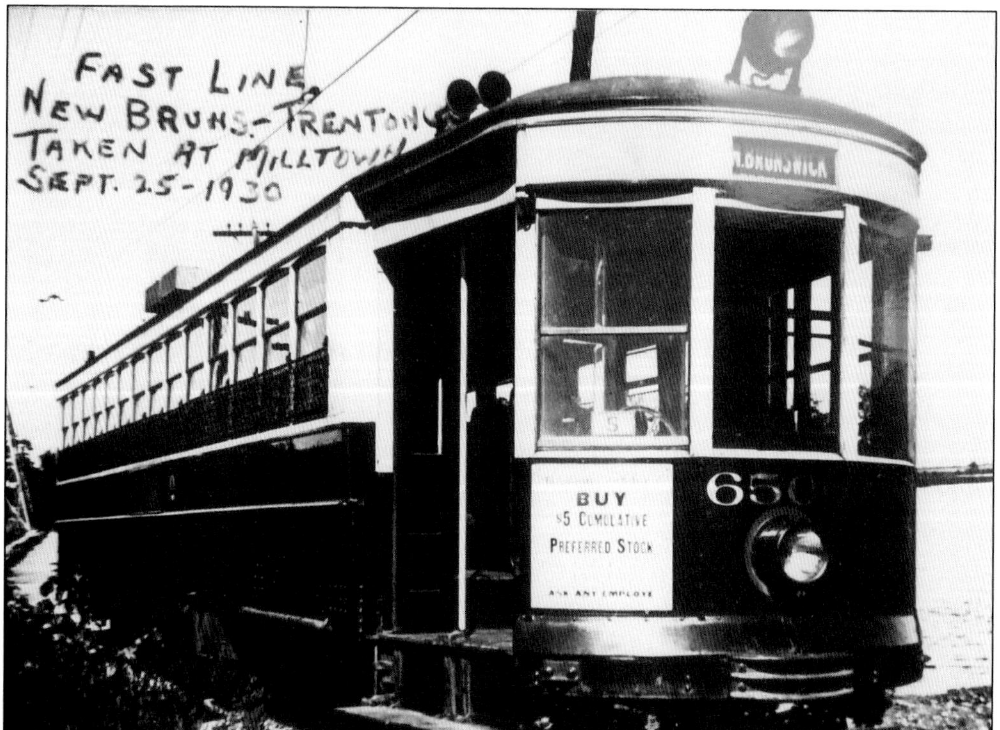

Public Service's "Fast Line" car, which serviced Milltown. This photograph was taken in September 1930. (Courtesy of Charlie Nenninger.)

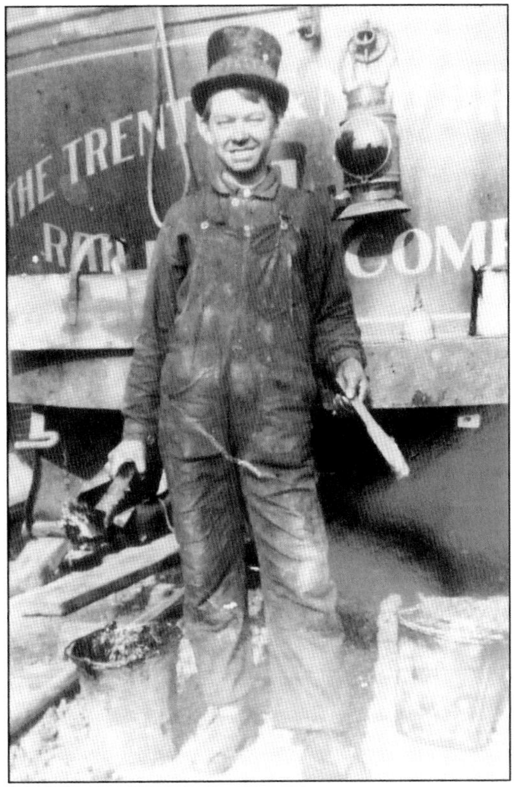

This man was employed as a "grease monkey" on the "Fast Line," which ran along the high-tension wires from New Brunswick to Trenton. (Courtesy of Rita Carina.)

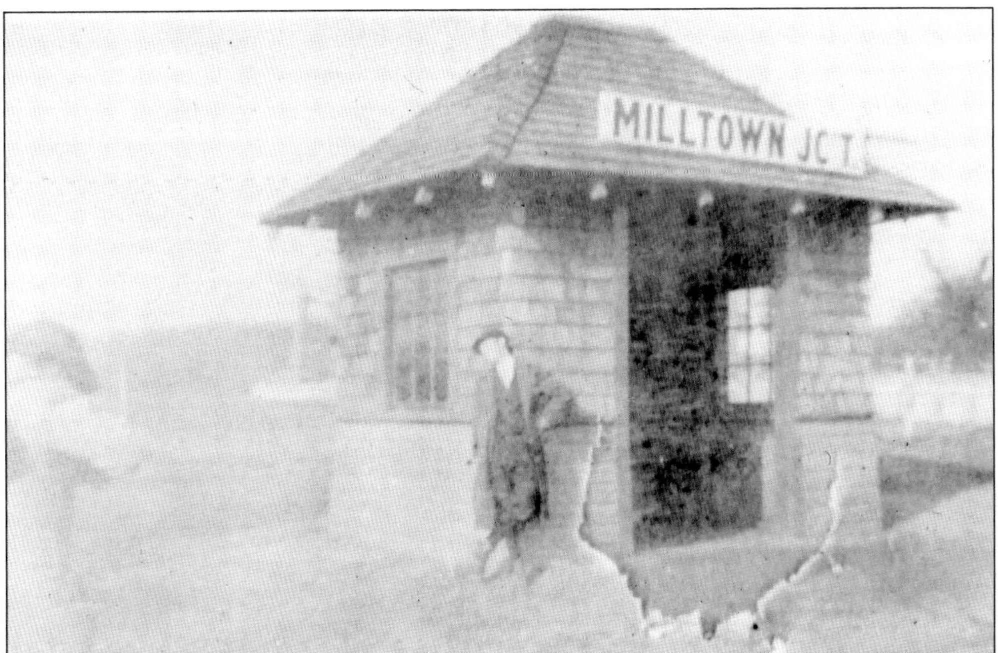

The "Fast Line" trolley station was located off North Main Street, at the junction of the local trolley tracks, near the high-voltage power lines. (Courtesy of C. Harrison Hill.)

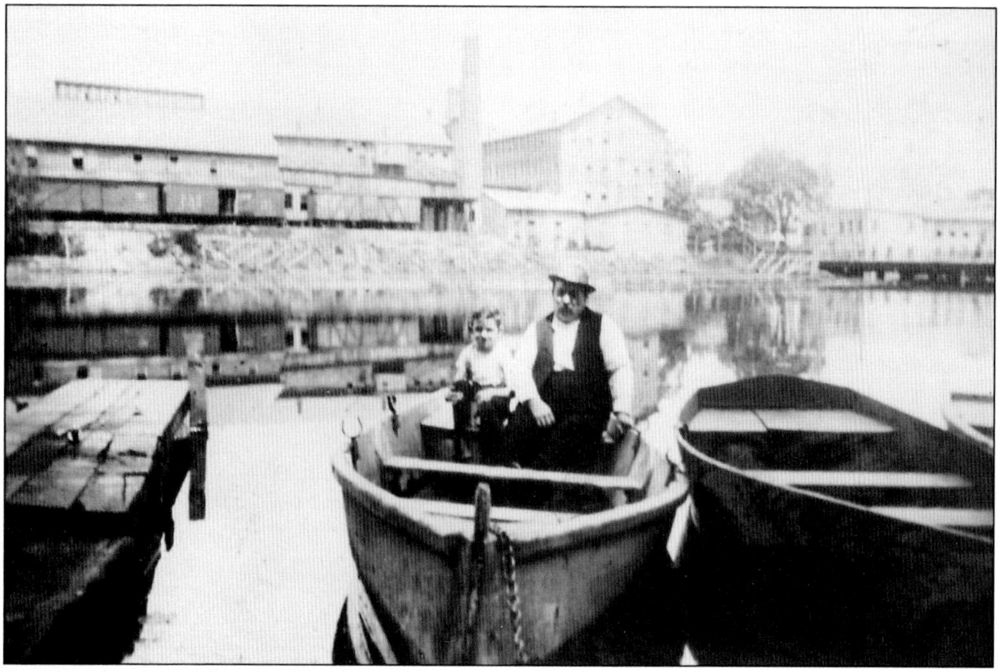

Roy Denhard and his uncle, Phil Kline, boating on the Mill Pond in the 1920s. In the background can be seen the Michelin Tire Company and the Rinky Dink. (Courtesy of Hazel Jacobsen Denhard.)

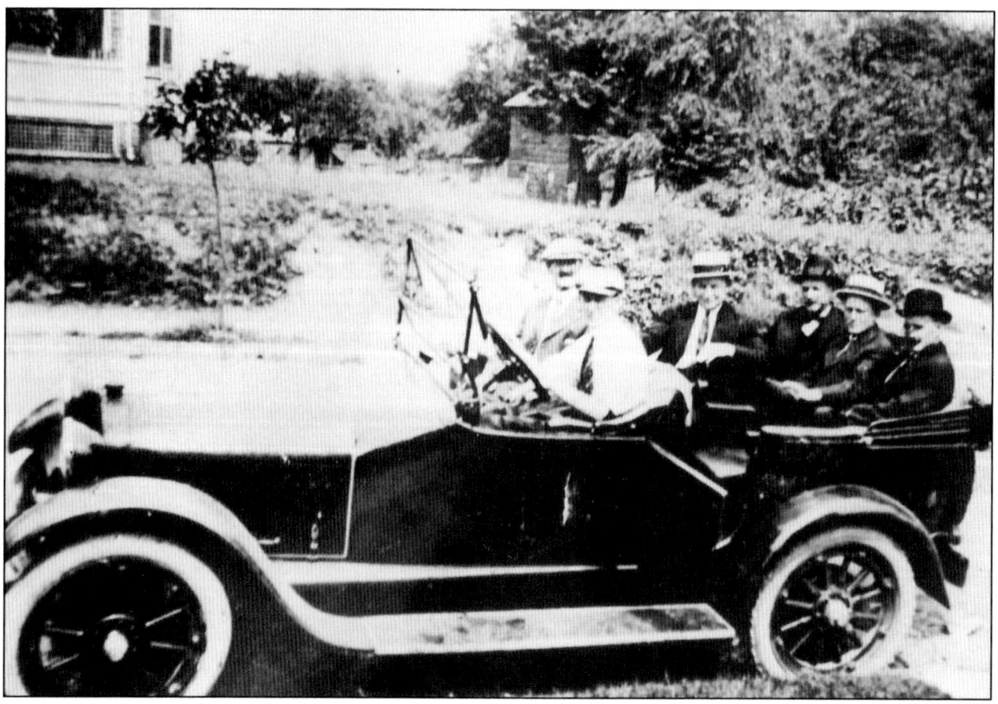

Bill Booream is driving next to "Cooney" Kuhlthau. The identities of the other men are unknown. (Courtesy of Irma Lown.)

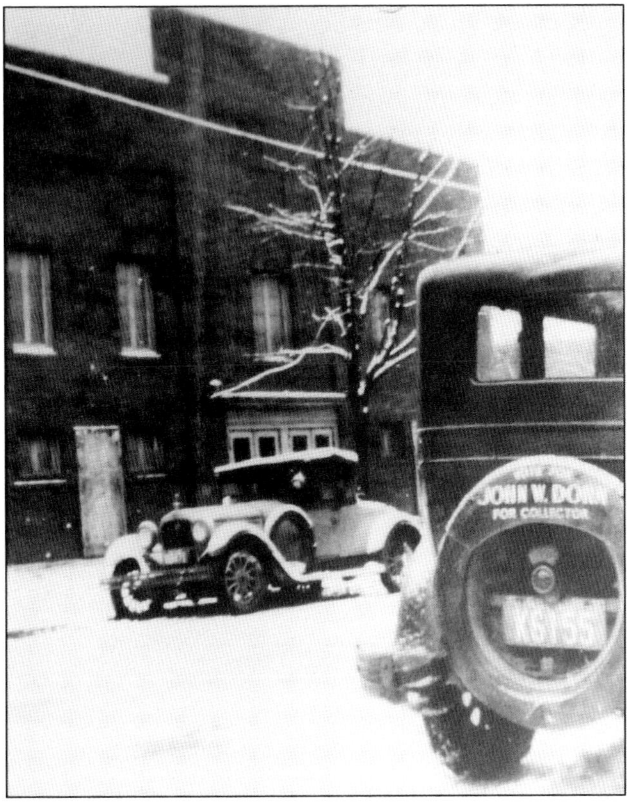

Vintage automobiles, pictured in front of the Community House on North Main Street, 1930. (Courtesy of Rita Carina.)

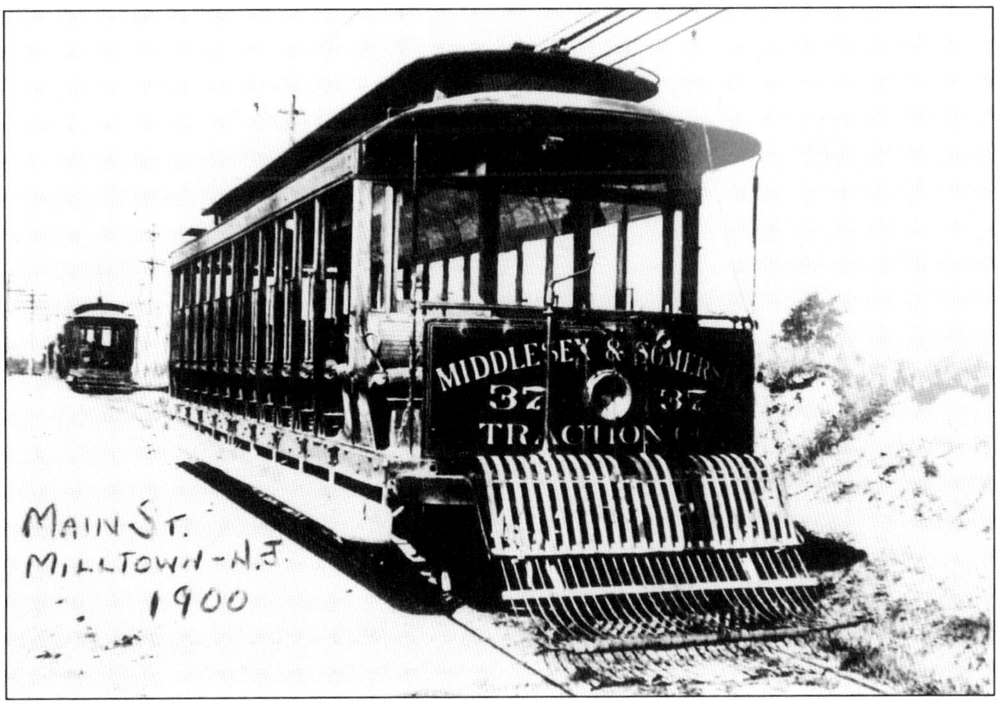

Main Street trolleys, 1900. (Courtesy of Charlie Nenninger.)

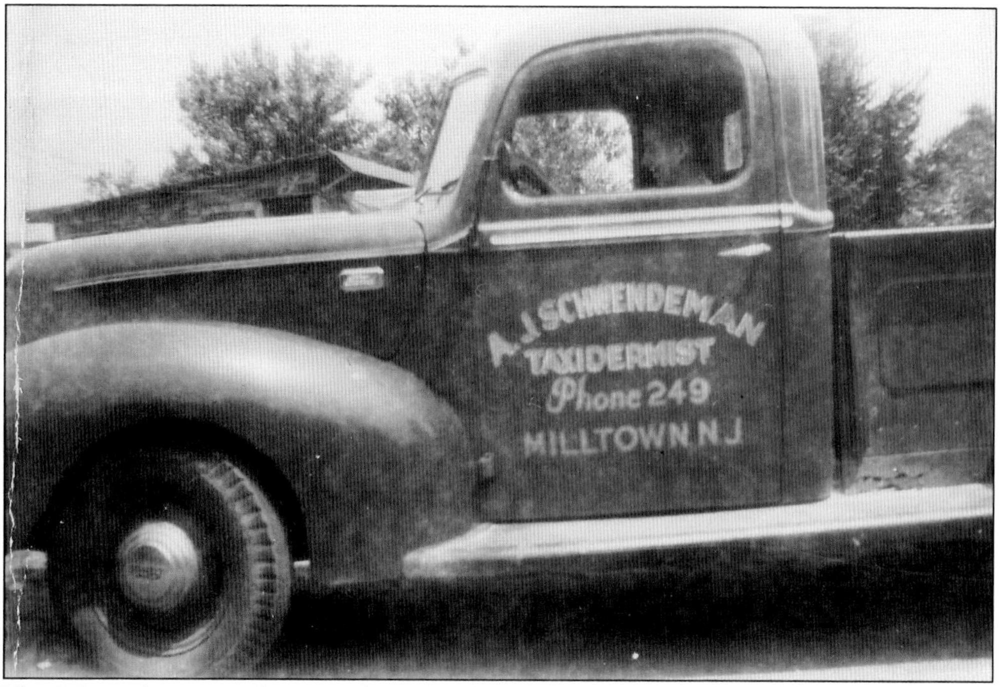

The Schwendeman taxidermy truck, *c.* the 1940s. (Courtesy of the Schwendeman family.)

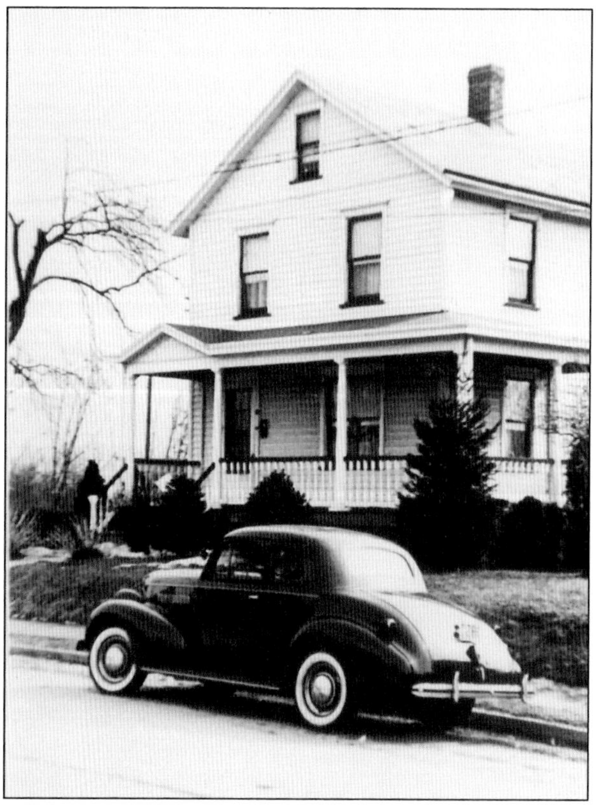

A family car, on 82 Van Liew Avenue, 1945. (Courtesy of Ken Selover.)

Two

Batter Up!

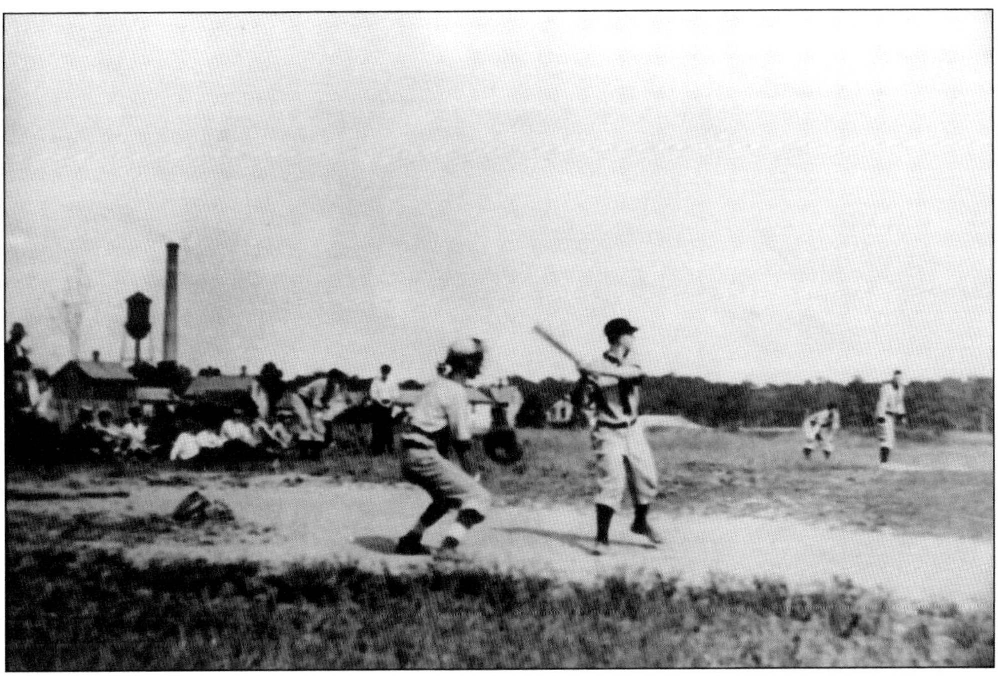

Michelin Athletic Field, 1907. (Courtesy of Rita Carina.)

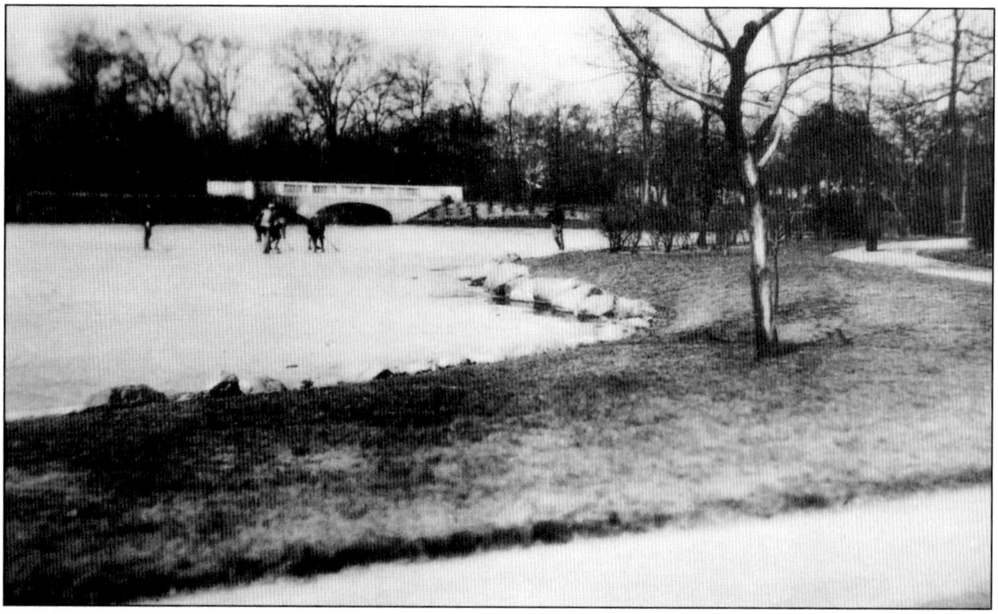

Ice skating on Sucker Brook, *c.* 1930. The second Riva Avenue Bridge is in the background. (Courtesy of Rita Carina.)

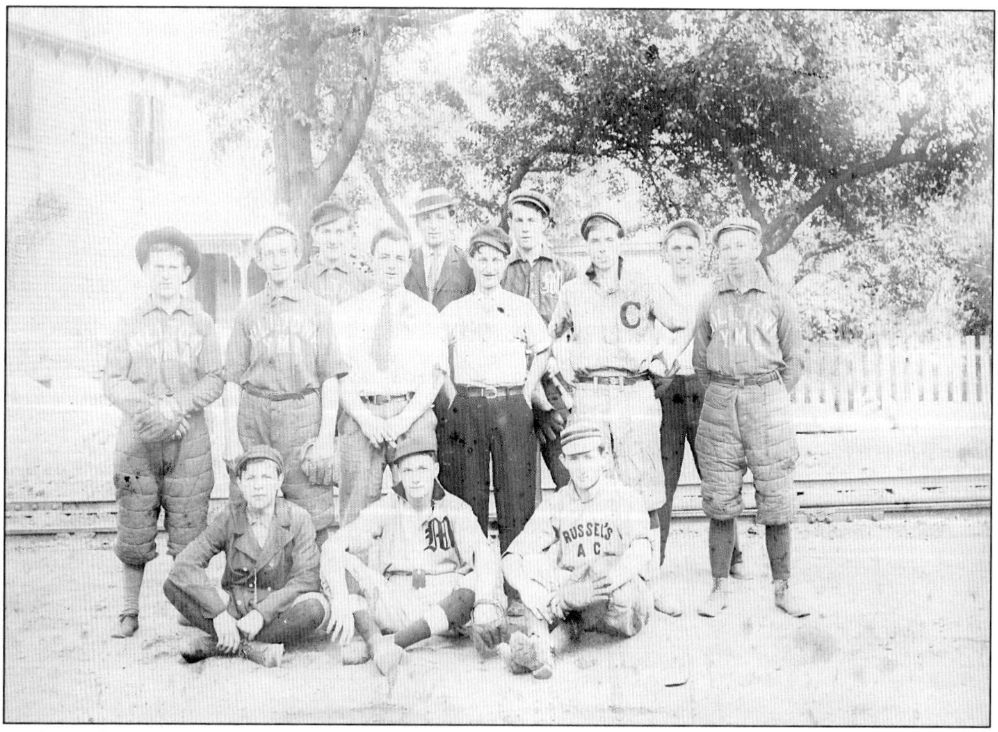

Early Milltown baseball players pose by the tracks. Among those pictured are: (second row) George Buhl (far left) and Henry Willenbrock (sixth from left); (back row, third from left) George Hofer. (Courtesy of Milltown Historical Society.)

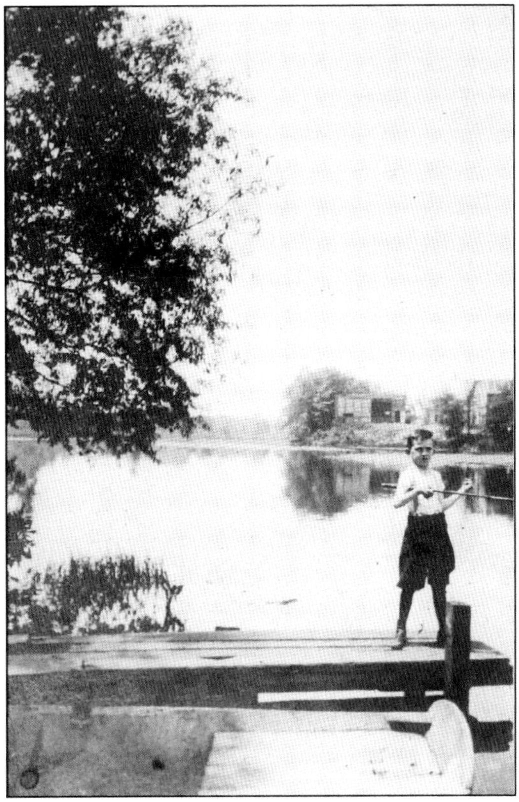

Ferdinand Denhard, fishing in the Mill Pond, *c.* 1915. (Courtesy of Hazel Jacobsen Denhard.)

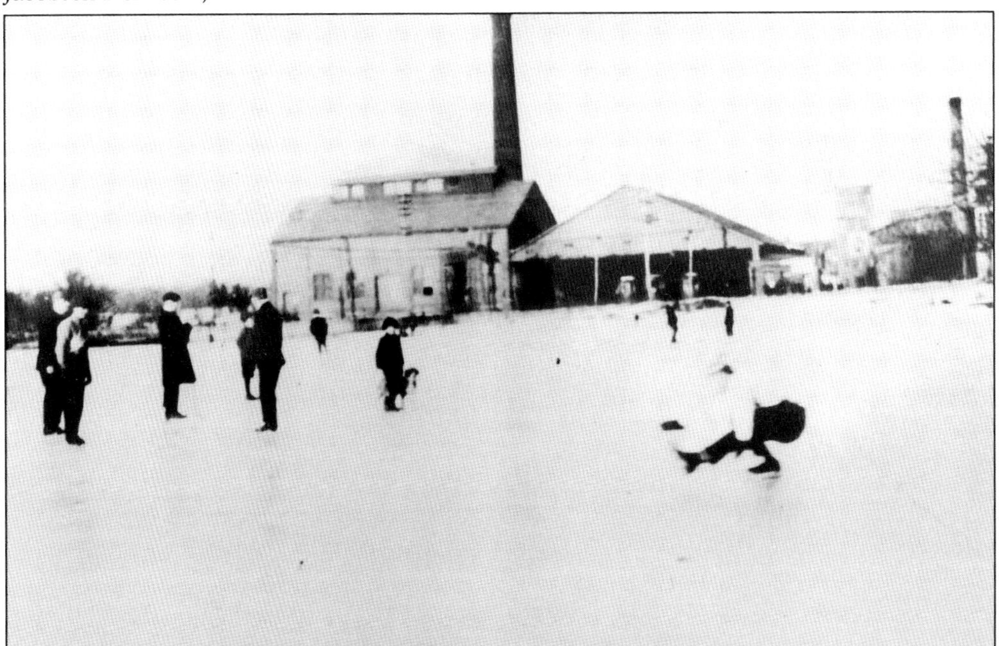

The fancy skater on the right is Reuben Holzer. In the background can be seen, from left to right: the power house, the car barn, the Russell Playing Card factory, and Sayre's Hotel. (Courtesy of Rita Carina.)

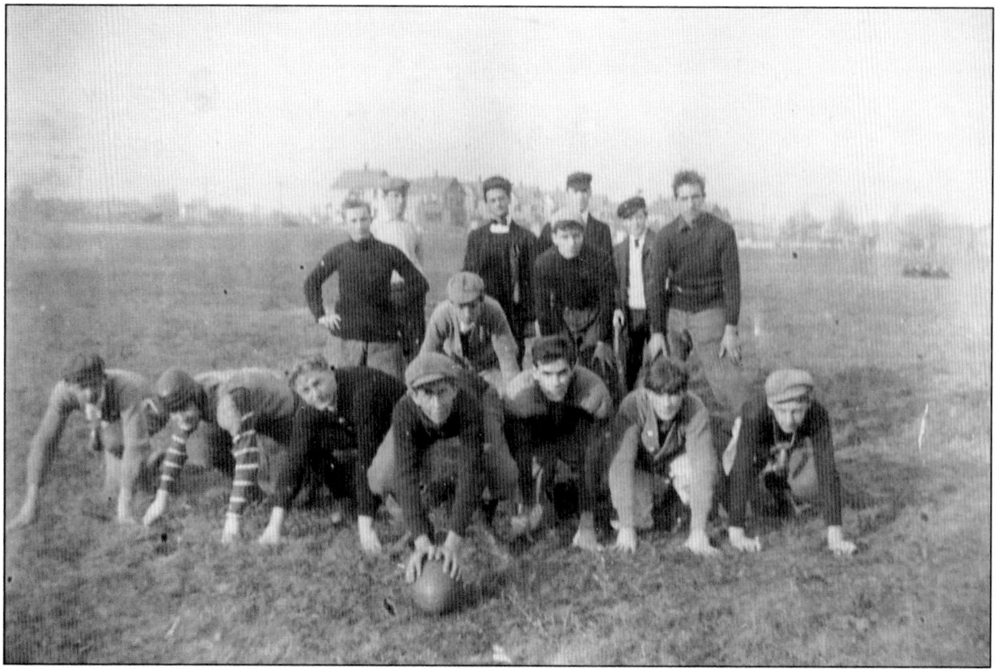

Les Snedeker, Joe Crabiel, Frank Hodapp, and Ted Snedeker are some of the young men playing football in this field. (Courtesy of Irma Lown.)

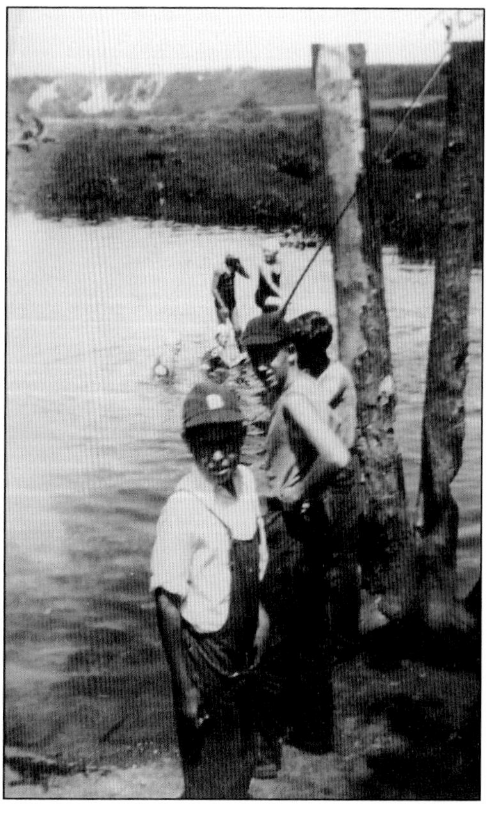

Fishing in Milltown, *c.* 1930s. The boy in the middle is J. Edward Crabiel. He would go on to enjoy a long, successful political career as mayor (1948–51), assemblyman (1954–66), state senator (1966–74), and New Jersey Secretary of State (1974–77). (Courtesy of Paulette Crabiel Wahler.)

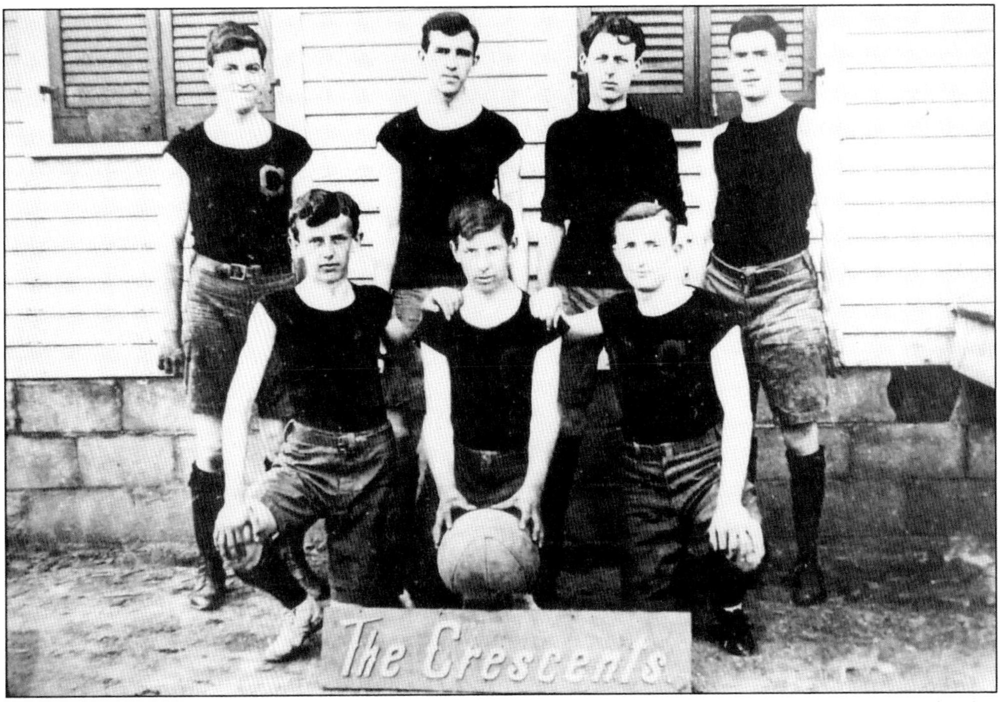

The Crescents basketball team, *c.* 1910. Pictured here are, from left to right: (front row) Charles Crabiel and John Junker; (back row) unknown, Joe Crabiel, Lew Booream, and Bill Evans. (Courtesy of Charlie Nenninger.)

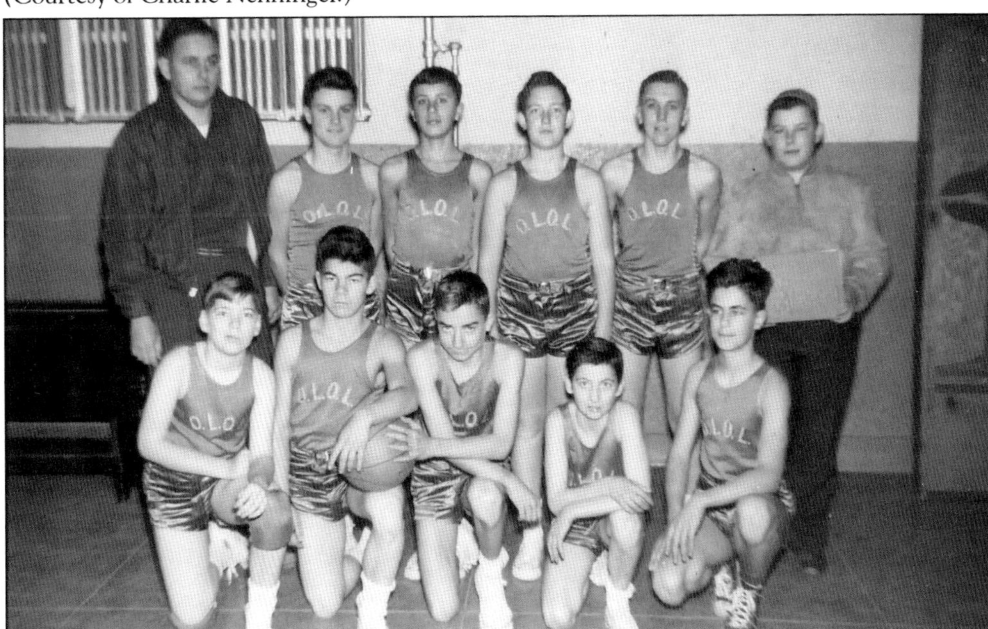

Our Lady of Lourdes basketball team, 1957. Seen here are, from left to right: (front row) Paul Clark, Frances D'Andrea, Billy Rhinehart, and Robert Shank; (back row) Richard Loomis (coach), Jimmy Heffernan, Pete Jablonski, George H. Stilwell Jr., Rich Wysocki, and Joe Rademacher. (Courtesy of George H. Stilwell Jr.)

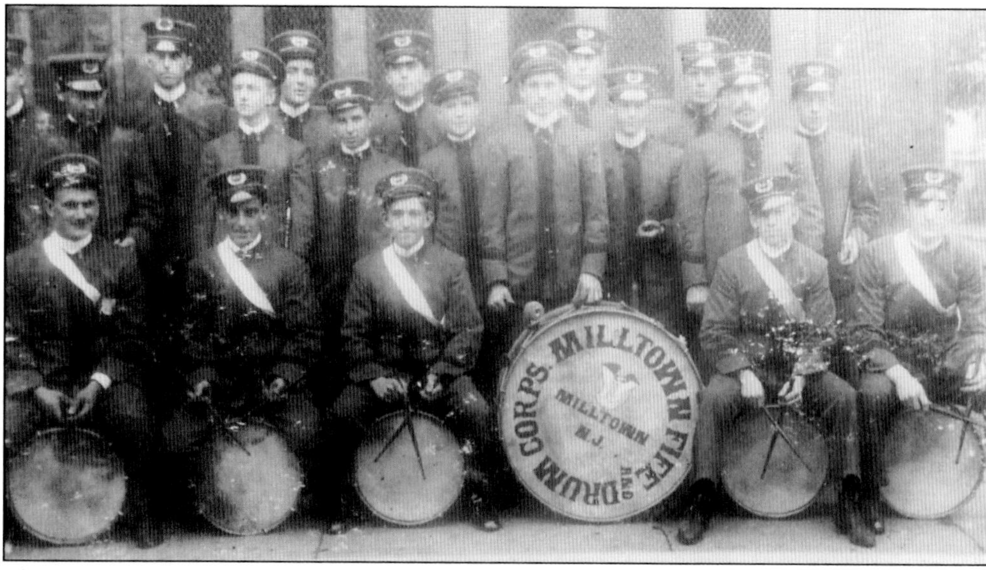

The Milltown Fife and Drum Corps, 1907. Posing here are, from left to right: (front row) Henry Hammond, William Lins, John Heyl, William Willenbrock, and Charles Hodapp; (back row) William Evans, Oscar Christ, Fred Kautz, Chris Jensen, Henry Christ, John Bauries, Hector LeJoy, John Hartlander, John Heimel, Frank Hodapp, John Deiner, Andrew Beecher, Conrad Kuhlthau (director), and Fred Hartlander. (Courtesy of Rita Carina.)

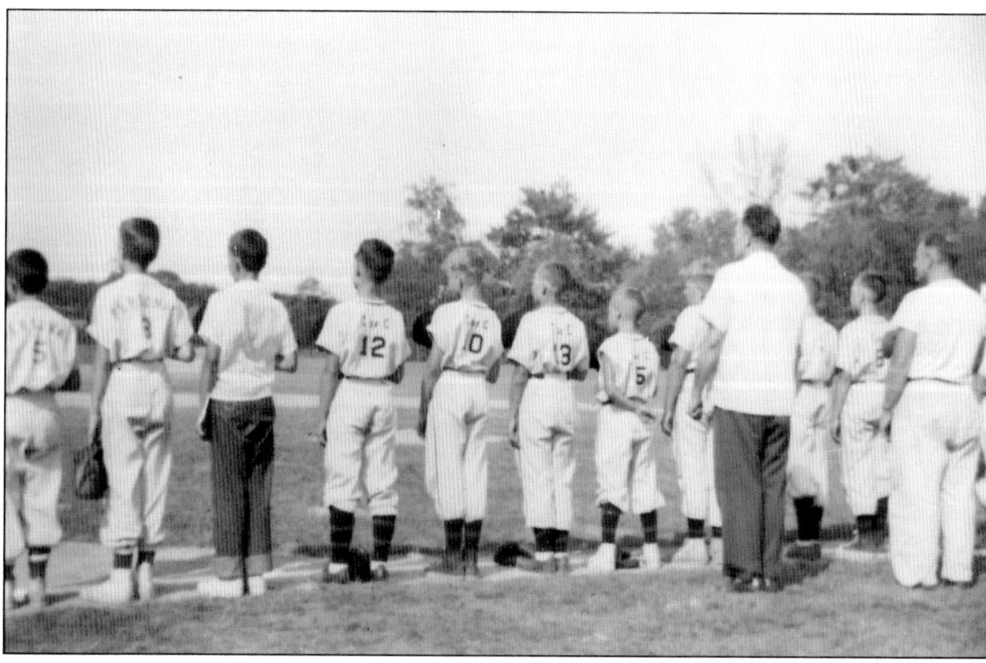

Opening Day ceremonies, Milltown Little League, *c.* 1950s. (Courtesy of George H. Stilwell Jr.)

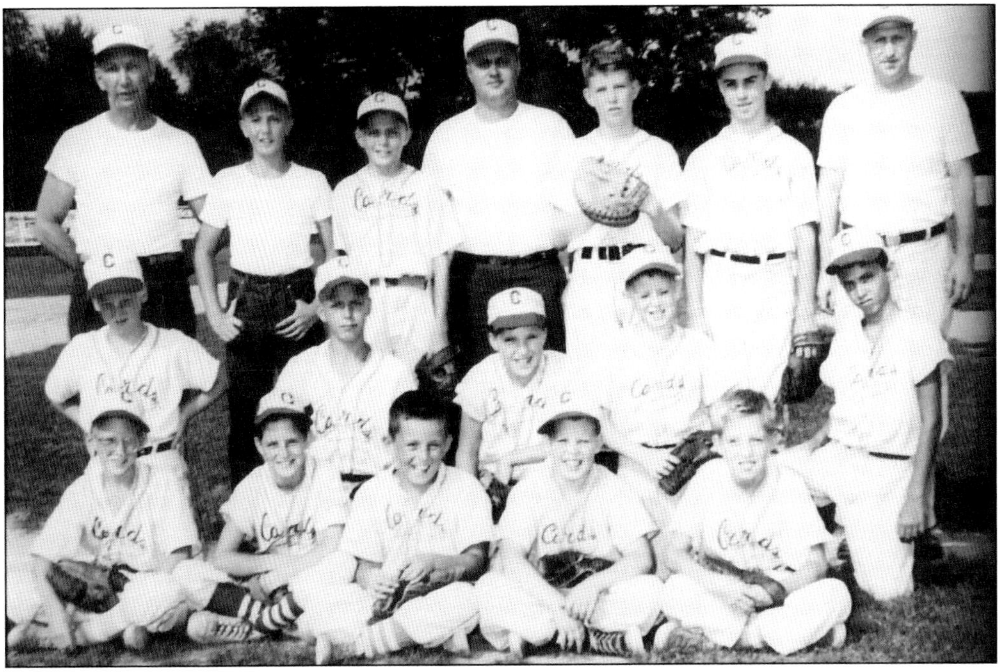

The 1959 Little League Cardinals were sponsored by the Milltown Rescue Squad. Seen here are, from left to right: (front row) Mick Leaver, Barry Reinhard, Jim Dunfee, Jim Allinder, and Robert Doerr; (middle row) Arnold Horvath, Joe Adochio, Walt Jakinitschuk, Mickey Shalayda, and Robert Volk; (back row) Leo Redding, Alan Rittman, Alan Smith, Del Cavanaugh, Jim Dwyer, Jim Wysocki, Joe Linderman. (Courtesy of Eve Redding.)

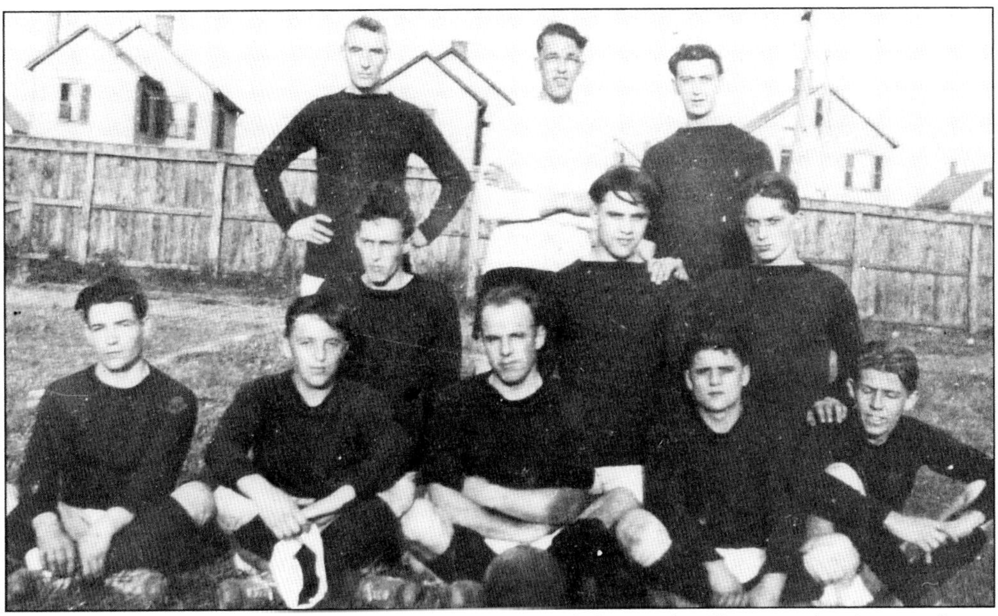

Soccer players, at Michelin Field. Seen here are, from left to right: (front row) unknown, Louis Movel, Andy Cooper, Yves Placard, and Louis Bordel; (middle row) Allen ?, Henri Navor, and Yves Fitamant; (back row) George Malabar, C. Osborne, and Gus Jacquemot.

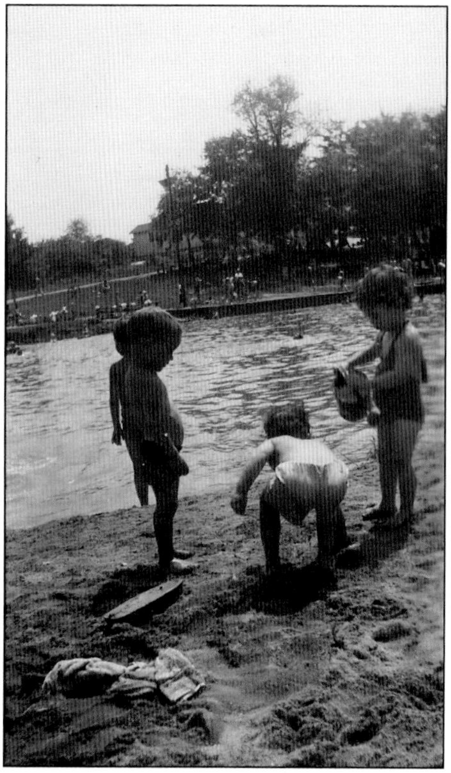

Richie Plantec, Richie Small (bending over), and Rosemary Phadden play at Milltown's "Ol' Swimmin' Hole", 1948. (Courtesy of Karen Small Harding.)

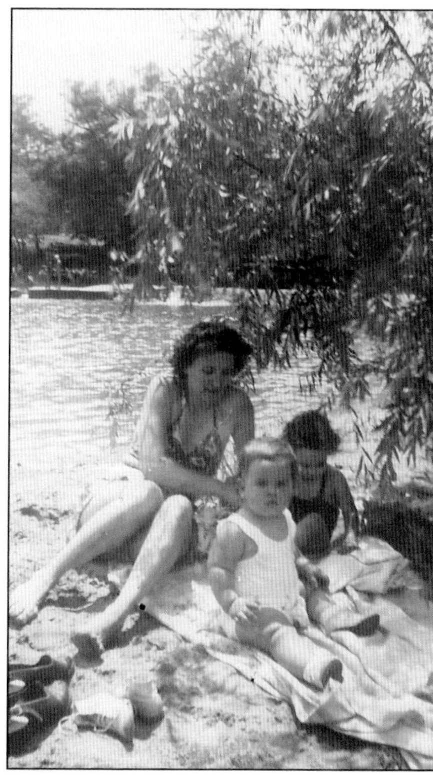

More fun on the same day in 1948. Pictured here are Mary Phadden (adult), Rosemary Phadden (at rear), and Karen Small (baby). (Courtesy of Karen Small Harding.)

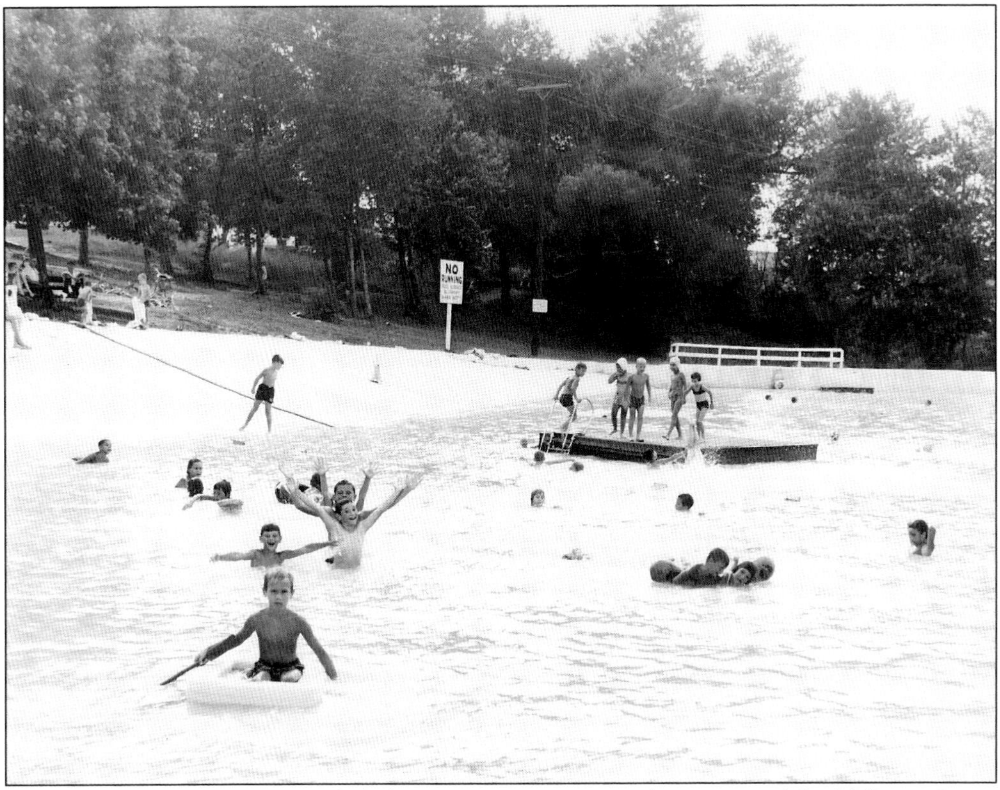

In 1958, Milltown's swimming hole became a swimming pool, courtesy of the Milltown Lions Club pool project, chaired by Harold L. Herbert. This picture was taken in 1964. (Courtesy of Edward V. Vetter Sr.)

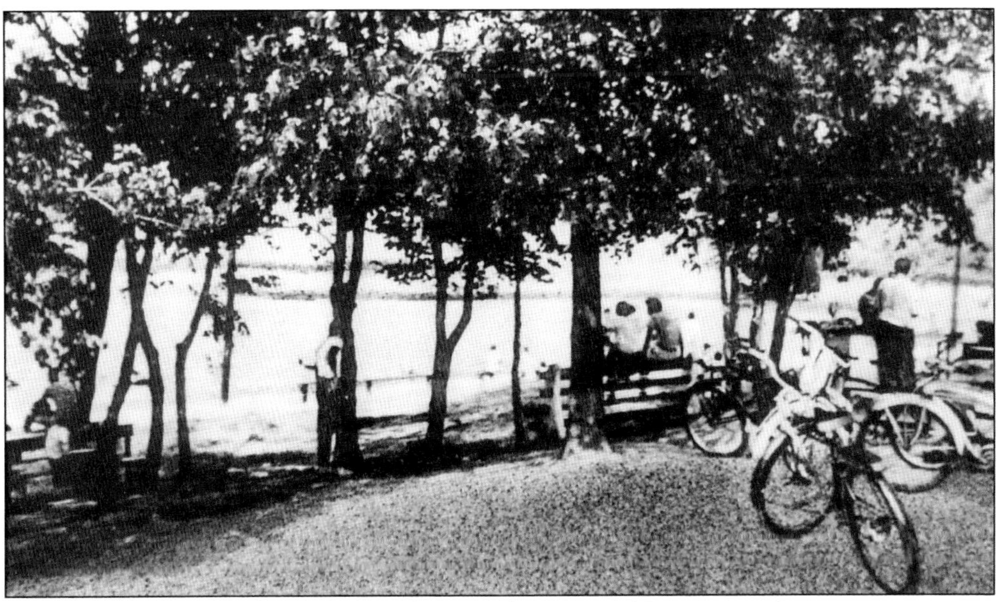

The Milltown Park and swimming pool, 1950s. (Courtesy of Brian Harto.)

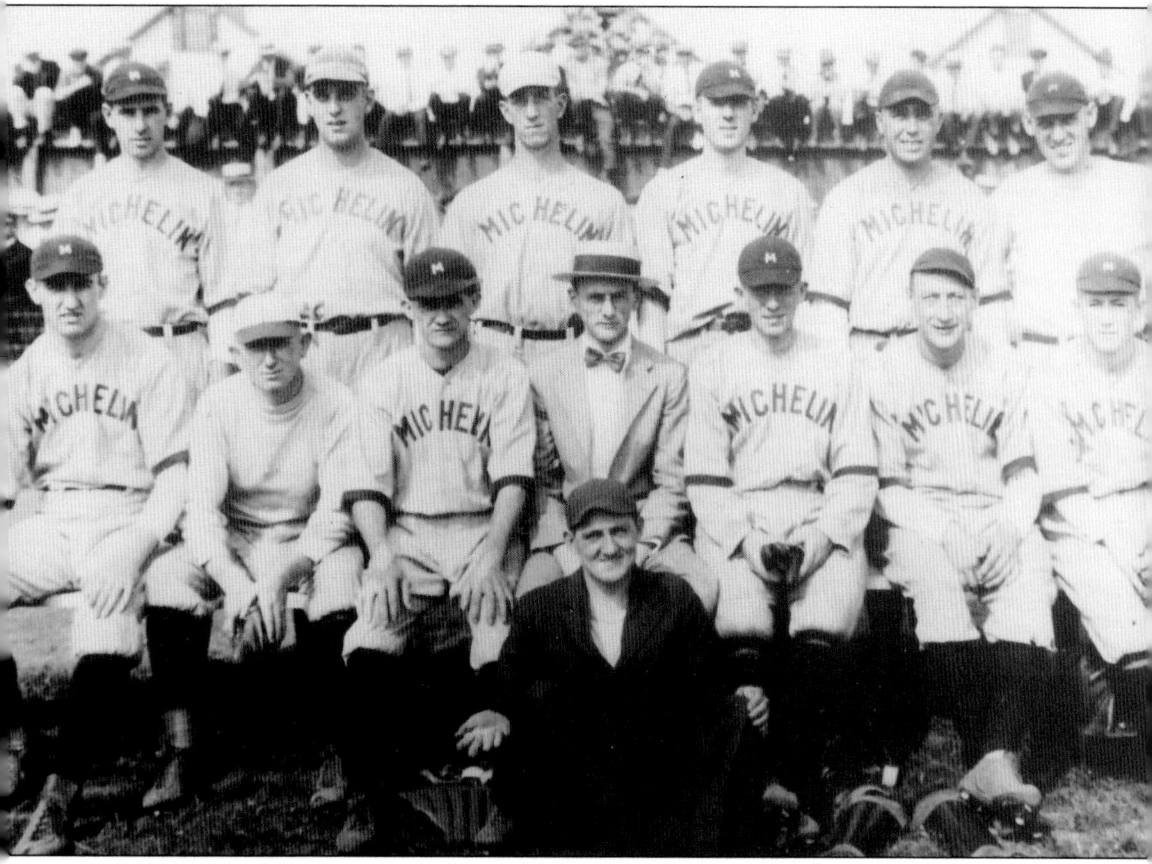

On July 31, 1920, the semi-professional Michelin Tire Company baseball team posed at the Michelin Baseball Field, prior to a game with "The House of David," a top-caliber, traveling team from Michigan. Michelin lost the game 6-1. The game was attended by 3,386 fans, who spent $1,700. Seen here are, from left to right: (front row) Clayton Smith, Murray Borlund, Fred Kohrherr, Lester Snediker, Leon Nixon, Herbert Hamann, and Lefty Lyons; (back row) Charles Crabiel, Carl Hermann, Ab Hermann, Russ Evans, Ed Spille, and Frank Dunn. The umpire is A.C. McMahon, of Brooklyn, New York. At the time the photograph was taken, he was a Rutgers University Varsity coach. Ab Hermann went on to play major league baseball, and is still the only major-leaguer to come from Milltown. He played for the Boston Braves in 1923 and 1924. In thirty-two games as an infielder, he batted .234 with 11 RBIs. The photograph was taken by O.B. Viken. (Courtesy of Rita Carina.)

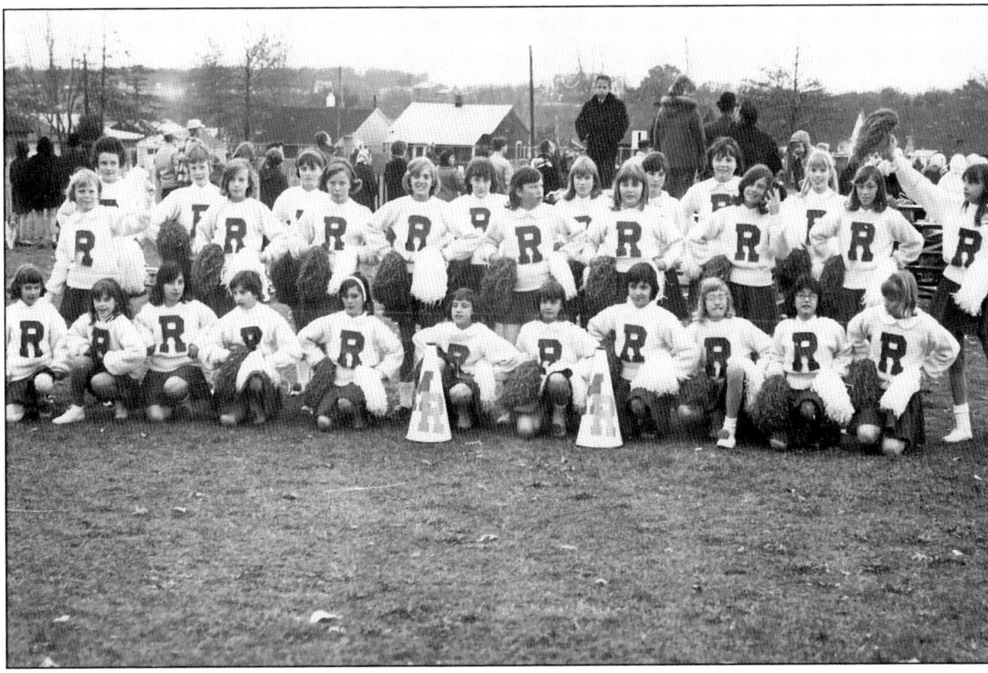

The Milltown Rangers cheerleaders, 1966. (Courtesy of Edward V. Vetter Sr.)

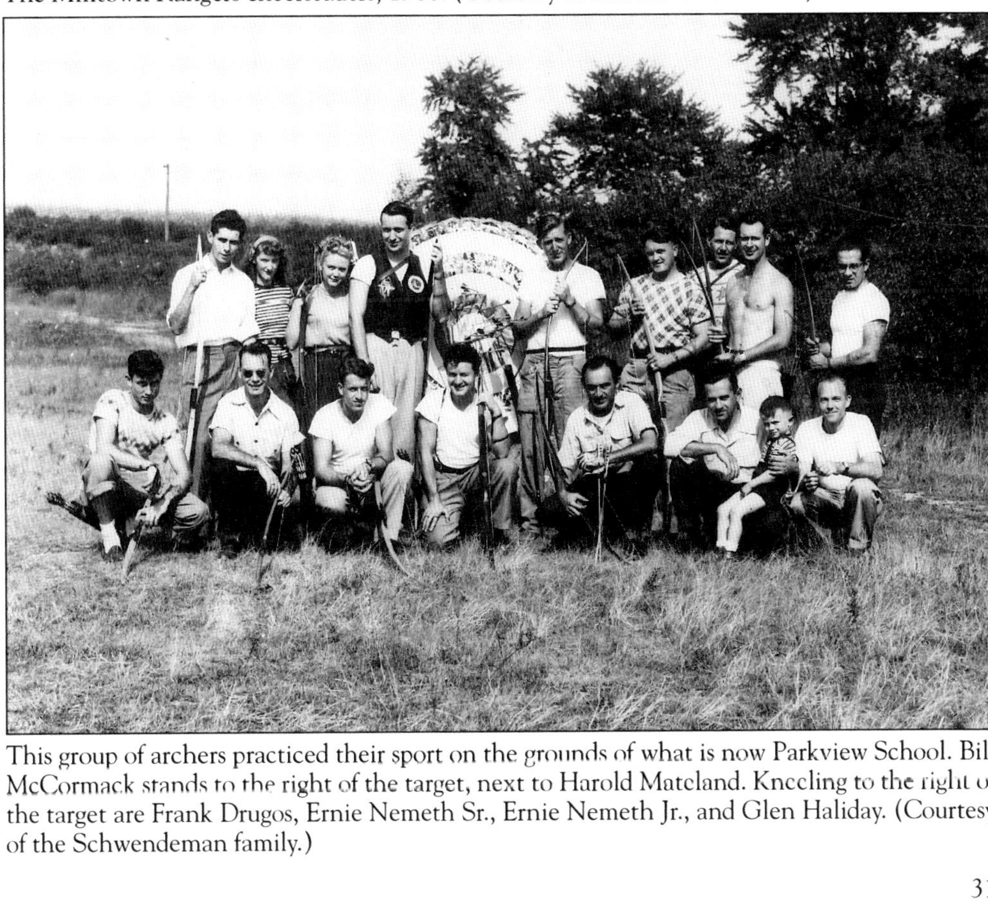

This group of archers practiced their sport on the grounds of what is now Parkview School. Bill McCormack stands to the right of the target, next to Harold Mateland. Kneeling to the right of the target are Frank Drugos, Ernie Nemeth Sr., Ernie Nemeth Jr., and Glen Haliday. (Courtesy of the Schwendeman family.)

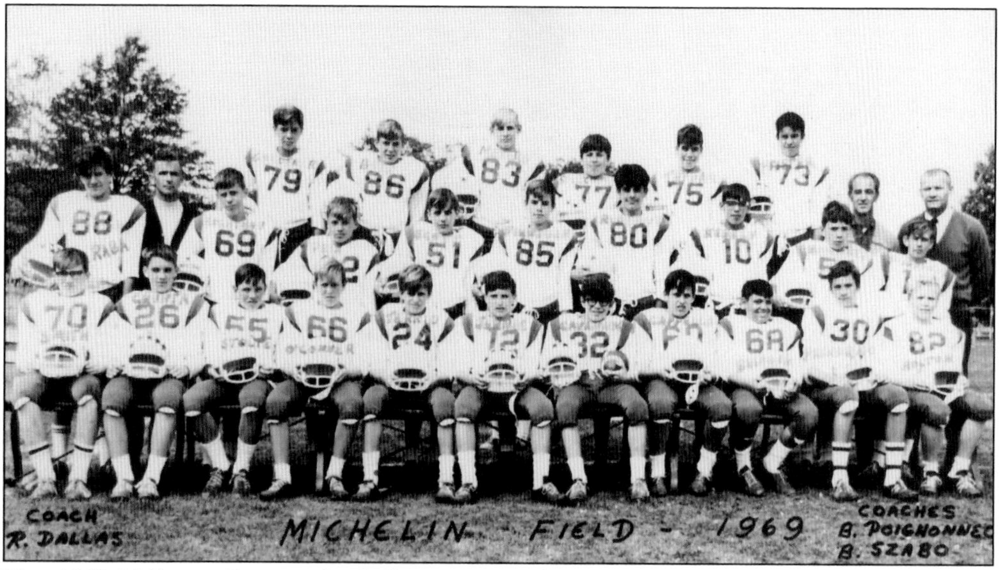

The 1969 Milltown Rangers football team were the National Division Midget Champions. They were coached by Rich Dallas, B. Poignonnec, and B. Szabo. (Courtesy of Joan Dallas.)

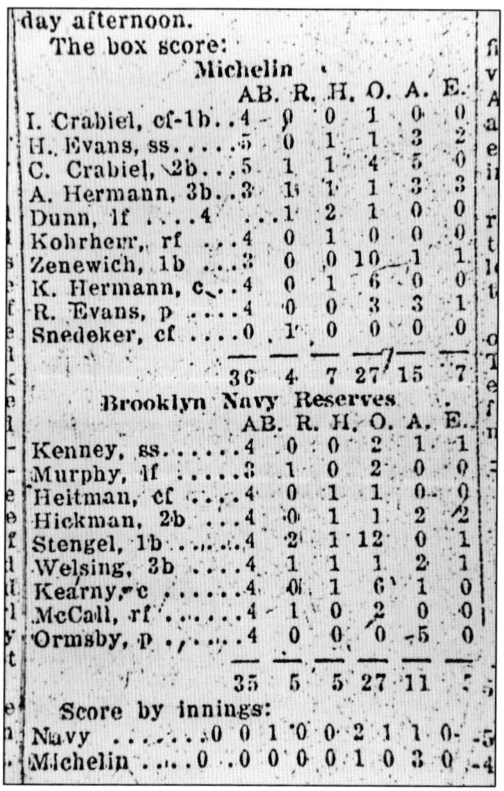
day afternoon.

The box score:

Michelin

	AB.	R.	H.	O.	A.	E.
I. Crabiel, cf-1b	4	0	0	1	0	0
H. Evans, ss	5	0	1	1	3	2
C. Crabiel, 2b	5	1	1	4	5	0
A. Hermann, 3b	3	1	1	1	3	3
Dunn, lf	4	1	2	1	0	0
Kohrherr, rf	4	0	1	0	0	0
Zenewich, 1b	3	0	0	10	1	1
K. Hermann, c	4	0	1	6	0	0
R. Evans, p	4	0	0	3	3	1
Snedeker, cf	0	1	0	0	0	0
	36	4	7	27	15	7

Brooklyn Navy Reserves

	AB.	R.	H.	O.	A.	E.
Kenney, ss	4	0	0	2	1	1
Murphy, lf	3	1	0	2	0	0
Heitman, cf	4	0	1	1	0	0
Hickman, 2b	4	0	1	1	2	2
Stengel, 1b	4	2	1	12	0	1
Welsing, 3b	4	1	1	1	2	1
Kearny, c	4	0	1	6	1	0
McCall, rf	4	1	0	2	0	0
Ormsby, p	4	0	0	0	5	0
	35	5	5	27	11	[illegible]

Score by innings:

Navy	0	0	1	0	0	2	1	1	0	5
Michelin	0	0	0	0	0	1	0	3	0	4

This box score is from a baseball game between Michelin and the Brooklyn Navy Reserves, *c.* 1920–25. This was a big day in town, for most of the locals hadn't seen players of this caliber. Casey Stengel and Jimmy Hickman both played for Brooklyn. Michelin pitcher Russell "Swifty" Evans pitched the entire game, even striking out the mighty Casey Stengel. (Coutesy of Brian Harto.)

Three

School Days

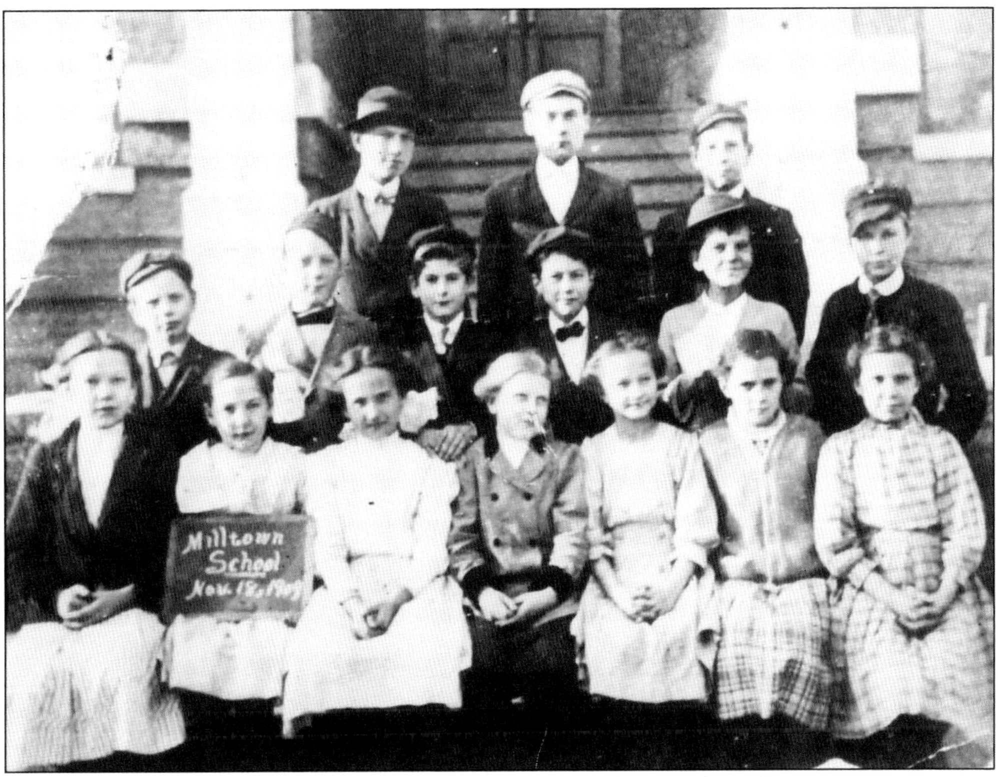

Milltown Public School, November 18, 1909. (Courtesy of Ken Selover.)

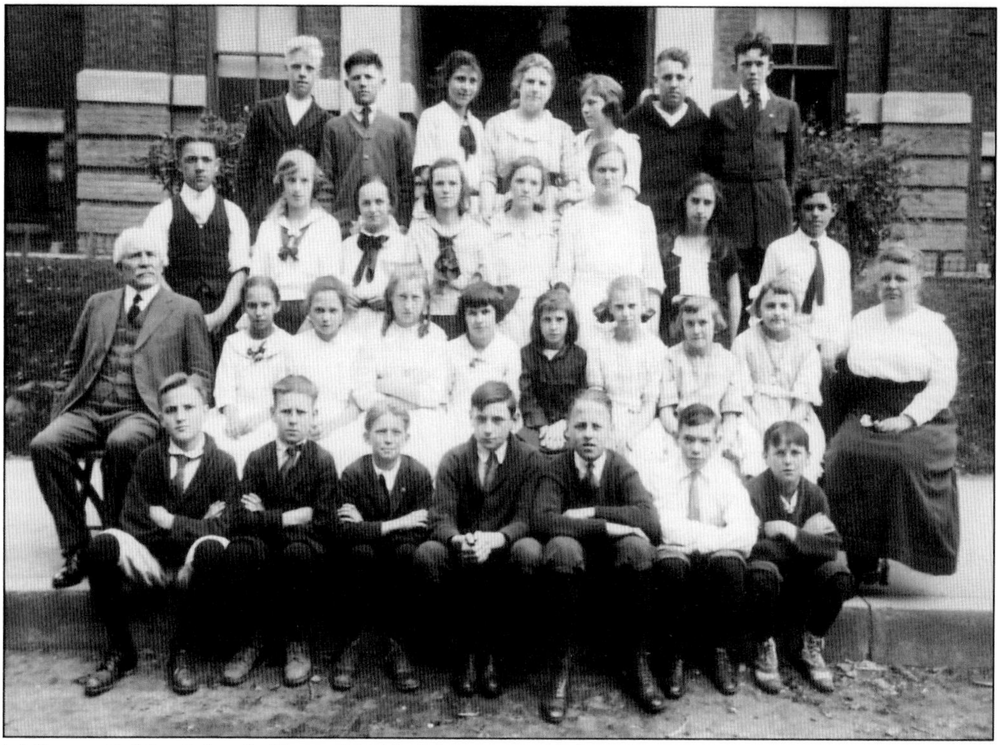

Milltown Public School, Class of 1922. (Courtesy of Edward V. Vetter Sr.)

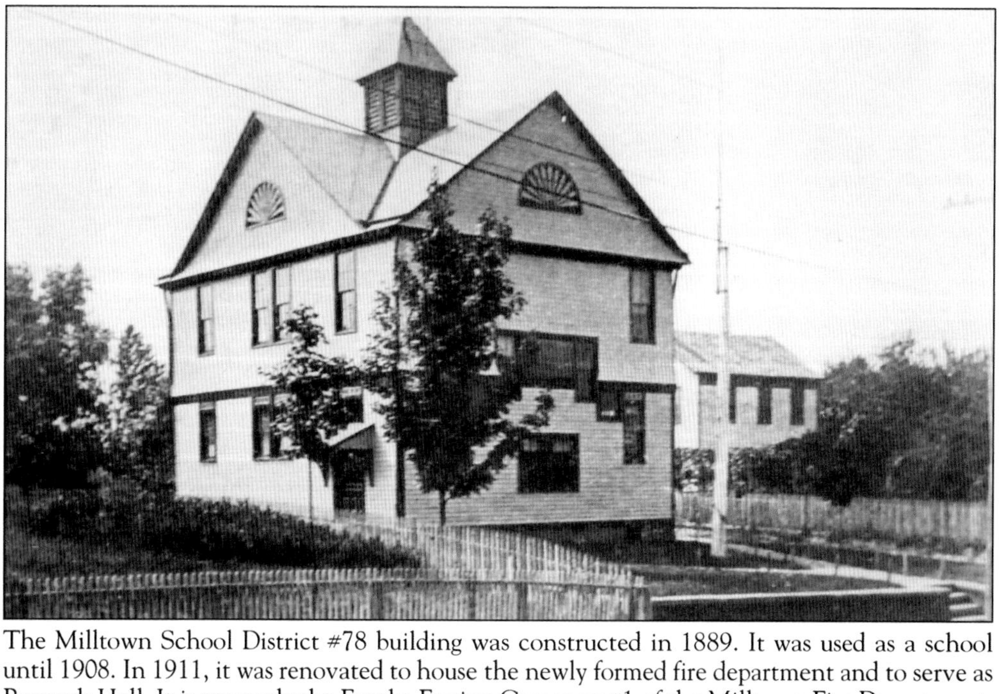

The Milltown School District #78 building was constructed in 1889. It was used as a school until 1908. In 1911, it was renovated to house the newly formed fire department and to serve as Borough Hall. It is currently the Eureka Engine Company #1 of the Milltown Fire Department. Some of the original blackboards can still be seen inside the firehouse. This photograph was taken *c.* 1905, by I.S. VanDerveer. (Courtesy of Brian Harto.)

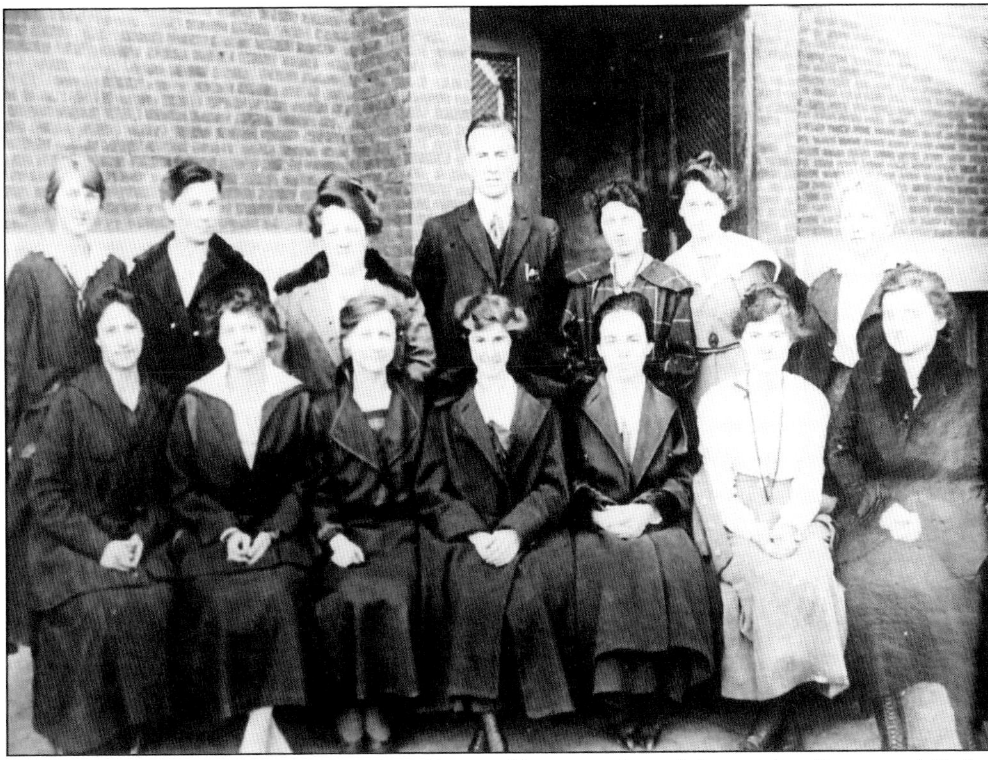

Milltown Public School teachers, 1919. Pictured here are, from left to right: (front row) Helen Glock, Emma Peters, Mame Glock, Irene Van Nois, Helen Cooper, Mabel Stevenson, and Emma Groner; (back row) Miss Robbins, Bessie Meyers, Mrs. G. LaFarge, Harry R. B. Meyers (principal), Flo Cory, Hazel Hughs, and Grace Shaw. (Courtesy of Ken Selover.)

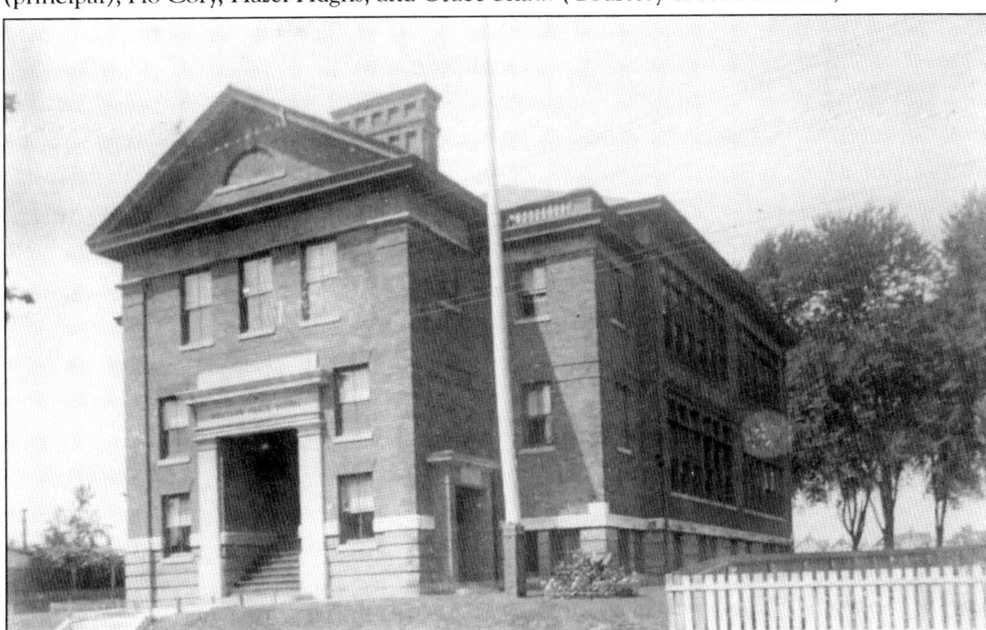

Milltown Public School, just after it was built in 1907. (Courtesy of Brian Harto.)

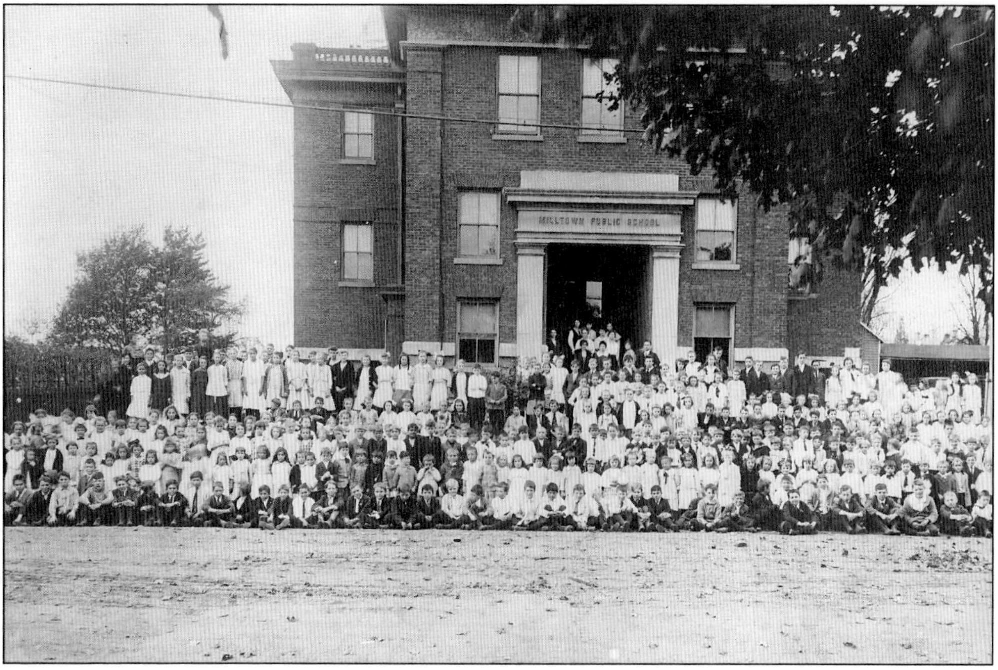

The entire student and teacher population of the Milltown Public School, *c.* 1920s. (Courtesy of Milltown Historical Society.)

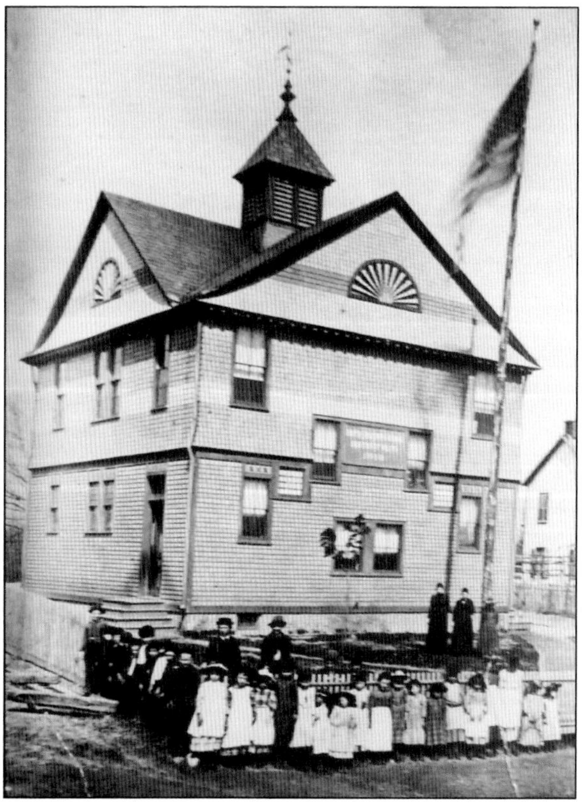

Another view of Eureka Engine Company #1 of the Milltown Fire Department, *c.* 1905. (Courtesy of Eureka Engine Company #1.)

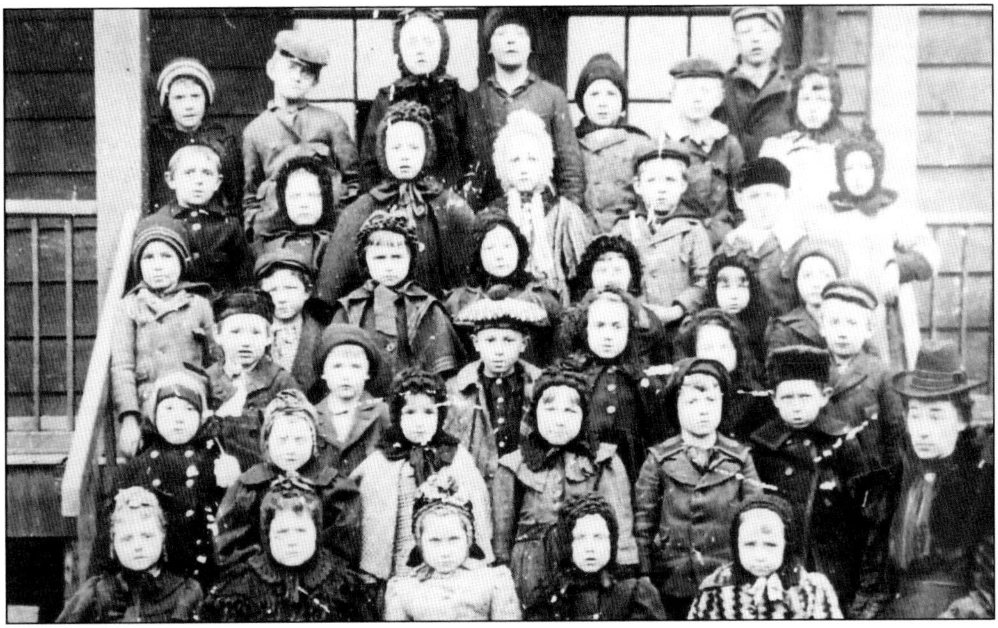

A Milltown Public School, 1897. This picture was most likely taken at one of the two North Side schools used during the era. Seen here are, from left to right: (front row) Anna Miller, Edith Kohlhepp, Amy Hamman, May Nevius, and Lil Willenbrock; (second row) Clarkson Steele, Bessie Henderson, Ethel Thompson, Martha Boessing, Harold Kuhlthau, and LeRoy Thompson; (third row) Henry Baier, Willard Thompson, Art Beecere, Leona Bauries, Mary Beatty, and Ted Baier; (fourth row) Ed Nevius, Pete Zenewich, Mary Zenewich, Delia Adams, unknown, Viola Thompson, and Herbert Schaeffer; (fifth row) Joe Crabiel, Hattie Evans, Elizabeth Lins, Anna Hoelzer, Clarence Johnson, Oscar Christ, and Magdaline Crabiel; (back row) William Evans, Tot Noyes, Sadie Noyes, Matthew Herr, William Lins, Frank Hodapp, Lou Adams, and Mena Lins. (Courtesy of Ken Selover.)

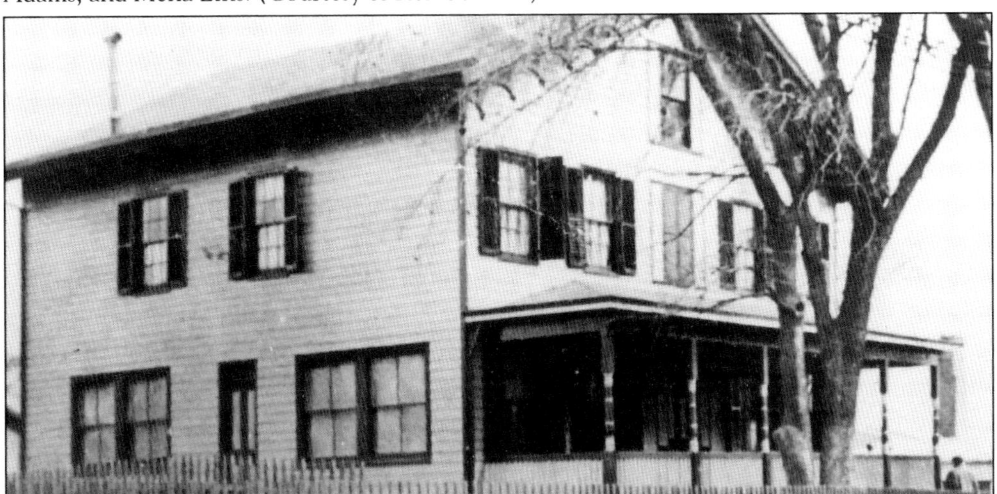

The French School, pictured in 1912, was opened by the Michelin Tire Company, and held classes from 1910 until June 1930. Classes were conducted in French four days a week, and in English one day a week. The school building stood across from the plant, on the spot now occupied by the First Fidelity Bank. (Courtesy of Rita Carina.)

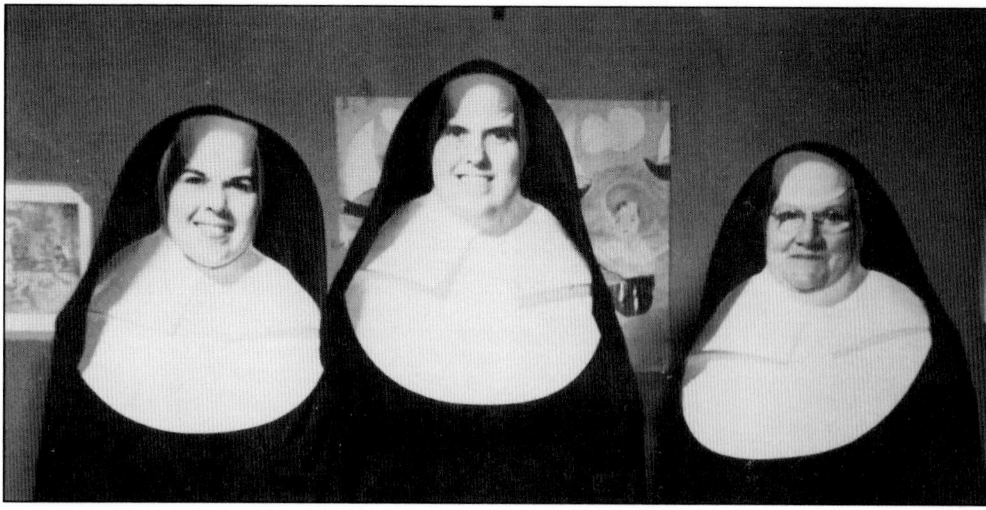

Pioneer sisters of Our Lady of Lourdes School. From left to right are Sister M. Lawrence, Sister M. Jeremiah, and Sister M. Amadeus. (Courtesy of Rita Carina.)

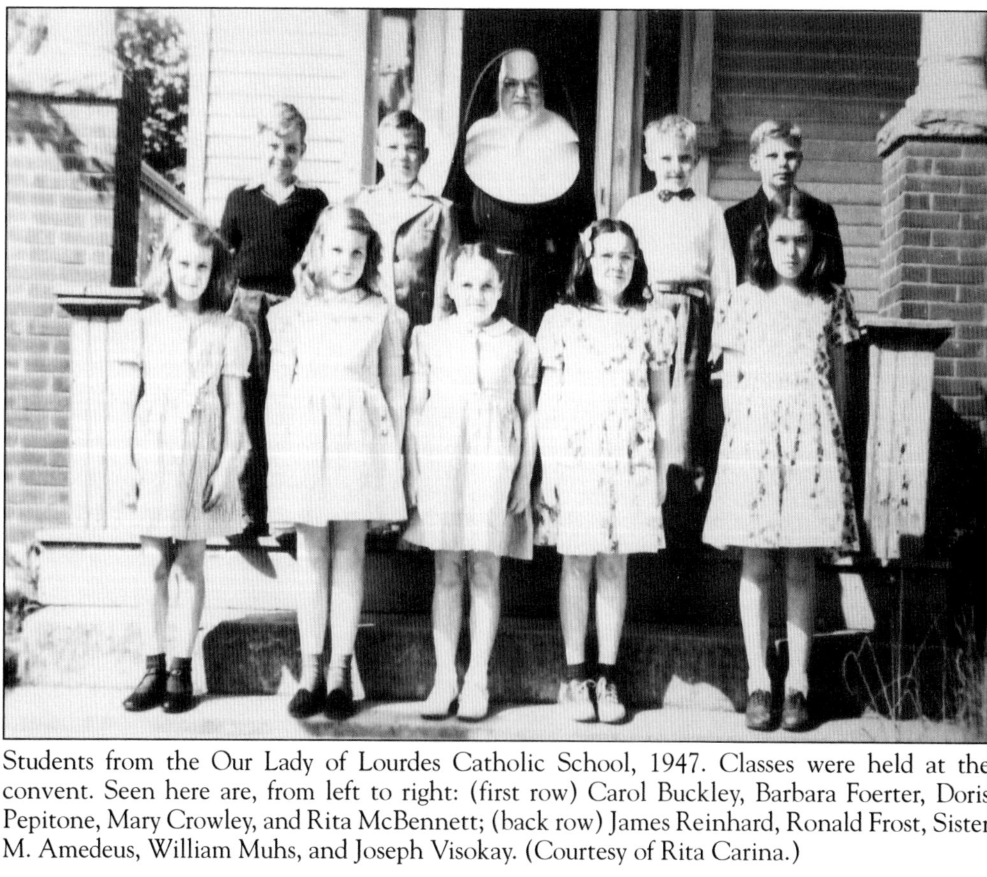

Students from the Our Lady of Lourdes Catholic School, 1947. Classes were held at the convent. Seen here are, from left to right: (first row) Carol Buckley, Barbara Foerter, Doris Pepitone, Mary Crowley, and Rita McBennett; (back row) James Reinhard, Ronald Frost, Sister M. Amedeus, William Muhs, and Joseph Visokay. (Courtesy of Rita Carina.)

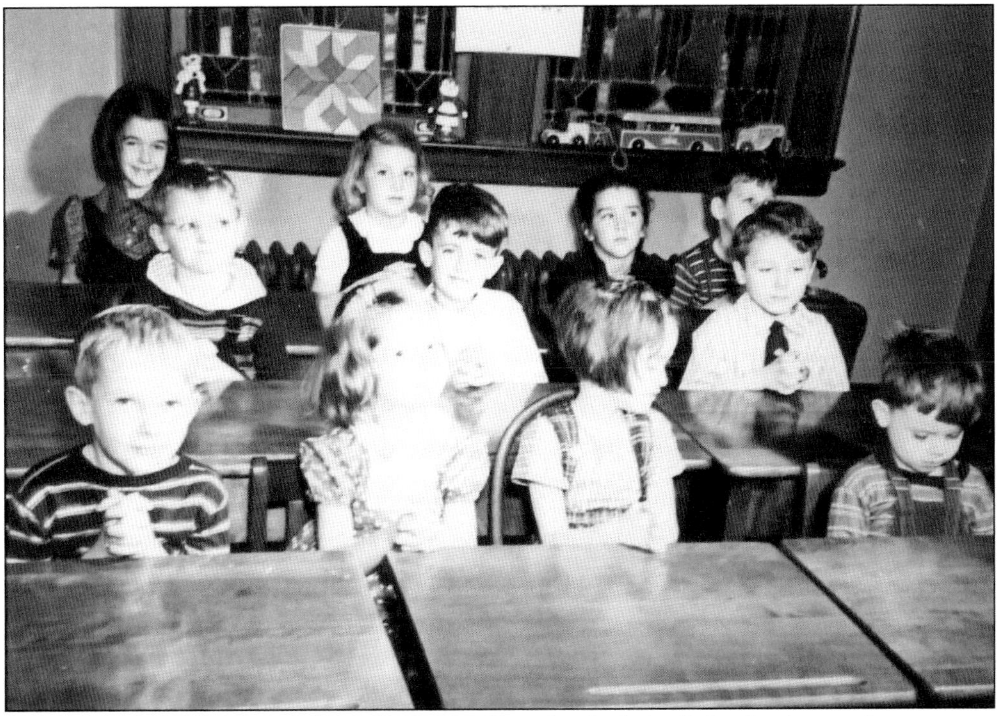

Kindergarten and the first grade of Our Lady of Lourdes Catholic School, taken at the rectory in October 1943. Pictured here are, from left to right: (front row) William Muhs, Eleanor Pollard, Margaret McBennett, and William Rooney; (middle row) Paul Lyons, John McBennett, and Thomas Mulhern; (back row) Rita McBennett, Barbara Foerter, Mary Crowley, and James Reinhard. (Courtesy of Rita Carina.)

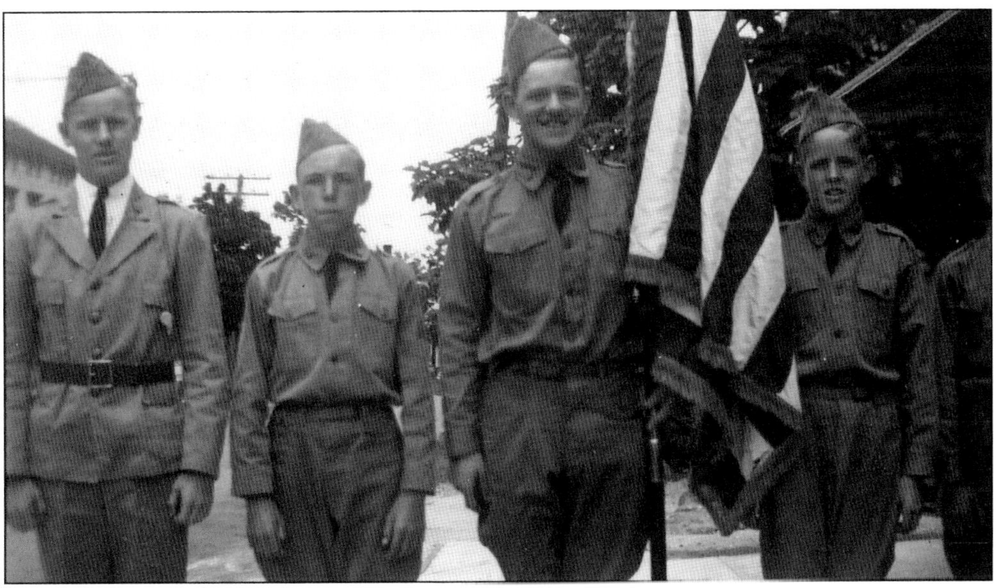

The Columbus Cadets, a Catholic youth group, in 1938. Seen here are, from left to right, Arthur J. Schwendeman II, Mickey Hoffman, George Krause (holding flag), and David J. Schwendeman. (Courtesy of the Schwendeman family.)

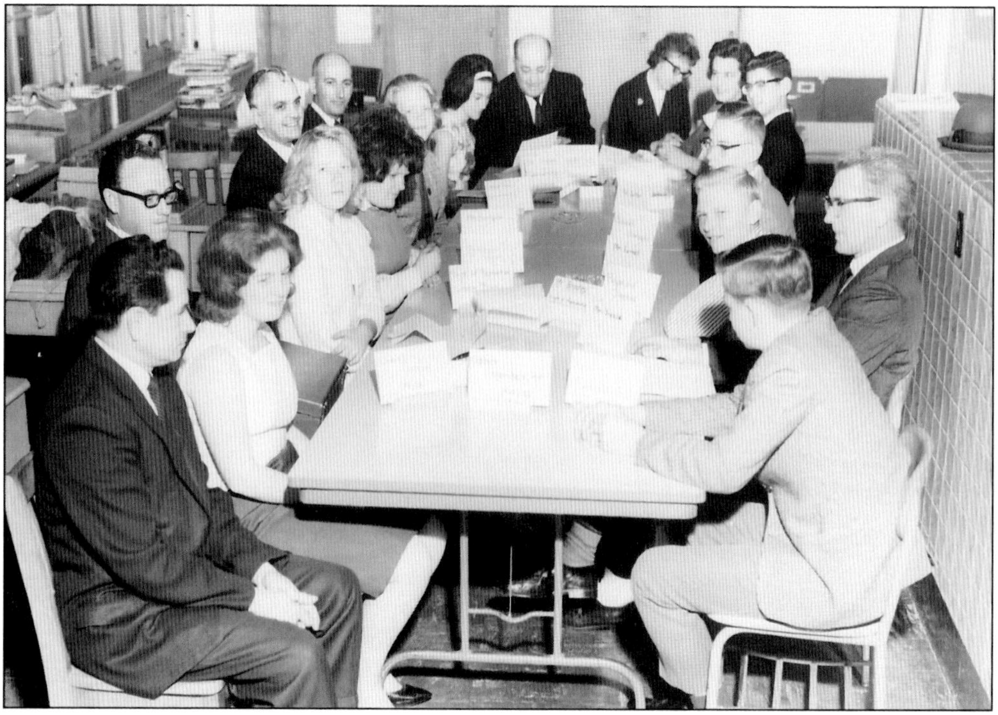

Youth in government, 1967. Seen here are, beginning in the lower left corner, Mayor John Vandeputte, Diane Cushing, Edward Bradley, Linda Riva, Allison ?, unknown, Councilman Jack Georgiana, Councilman Don Astor, unknown, unknown, Police Chief Bill Riha, unknown, Thelma Pondl, unknown, Robert Shalayda, Raymond Rahon, Mr. Breese, and Councilman Robert C. Potte. (Courtesy of Edward V. Vetter Sr.)

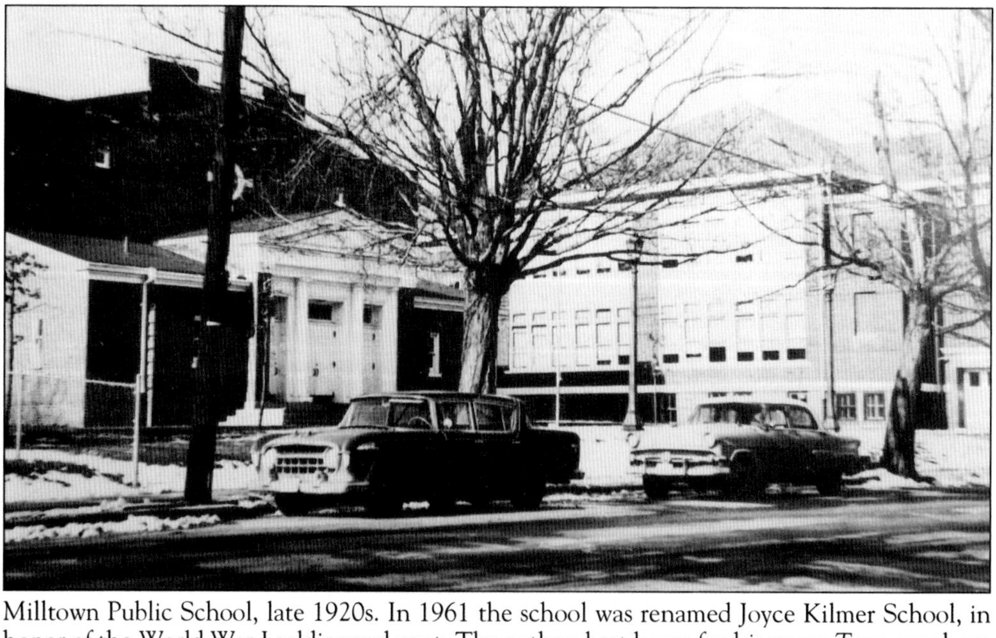

Milltown Public School, late 1920s. In 1961 the school was renamed Joyce Kilmer School, in honor of the World War I soldier and poet. The author, best know for his poem *Trees*, was born in nearby New Brunswick. (Courtesy of Ken Selover.)

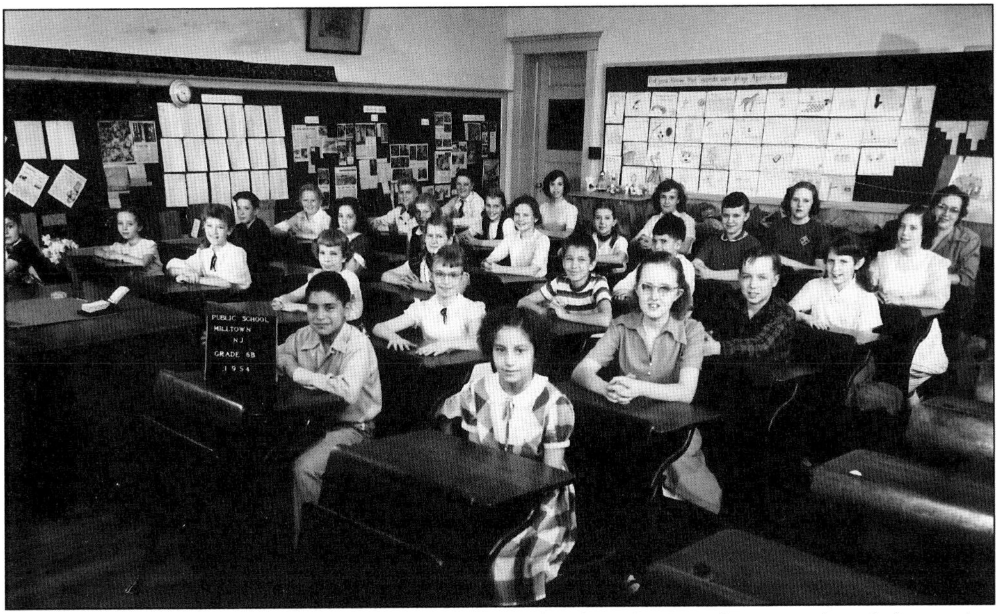

Mrs. Baird's sixth grade class, at Milltown Public School, 1954. Seen here are, from left to right: (front row) Joyce Simko, Lynn Harrison, James Kohlhepp, Jerilyn Burke, Laura Grover, and Mrs. Baird; (second row) Carl Subila, Lynda Crabiel, Jeffrey Lins, Jack Mula, Carolee Gebhardt, and Maryann Allen; (third row) Joanne Junker, Maryann Takas, Patty Keller, Judy Miller, and Beverly Betzler; (fourth row) Diane Borieza, Diane Roma, Marilyn Auer, Sharon Gatewood, and Diane Decker; (back row) David Masters, Betty Ann Crawford, Edward Goff, Glen Lane, Fred Broxmeyer, and Fred Allen. (Courtesy of Lynda Crabiel Cummings.)

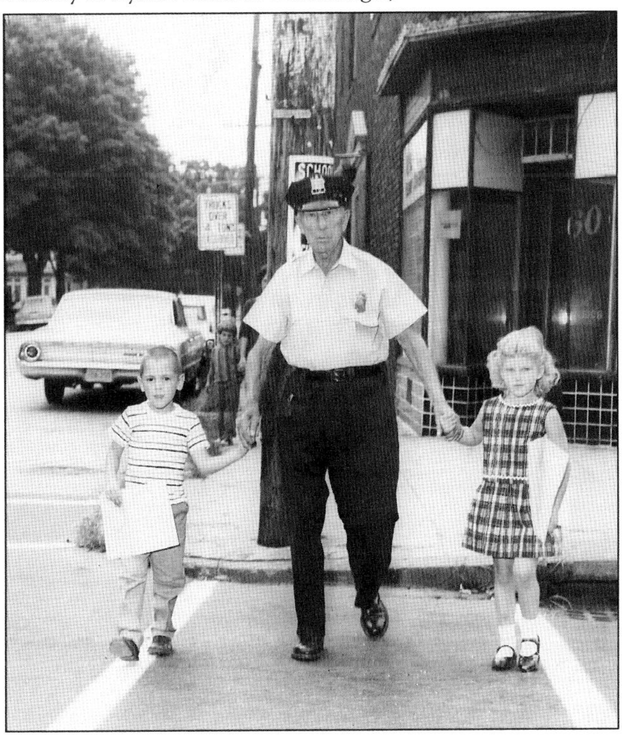

Crossing guard Nicholas Young, with Frank Torok and Monica Liebniewski, at the corner of West Church and South Main Streets, 1965. (Courtesy of Edward V. Vetter Sr.)

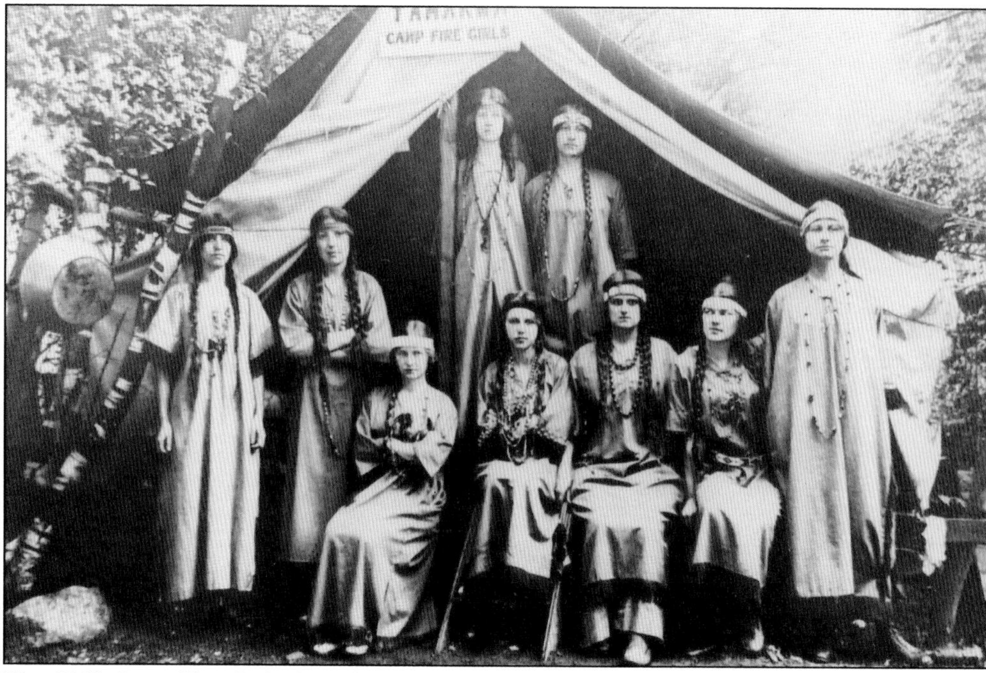

The 1913 Camp Fire Girls. Seen here are, from left to right: (front row) Emma Kaiser Roeser, Alma Kuhlthau Booream, Barbara Heyl Dorn, Blanche Cremming, Myra Brown Cremming, Edith Kohlhepp Rickhardt, and Mamie Glock; (back row) Vi Thompson Crabiel and Helen Glock Crabiel. (Courtesy of Rita Carina.)

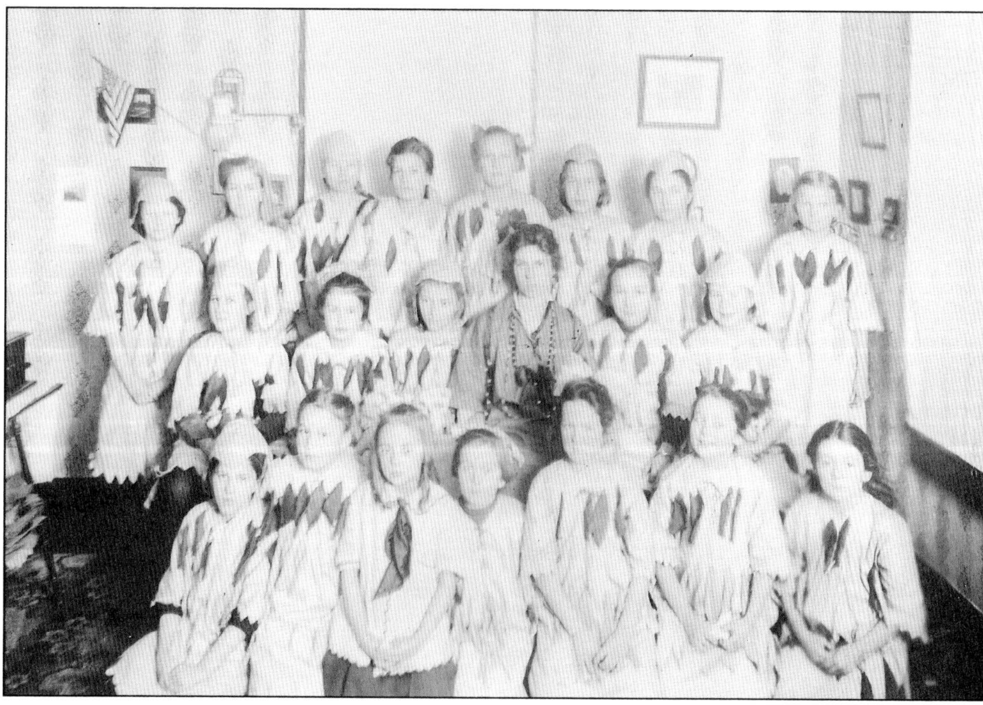

Camp Fire Girls, around 1917–18. In the upper right corner is Grace Crawford Laterre. Seated to the left of the leader is Edna Reeves. (Courtesy of Milltown Historical Society.)

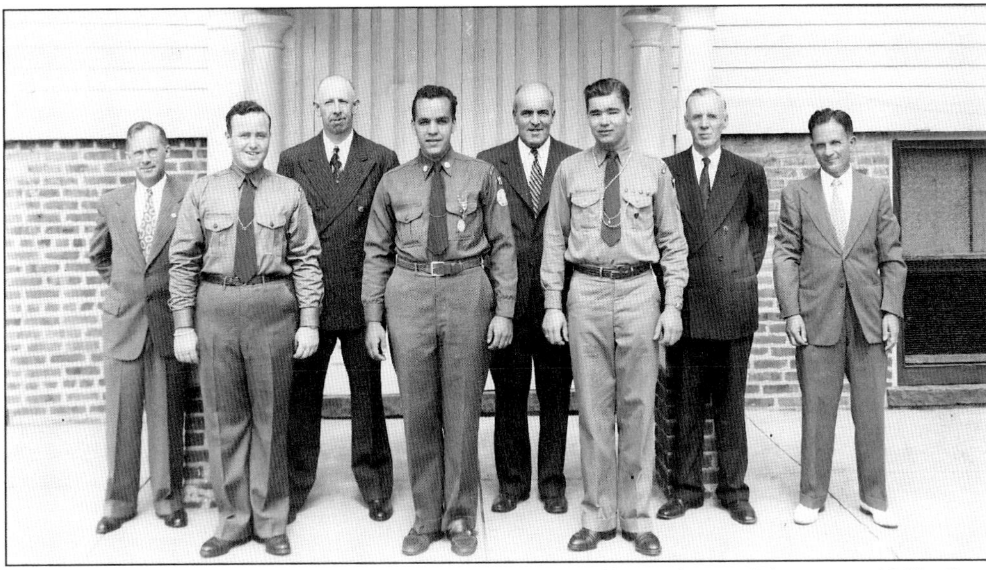

Boy Scout leaders and committee, in front of Fellowship Hall on Lakewood Avenue, *c.* 1940s. Seen here are, from left to right: (front row) Charles Betzler, Harold Fealey, and Donald Whitehead; (back row) Harry Barbehenn, Fred Miller, Robert Cleland, Fred Grutter, and Harry Hartman.

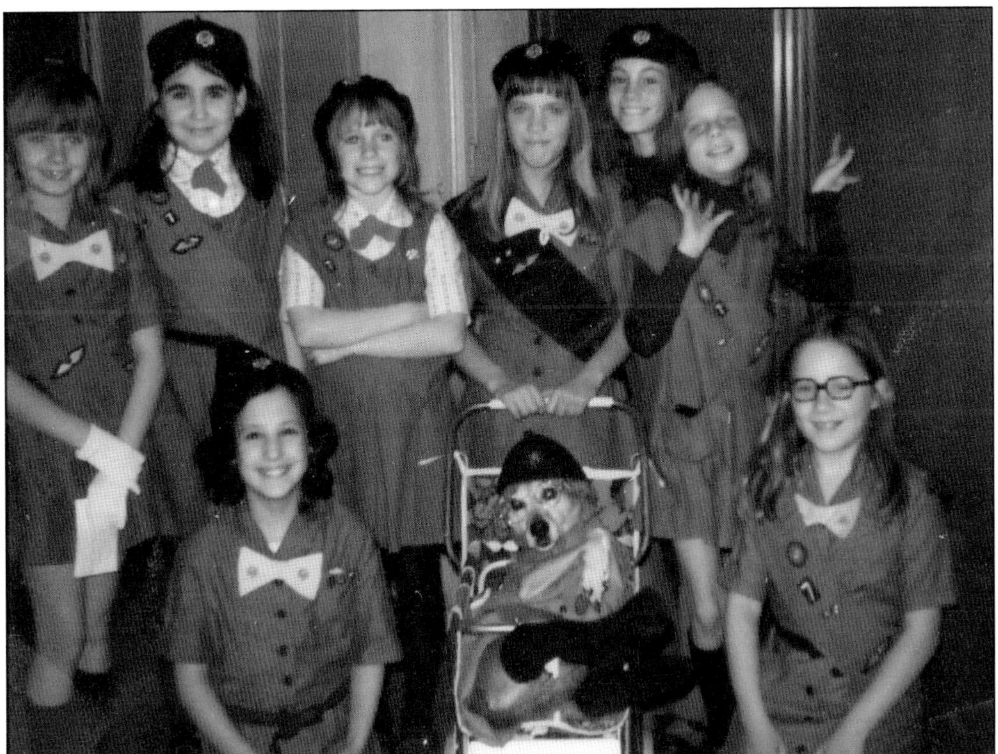

Girl Scouts, 1975. Seen here are, from left to right: (front row) Stephanie Bruno, "Sandy," and Lisa Bradley; (back row) Kym Zsamba, Kelly Lynch, Holly Snell, Margie Varga, Michelle Bennet, and Paulette Crabiel. (Courtesy of Paulette Crabiel Wahler.)

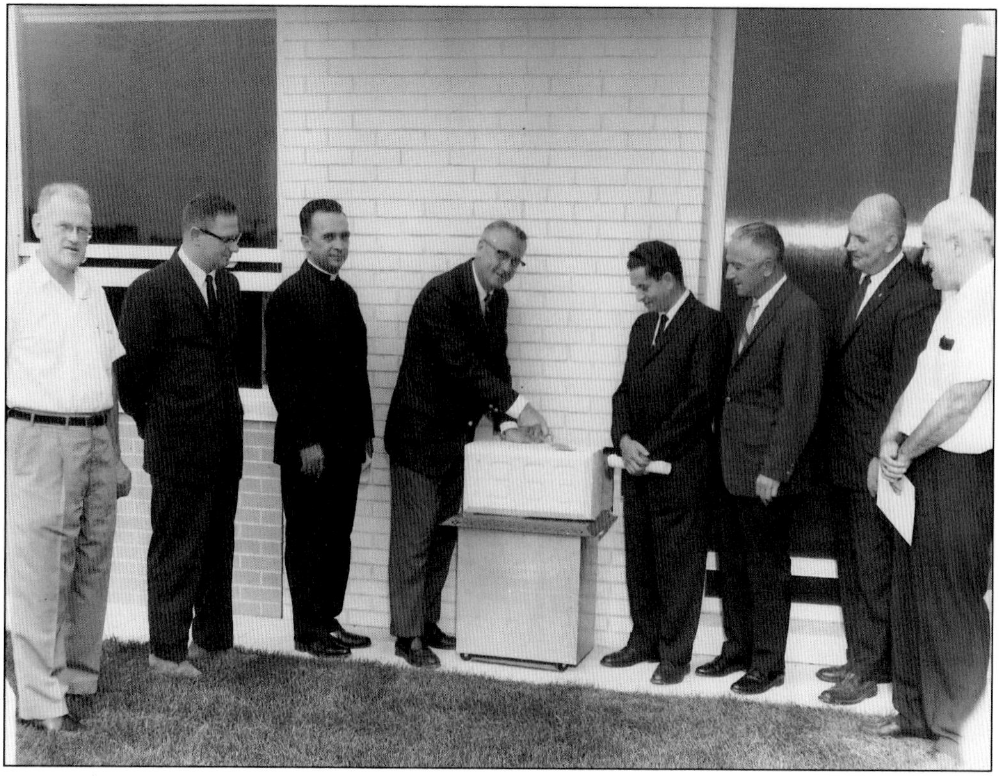

Laying the cornerstone for the Parkview School in 1963. Pictured here are, from left to right, Richard Potter, Ken Steeber Sr., Reverend Gerhart, Mayor John Vandeputte, Superintendent Ed Rickards, unknown, and unknown, and Robert Cleland. (Courtesy of Edward V. Vetter Sr.)

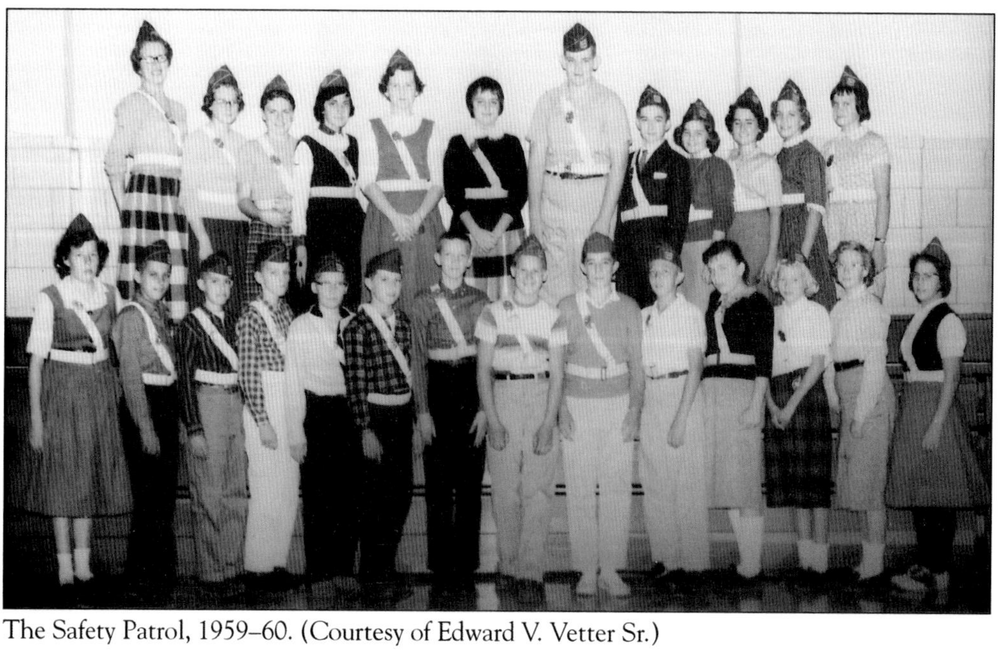

The Safety Patrol, 1959–60. (Courtesy of Edward V. Vetter Sr.)

Four

No Place Like Home

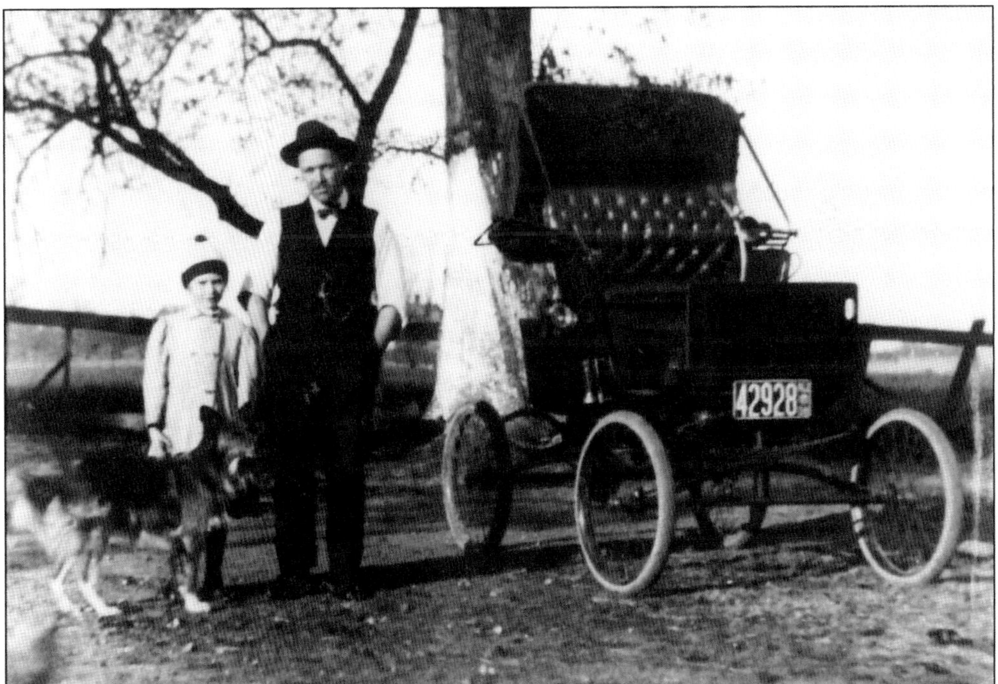

Miss Evelyn Lindstrom and her father, Oscar F., at their farm in 1908, with one of Milltown's first automobiles. The Lindstrom farm was located off Clay Street. Their house still stands on Lindstrom Court. (Courtesy of the estate of Evelyn Lindstrom.)

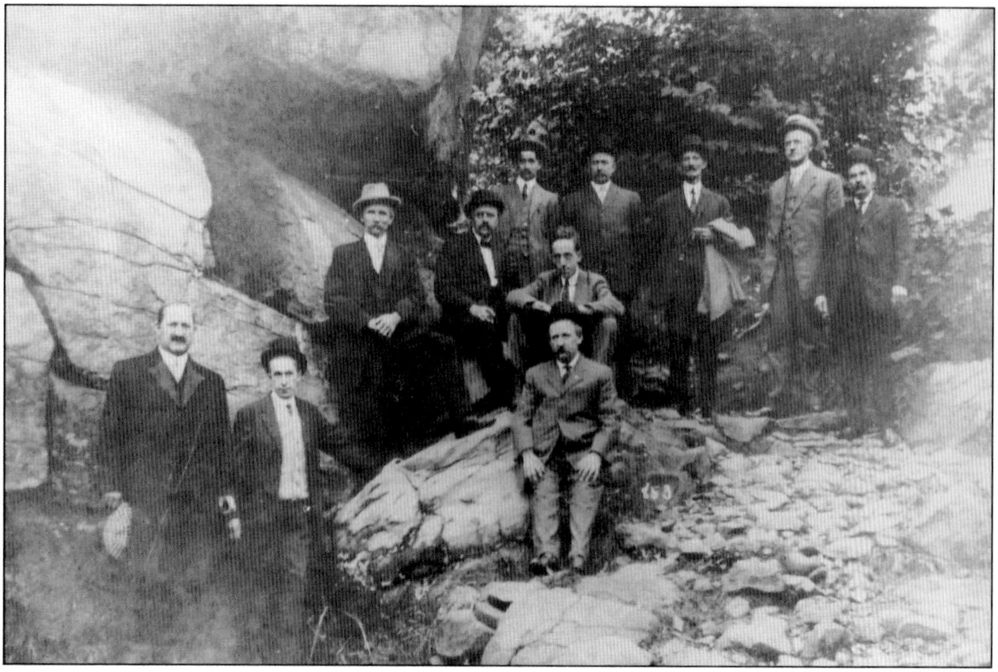

These Milltown men took a road trip to Devil's Den at Gettysburg, Pennsylvania, in the early 1920s. Seen here are, from left to right: (front row) C.W. Kuhlthau, William Junker, and Charles Junker Sr.; (middle row) William Heyl, Peter Jensen, and Cliff Waddington; (back row) Milton Brindle, Henry Kuhlthau, John Van Liew Booream, William Kuhlthau, and Charles Bauries. (Courtesy of Rita Carina.)

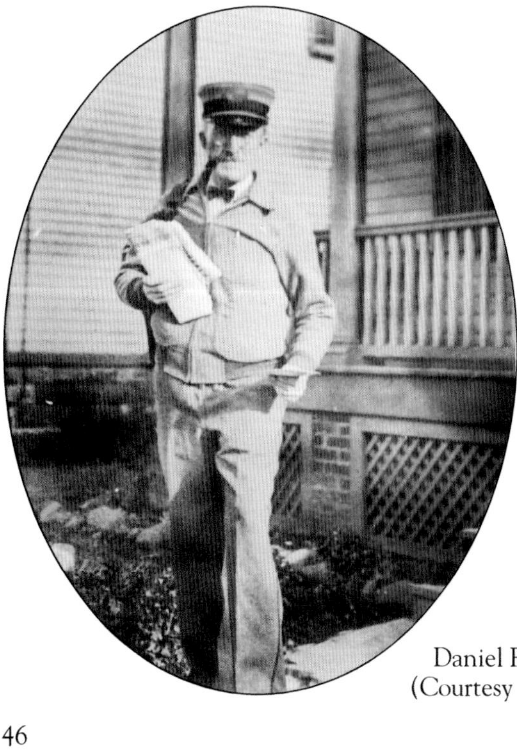

Daniel Reuse delivers mail on South Street, in 1935. (Courtesy of Rene Reuse.)

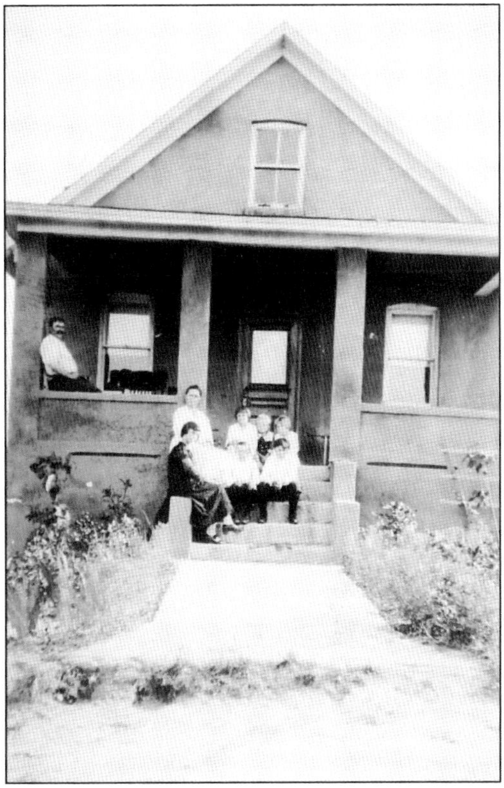

The Kinelski family, on the porch of their home at 294 Washington Avenue, in 1924. Sitting on the porch are: Francis (father); Mary (mother), on the top step; and children Mary, Frank, and Francis. On the bottom steps are Mary Gashinski (cousin), Stanley Kinelski, and Michael Kinelski. (Courtesy of Frank Kinelski.)

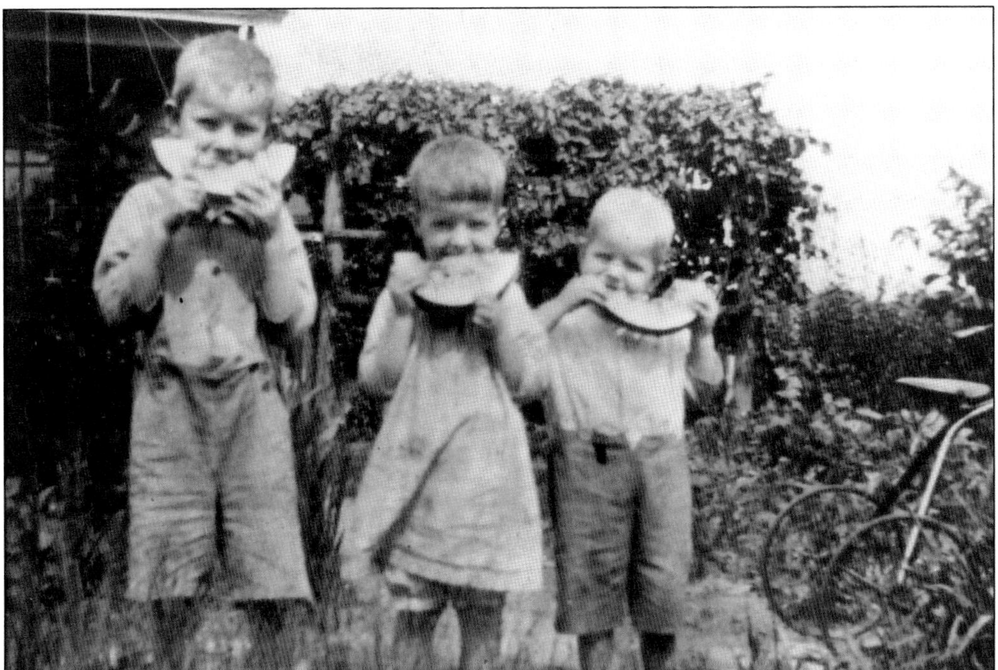

Arthur J. Schwendeman II, Helen Schwendeman, and David J. Schwendeman, eating watermelon at 119 South Main Street, in 1927. (Courtesy of the Schwendeman family.)

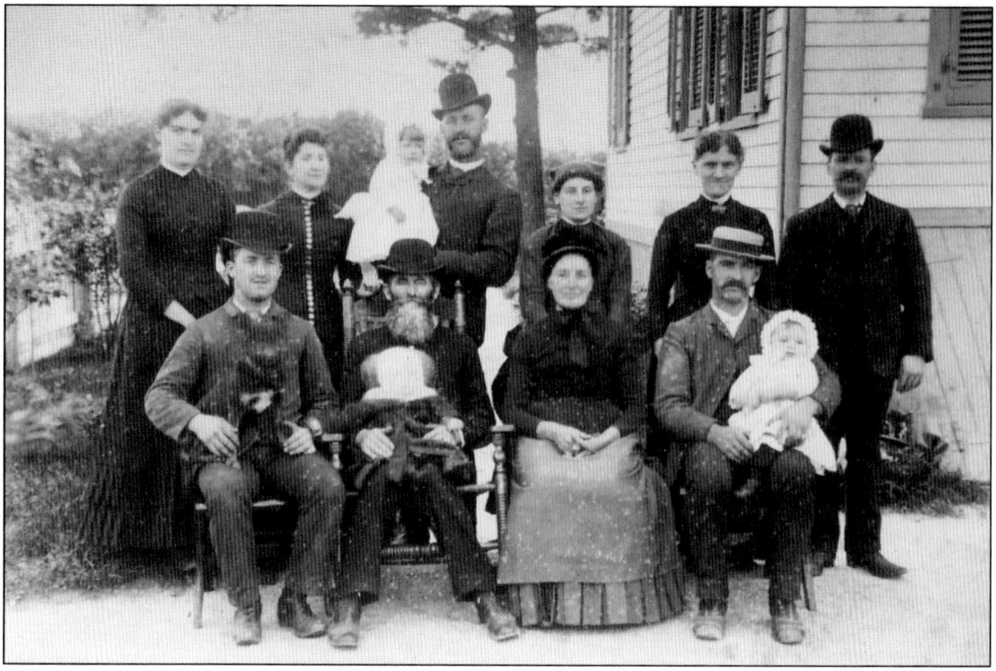

The Kuhlthau family in the 1880s. Pictured here are, from left to right: (front row) Conrad, Phillip (holding Catherine), Mabel Snediker Huff, and Phillip Jr. (holding Aubrey);.(back row) Catherine Snediker, Ameila, John (holding Mae), Ella Mamie, and Henry Kohlhepp. (Courtesy of Milltown Historical Society.)

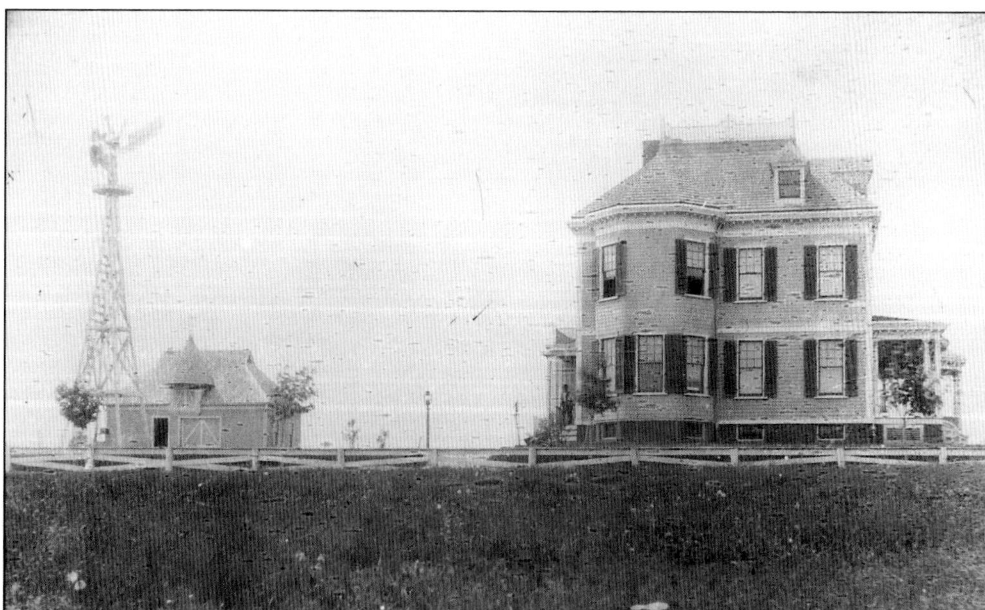

Dr. Ferdinand Riva set up practice in Milltown in 1888, and built this house, located at 170 North Main Street. It is currently the Crabiel Home for Funerals. The windmill is gone, but the carriage house remains. Riva Avenue is named for Dr. Riva. (Courtesy of Milltown Historical Society.)

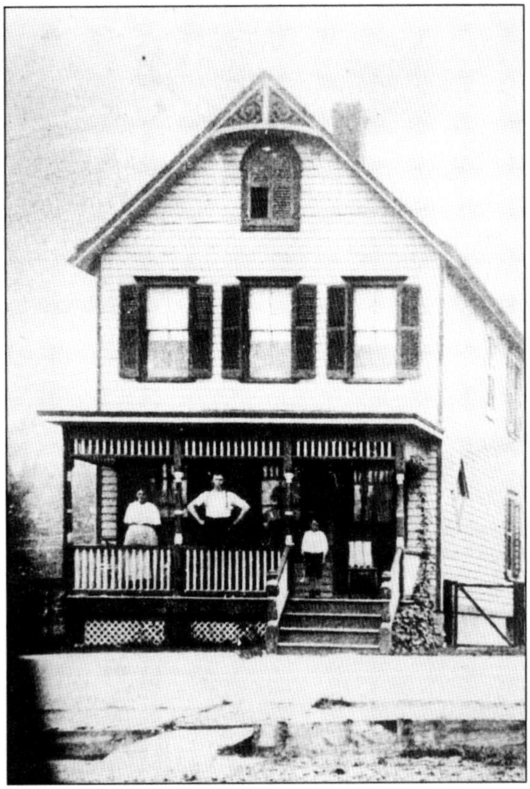

The Fine family residence on South Main Street, opposite Kuhlthau Avenue, 1910. (Courtesy of Irma Lown.)

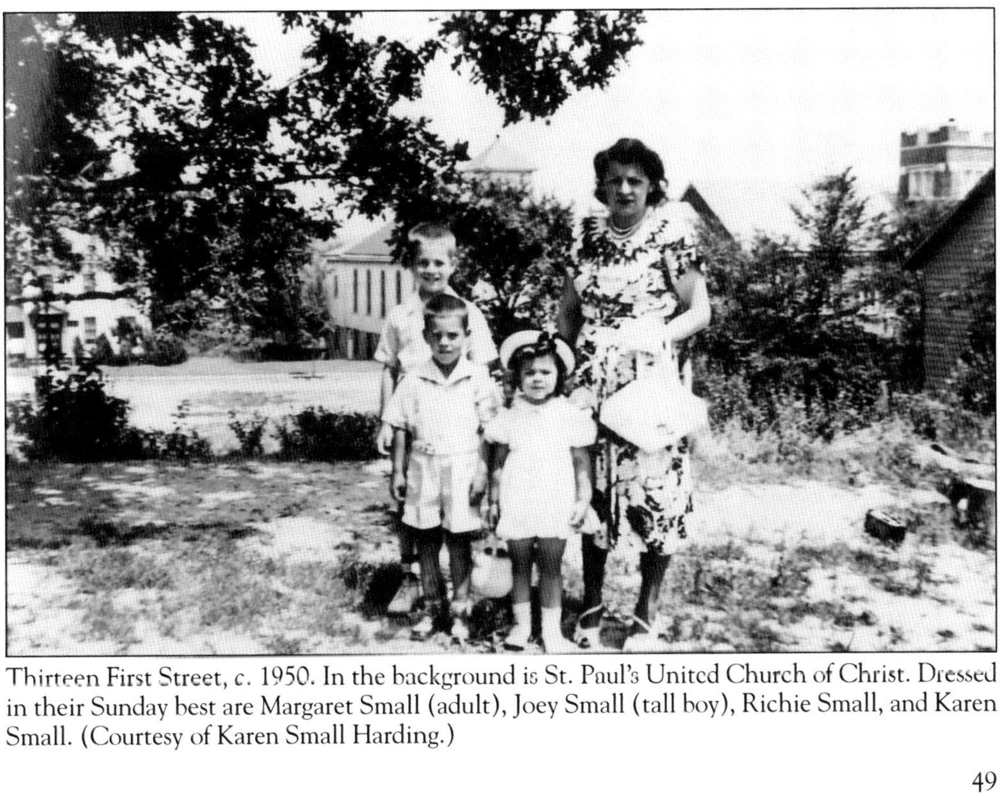

Thirteen First Street, c. 1950. In the background is St. Paul's United Church of Christ. Dressed in their Sunday best are Margaret Small (adult), Joey Small (tall boy), Richie Small, and Karen Small. (Courtesy of Karen Small Harding.)

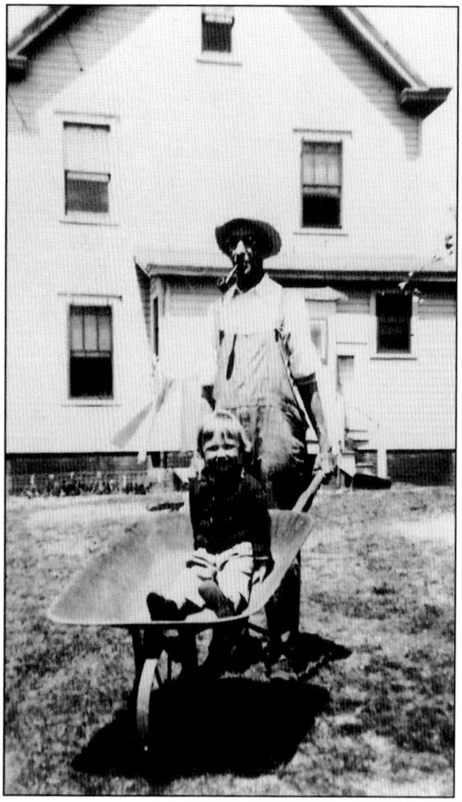

Hartvig Thompson and grandson George H. Stilwell Jr., in the yard of 86 Kuhlthau Avenue, c. 1945. (Courtesy of George H. Stilwell Jr.)

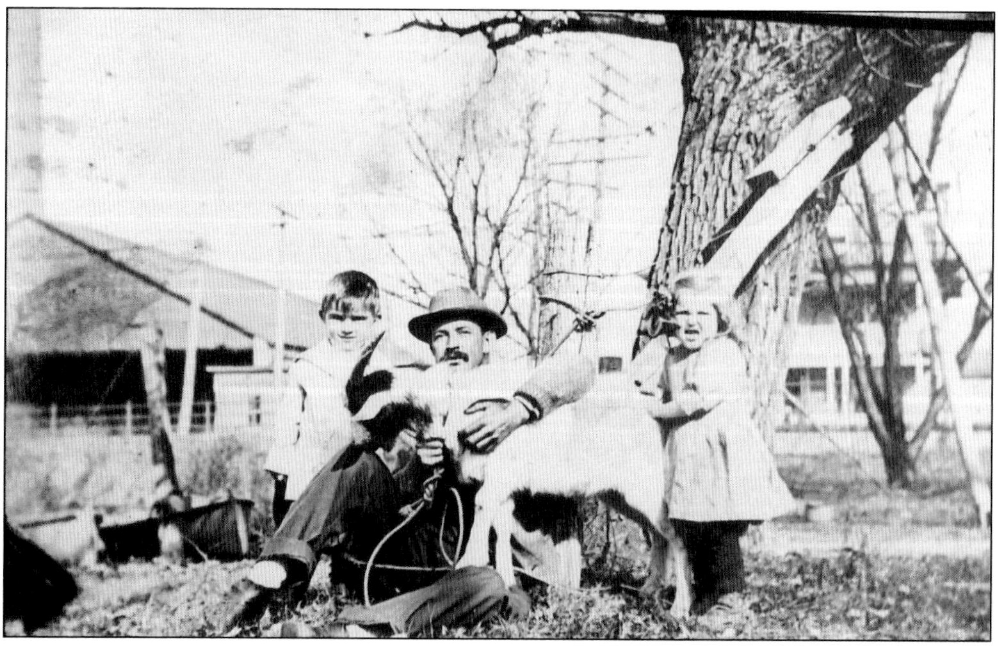

Charles Denhard, with son Ferdinand and niece Winifred Majors, and their goat, near the car barn, c. 1920s. (Courtesy of Hazel Jacobsen Denhard.)

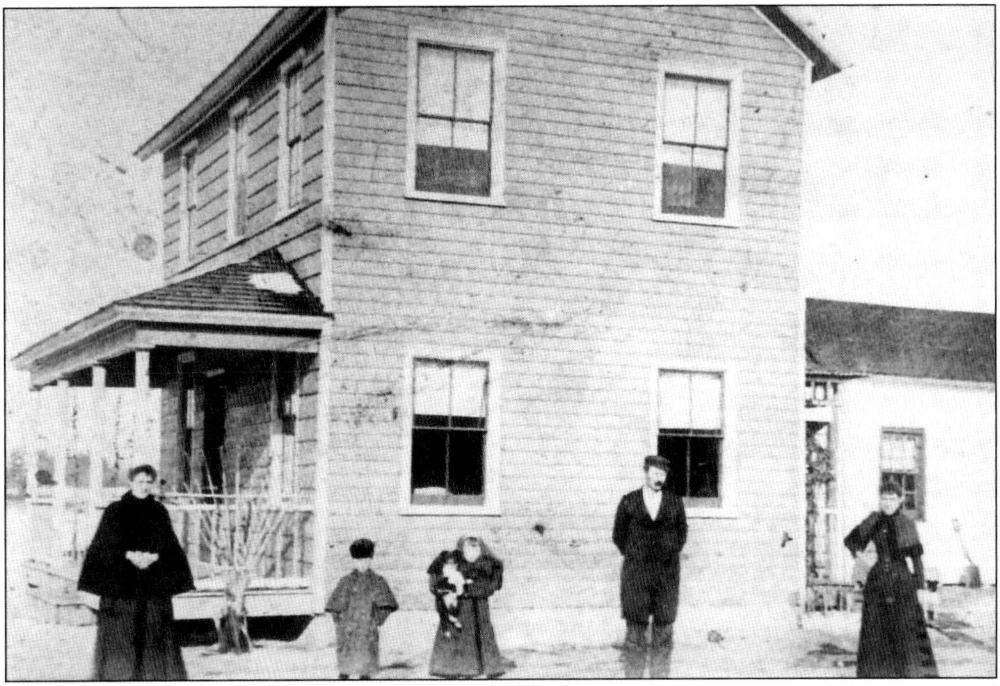

Carrie Van Duersen Booream Johnson, Howard Booream, Edna Booream, Will Booream, and Sarah Van Duersen. (Courtesy of Irma Lown.)

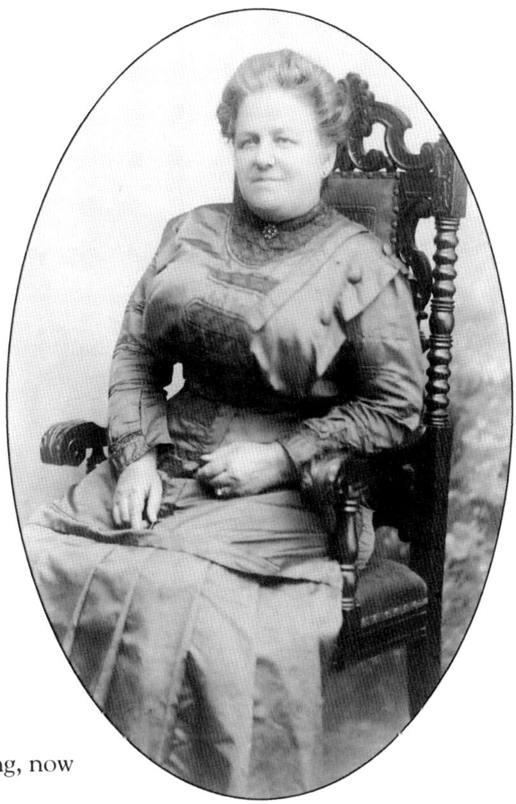

Marguerite Sayre, owner of Sayre's Hotel Marguerite on Main Street and Washington Avenue, with her husband Elmer. The building, now the Golden Lion Inn, was built in 1907.

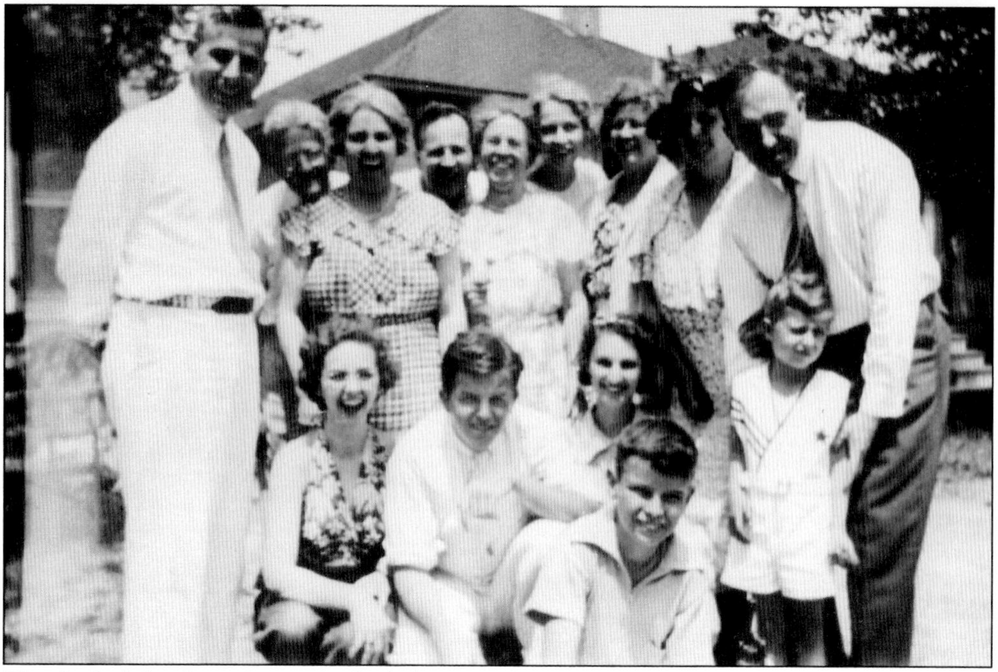

The Crabiel family, at Irving Crabiel's home, July 4, 1935. Seen here are, left to right: (front row) Charles D. Crabiel (kneeling), Marjorie Snedeker, J. Edward Crabiel, Doris Young, and David B. Crabiel; (back row) Charles B. Crabiel, Lester and Maugerite Crabiel Snedeker, Irving Crabiel, Elsie Crabiel, Beulah Lindstrom Crabiel, Viola Thompson Crabiel, Helen Glock Crabiel, and Joseph M. Crabiel Jr. (Courtesy of Paulette Wahler Crabiel.)

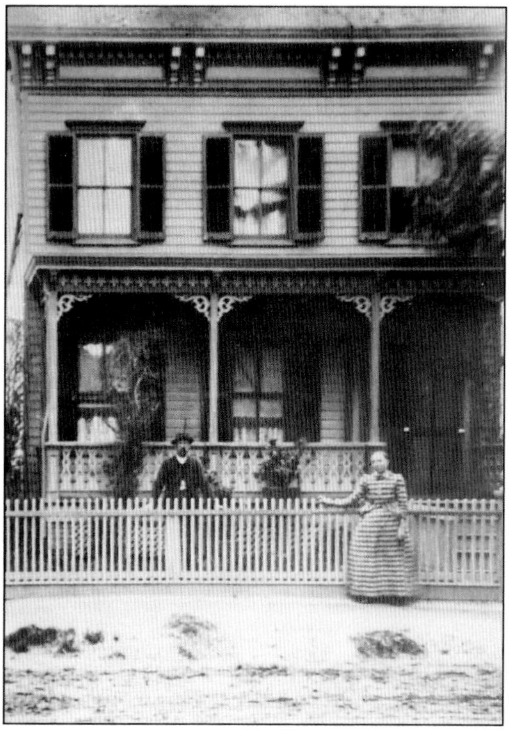

Mr. and Mrs. Ernest Schoppe, at their home at 46 North Main Street, *c.* 1900s. (Courtesy of Irma Lown.)

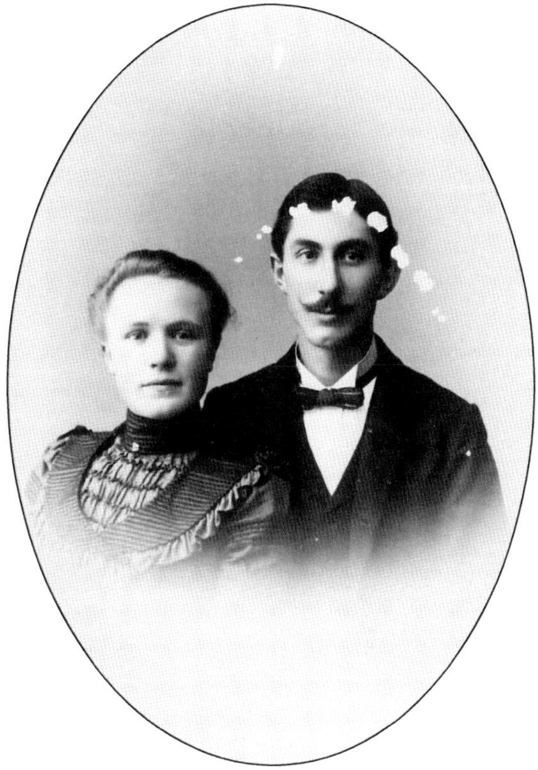

Elizabeth and Nick Young, *c.* early 1900s. (Courtesy of Milltown Historical Society.)

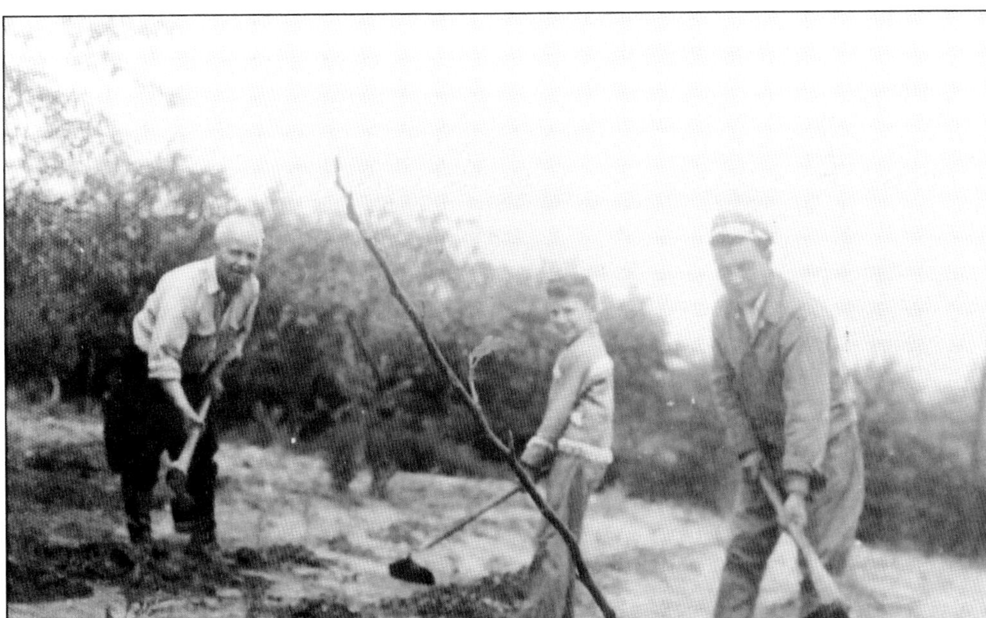

Ferdinand Manfredi, the oldest of thirteen, with his son Rosario (Roy), working their field with Uncle Umberto Gangi at their "summer home." This land became 72–76 JFK Drive and 2–6 William Street. (Courtesy of the Manfredi family.)

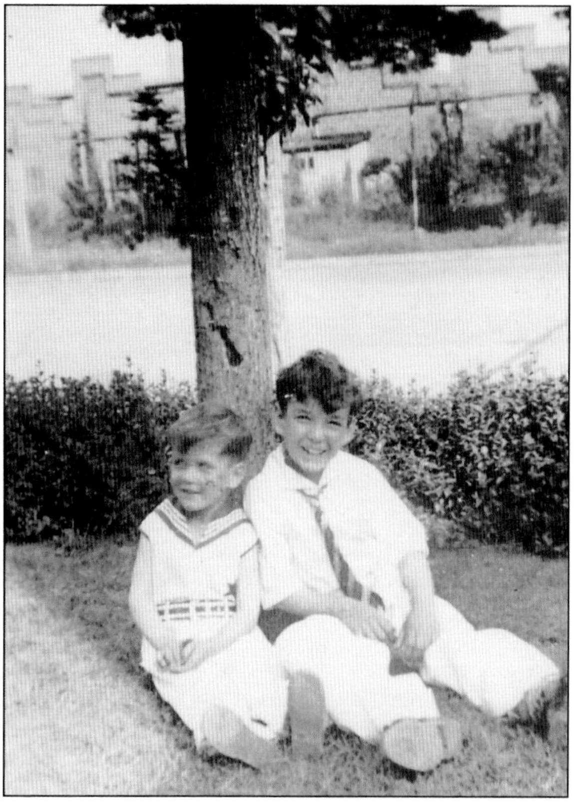

Edward and John Harto, outside their home at 47 Ford Avenue, *c.* 1936. (Courtesy of Edward Harto.)

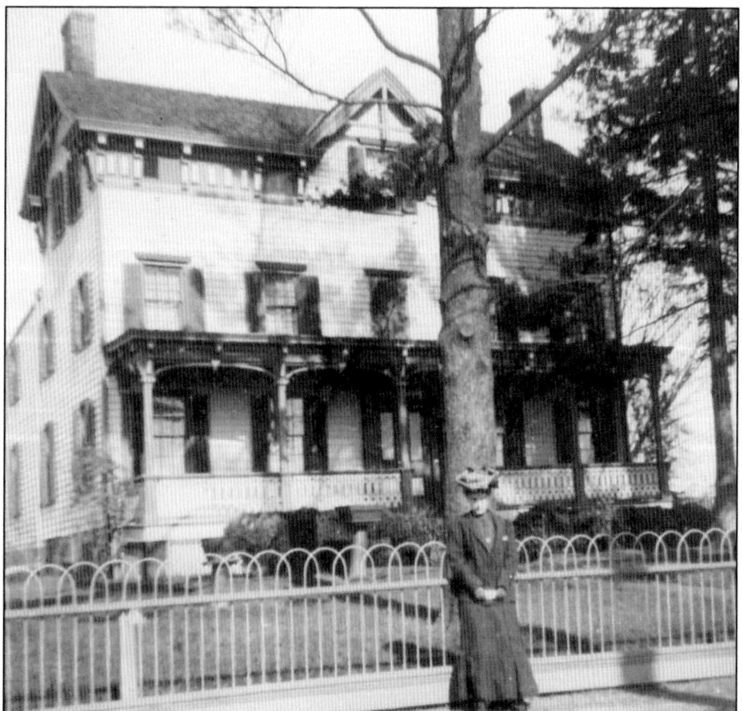

The Dennis Vanderbilt House, at 311 North Main Street, *c.* 1900s. (Courtesy of C. Harrison Hill.)

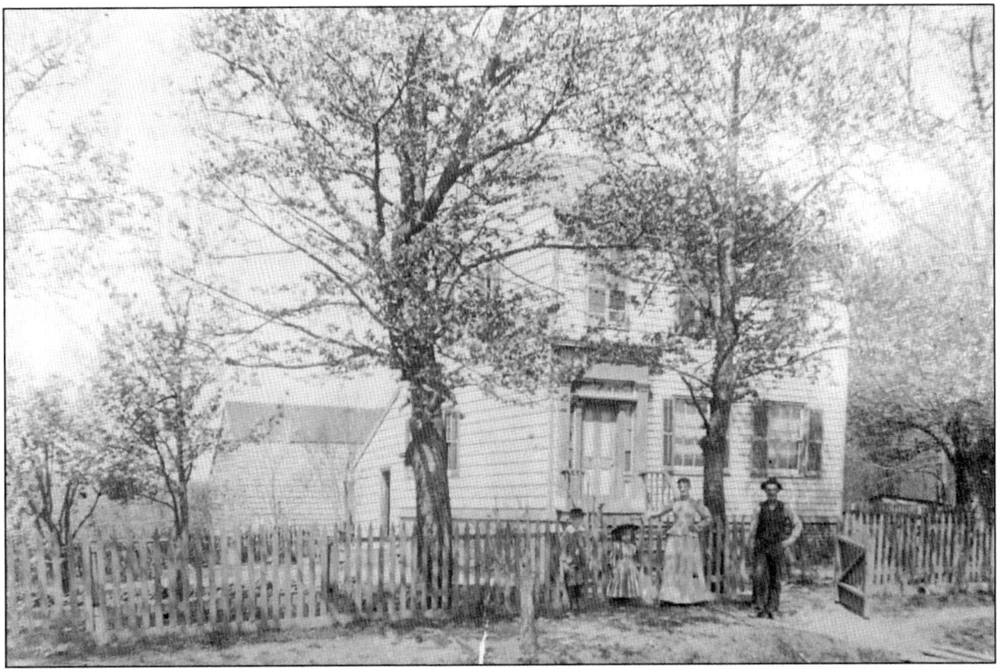

The residence of Mr. and Mrs. Robert A. Harkins, 334 North Main Street, 1897. The house was built between 1840 and 1850. Pictured here are, from left to right, twelve-year-old Oscar B. Harkins, eight-year-old Harriet A. Harkins, Mrs. Robert A. Harkins, and "Uncle Ben" Thompson. (Courtesy of C. Harrison Hill.)

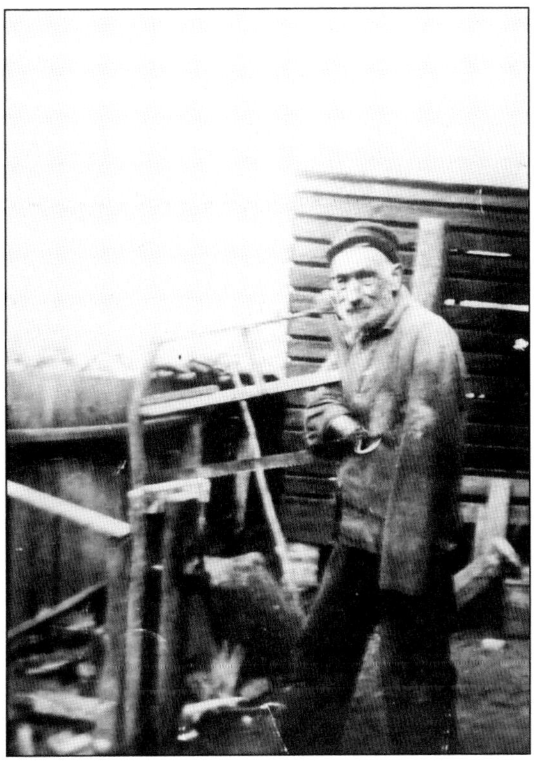

"Captain" John Fuchs lost both his arms in an accident at the Meyer Rubber Company. In this picture, he is seen sawing firewood. He was also an avid fisherman. His ability to manage with crude artificial arms made him a local celebrity. (Courtesy of Irma Lown.)

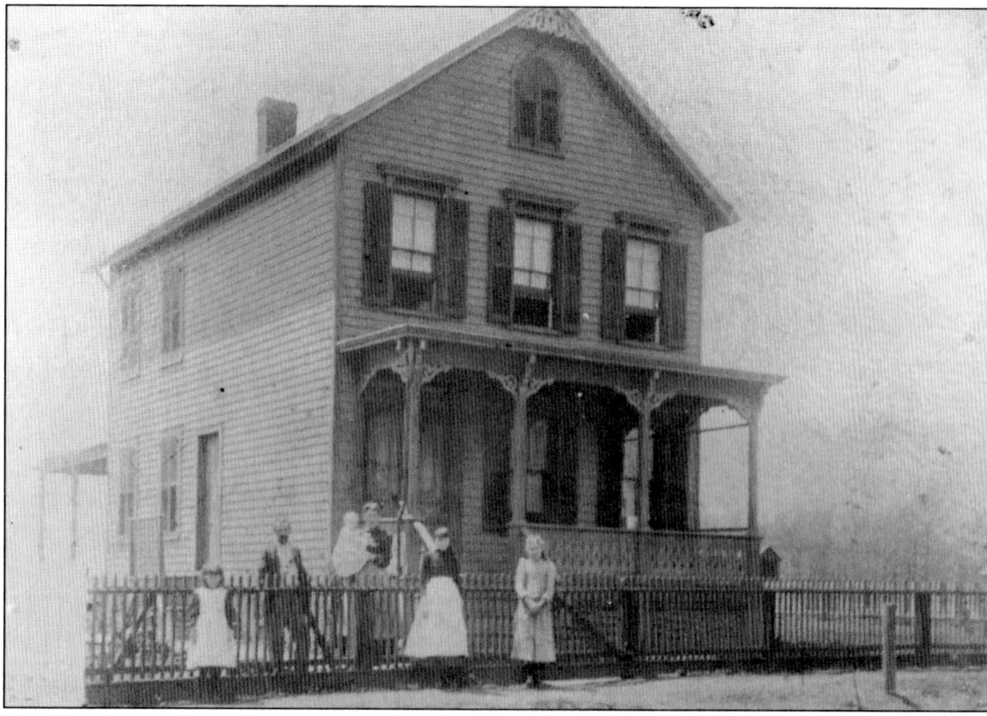

The Henderson family home, at 38 Clay Street, 1893. (Courtesy of Irma Lown.)

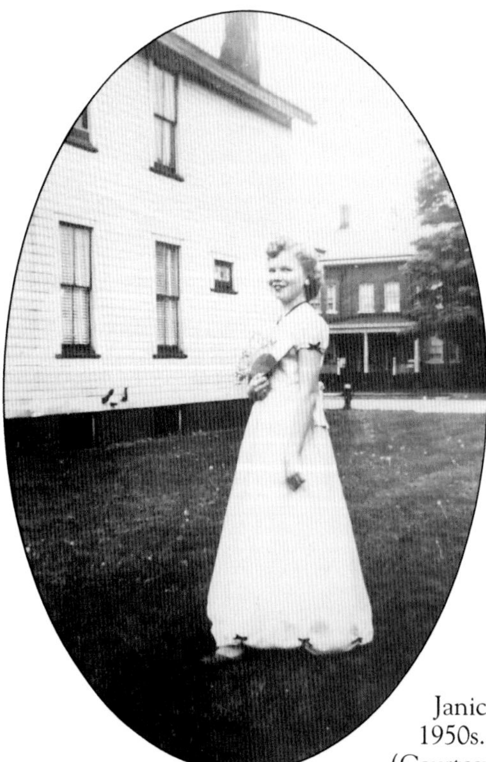

Janice Peterson Giles on her wedding day, in the 1950s. The picture was taken on Ford Avenue. (Courtesy of Ron Giles.)

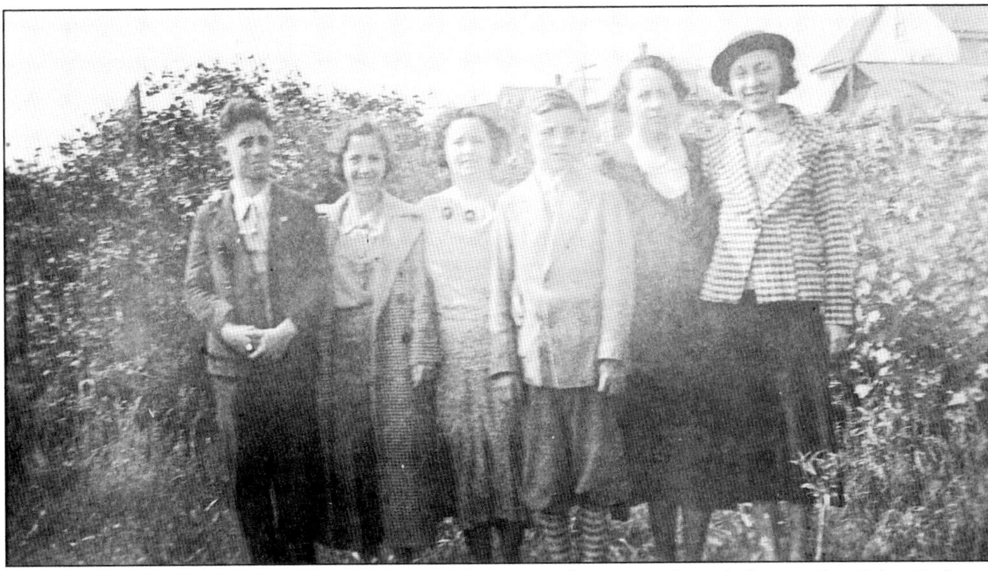

The Reuse family, at 78 South Street, c. 1930s. Seen here are, from left to right, John Poliero, Frances Poliero, Marie Poliero, Rene Reuse, Marcella Reuse, and Yvonne Reuse. (Courtesy of Helen Barus Moscar.)

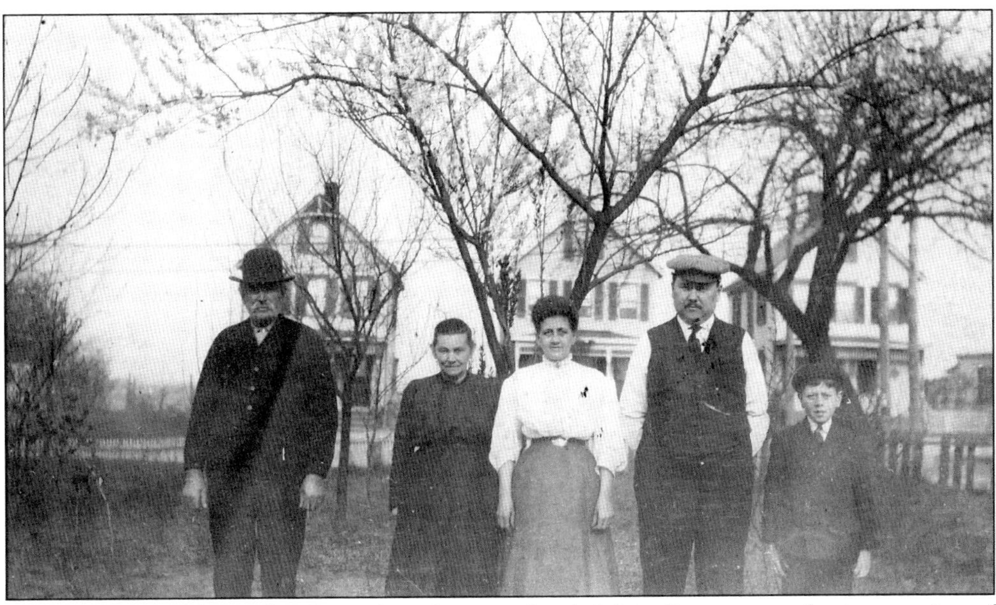

The William Kuhlthau family, at their farm on South Main Street, near the intersection of present-day Kuhlthau Avenue and South Main Street. Seen here are, from left to right, William Kuhlthau, Sara Doll Kuhlthau, Josephine Zimmerman Kuhlthau, William Kuhlthau Jr., and Russell William Kuhlthau. (Courtesy of Joan Herbert Whitman.)

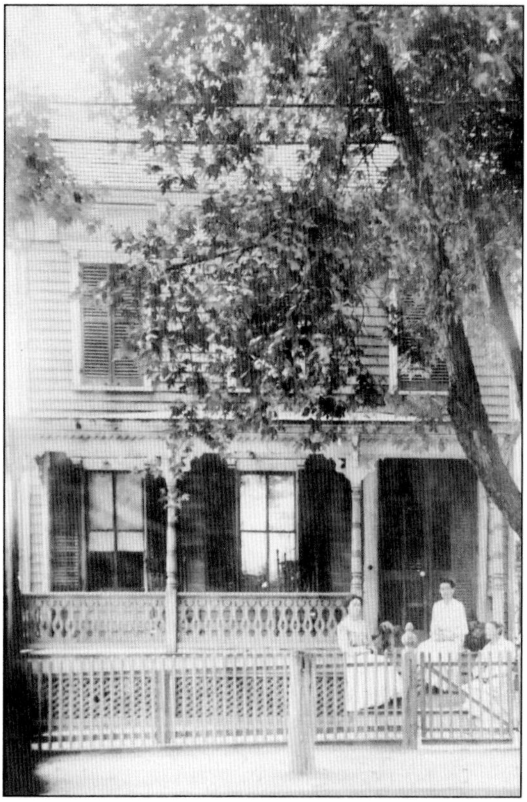

The Hofer homestead, at North Main Street, around the turn of the century. This house is located on the north side of Hanna's Florist. Pictured here are, from left to right, Hatie Hofer Lown, Kate Haefner, and Charlotte Hofer. (Courtesy of Irma Lown.)

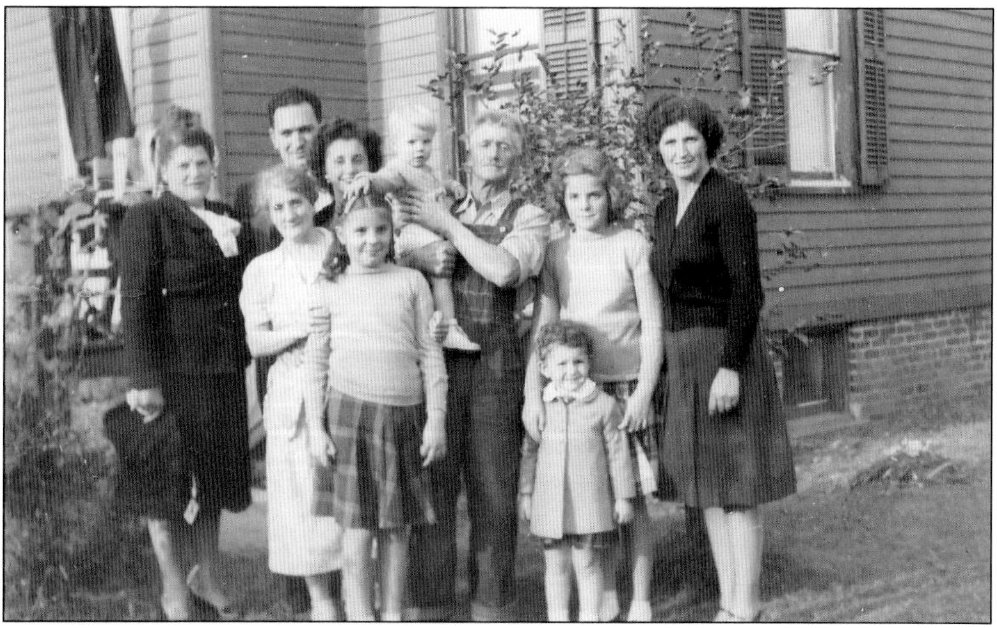

A family gathering at 70 South Street, 1945. Seen here are, from left to right, Ida Barus Tobino, John Tobino, Stella Barus, Rose Barus Roberts, Louise Schickner, Joseph Moscar (baby), Louis Barus, Sylvia Schickner Adochio, DeeDee Tobino, and Yolanda Barus Schickner. (Courtesy of Yolanda Barus Schickner.)

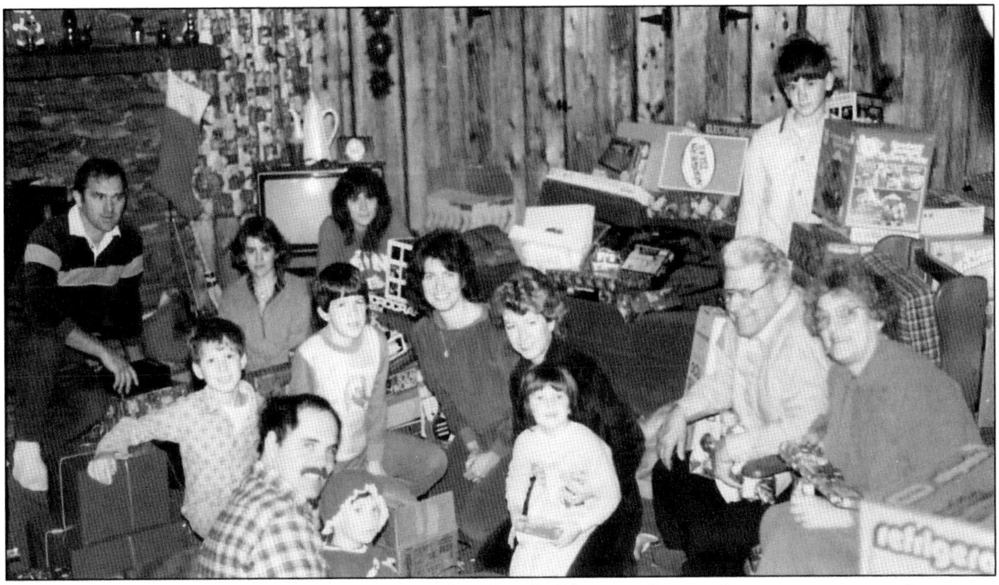

The civic-minded Herbert and Whitman families held many borough positions over the years. Here they pose at a holiday gathering, c. 1980s. Seen here are, from left to right: (front row) Harold D. Herbert and Sharon Herbert; (middle row) Scott Whitman, Harold D. Herbert II, Joan Herbert Whitman, Carol Herbert (holding niece), Kelly Herbert, Harold L. Herbert, and Edith Herbert; (back row) Jack Whitman, Debra Whitman, Sandra Whitman, and Jack S. Whitman (standing). The photograph was taken by William Herbert. (Courtesy of Joan Herbert Whitman.)

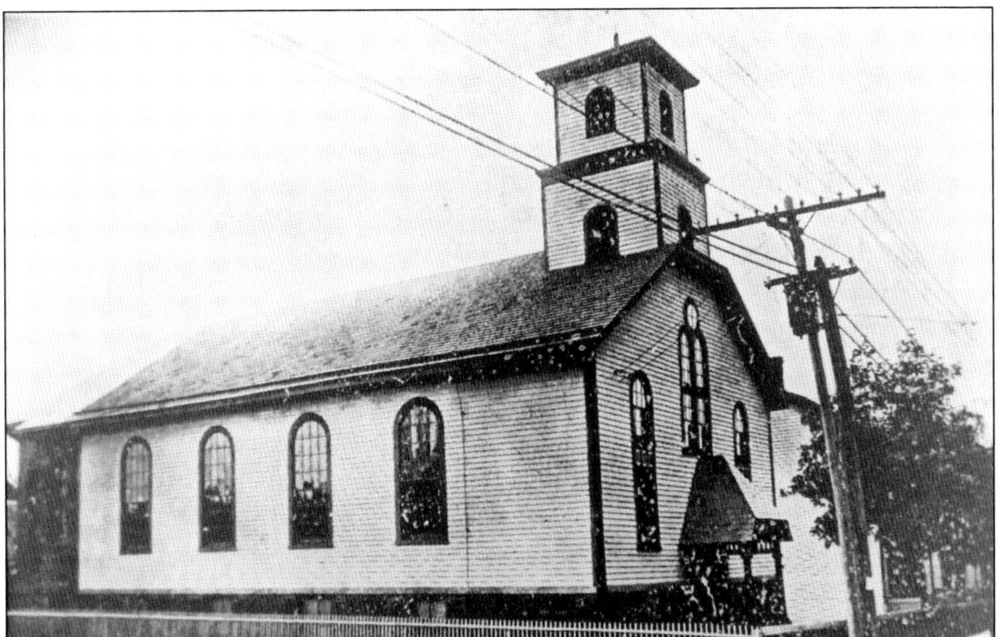

The German Reformed Church, now St. Paul's United Church of Christ, at South Main Street and Lakewood Avenue. The brick apse, on the back of the building, was added in 1910, and still remains in place on the newer building. (Courtesy of St. Paul's United Church of Christ.)

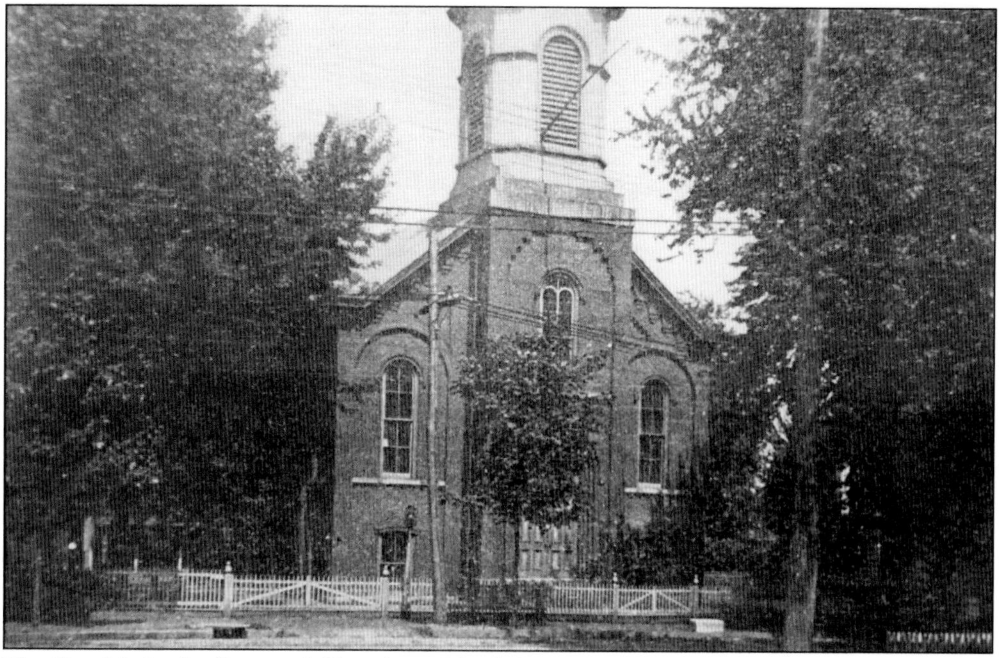

The First Methodist Episcopal Church, on North Main Street, *c.* 1908. The church was built in 1872. The stepping stone at the curb was given to the Milltown Historical Society and is located at the museum. The photograph was taken by I.S. Van Derveer. (Courtesy of Brian Harto.)

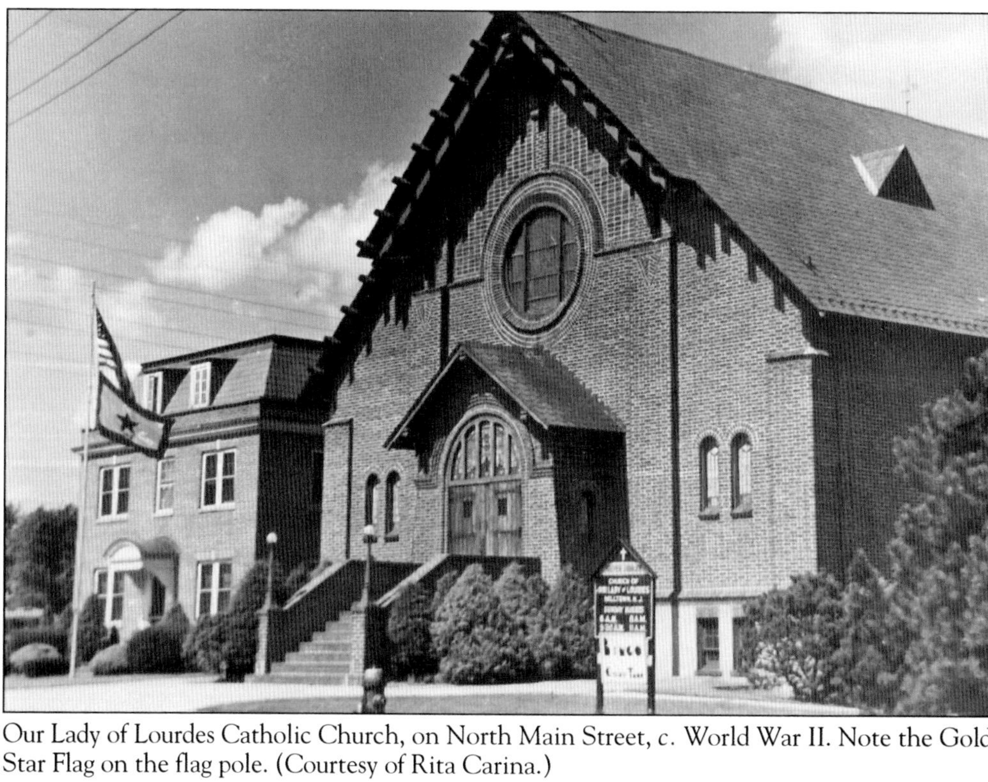

Our Lady of Lourdes Catholic Church, on North Main Street, *c.* World War II. Note the Gold Star Flag on the flag pole. (Courtesy of Rita Carina.)

Five

The French Connection

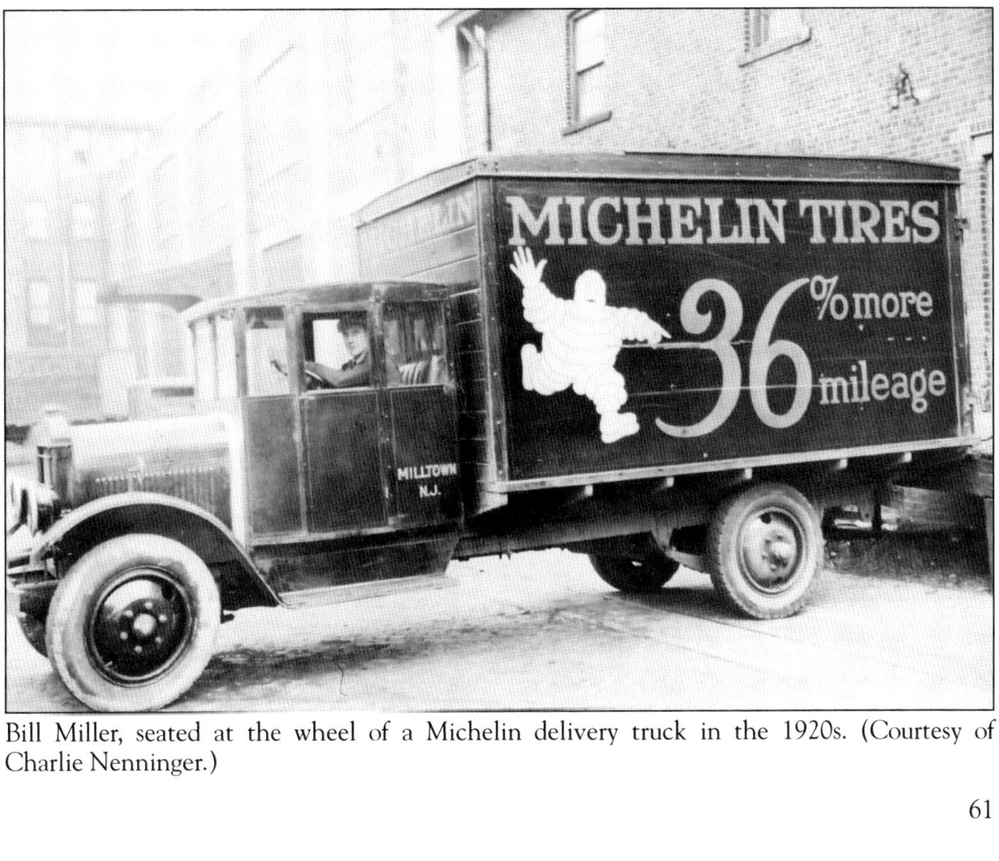

Bill Miller, seated at the wheel of a Michelin delivery truck in the 1920s. (Courtesy of Charlie Nenninger.)

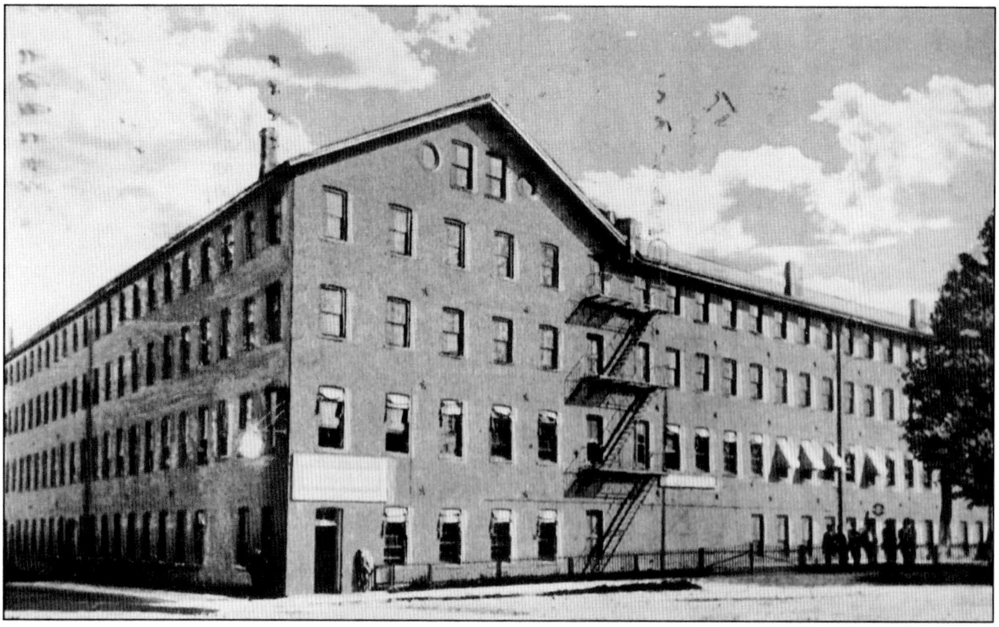

Building #1 of the Michelin Tire Company, at the corner of North Main Street and Ford Avenue, c. 1915. This photograph was taken by the Schneider brothers. (Courtesy of Brian Harto.)

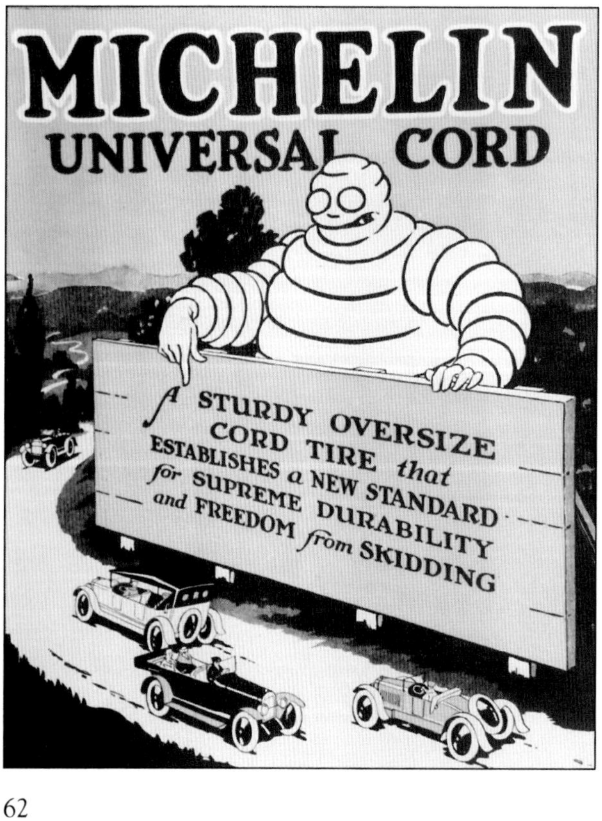

While their factory was located in Milltown, the Michelin Tire Company advertised in numerous magazines. Almost every issue of *The Saturday Evening Post* had a different advertisement. This example, originally printed in color, is from the November 13, 1920 issue. (Courtesy of Brian Harto.)

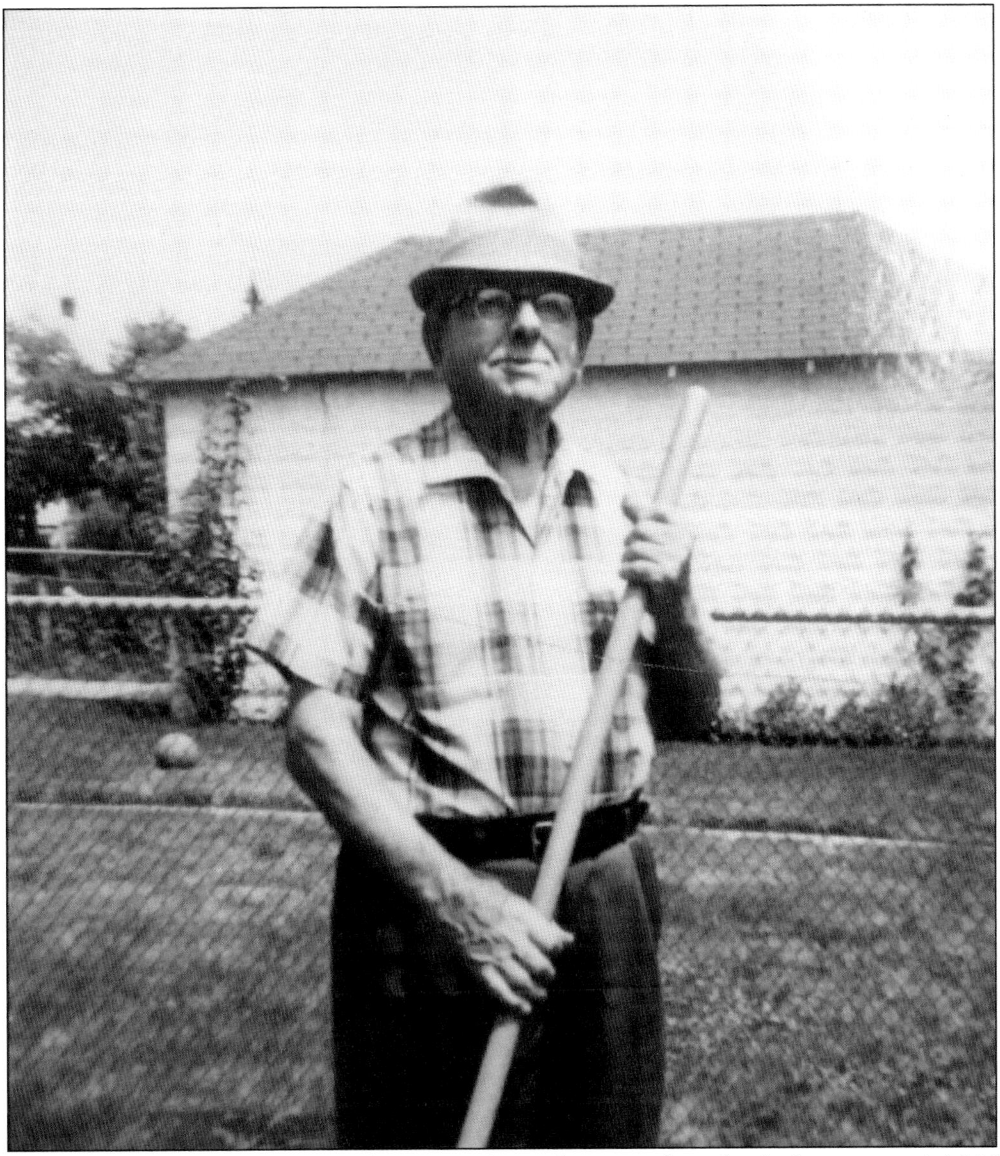

In 1906, at the age of fifteen, Joseph "Green" Carina began working for the International A&V Tire Company, on Ford Avenue. When the Michelin Tire Company moved into the plant in 1907, the first person they hired was Joe. He remained employed there until the plant closed in 1930. He then worked for the Michelin Realty Company until 1946. In addition, he worked at the Ford Avenue Algro Knitting Mills plant from 1937 until 1965. This meant that he worked in Milltown's Ford Avenue industrial complex for fifty-eight consecutive years. (Courtesy of Rita Carina.)

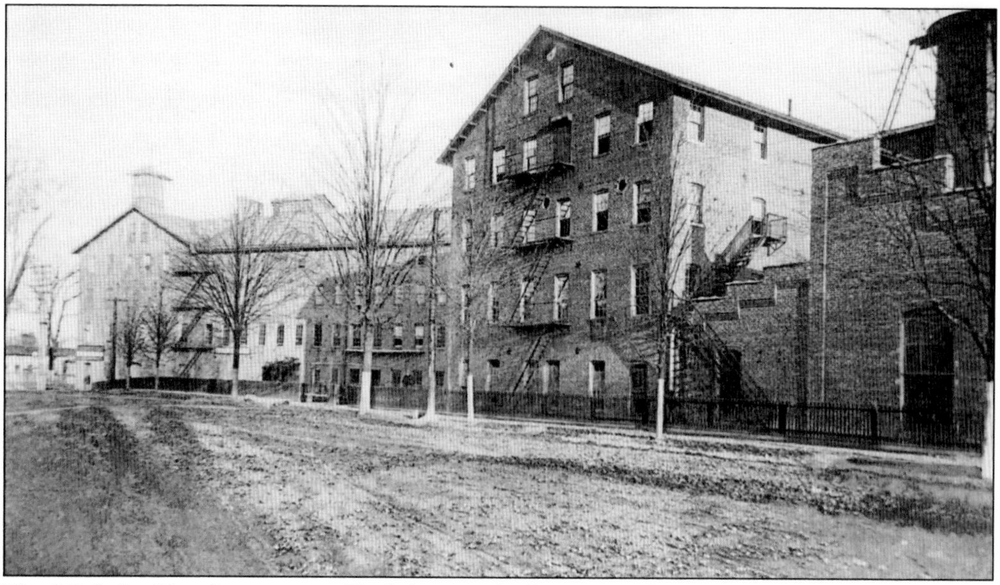

The Michelin Tire Company on Ford Avenue, looking toward Main Street, 1908. The cupola, on the building on the far left, was later blown down in a storm. This photograph was taken by Charles Hodapp. (Courtesy of Brian Harto.)

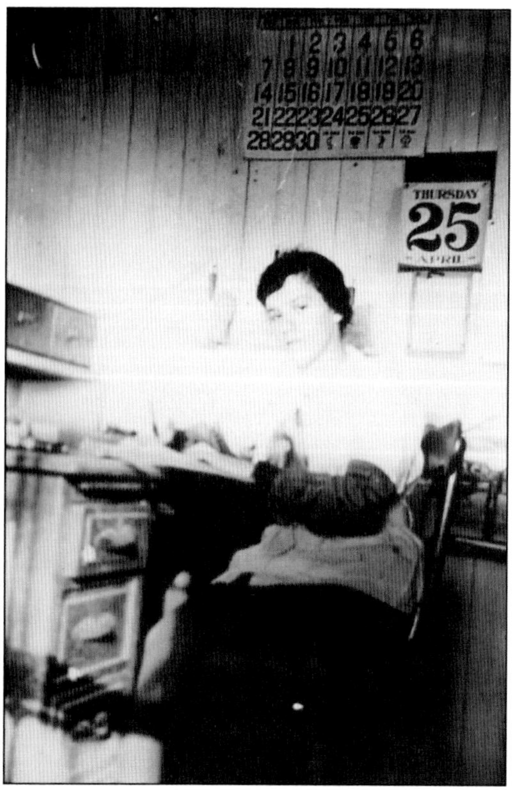

Miss Lillian Falk was a foreman at the Michelin Tire Company in 1918, much to the chagrin of her lesser-paid, male co-workers. (Courtesy of the Schwendeman family.)

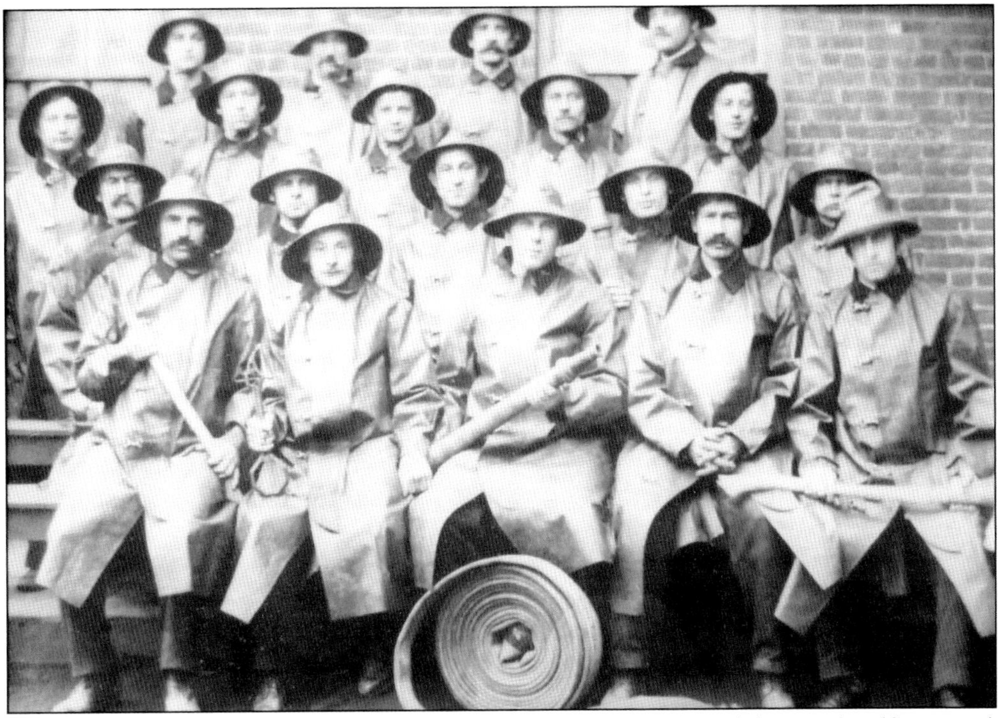

Michelin Tire Company firefighters, *c.* 1908. Seen here are, from left to right: (front row) unknown, Nick Singumard*, William Rupprecht, Charles Schmidt*, John Lins*; (second row) Emil Weber, Enos Huff*, George Lins*, Louis Pousie, William Kleen*; (third row) Nate Thompson, William Willenbrock*, Fred Kohrherr*, unknown, Fritz Hartlander*; (back row) Joe Rupprecht, Andrew Acker, Bernard Gil*, and Mr. Erikson. The men with the * next to their names later became Milltown firemen. (Courtesy of Eureka Fire Museum.)

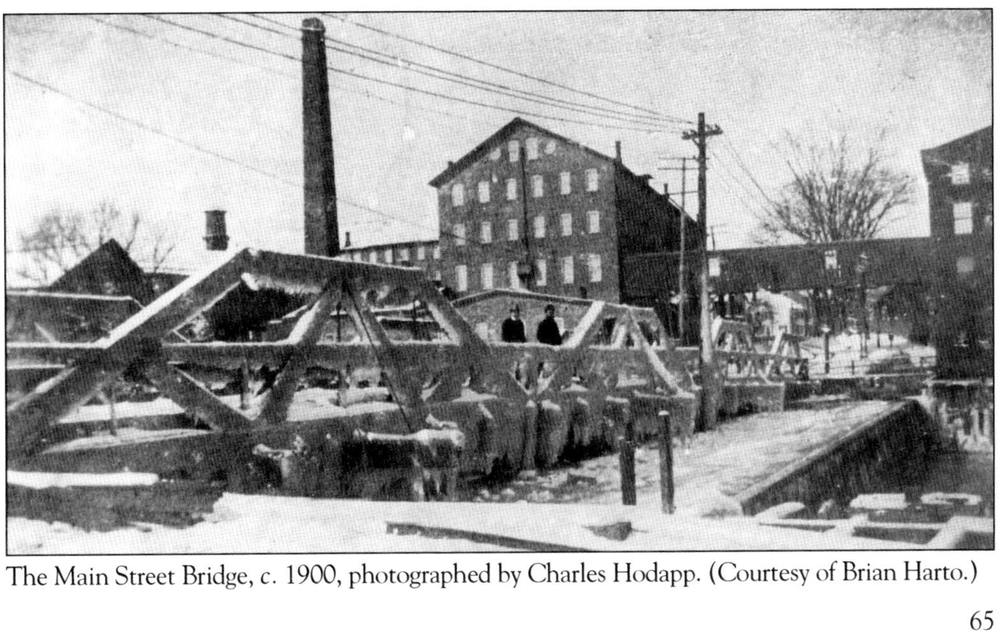

The Main Street Bridge, *c.* 1900, photographed by Charles Hodapp. (Courtesy of Brian Harto.)

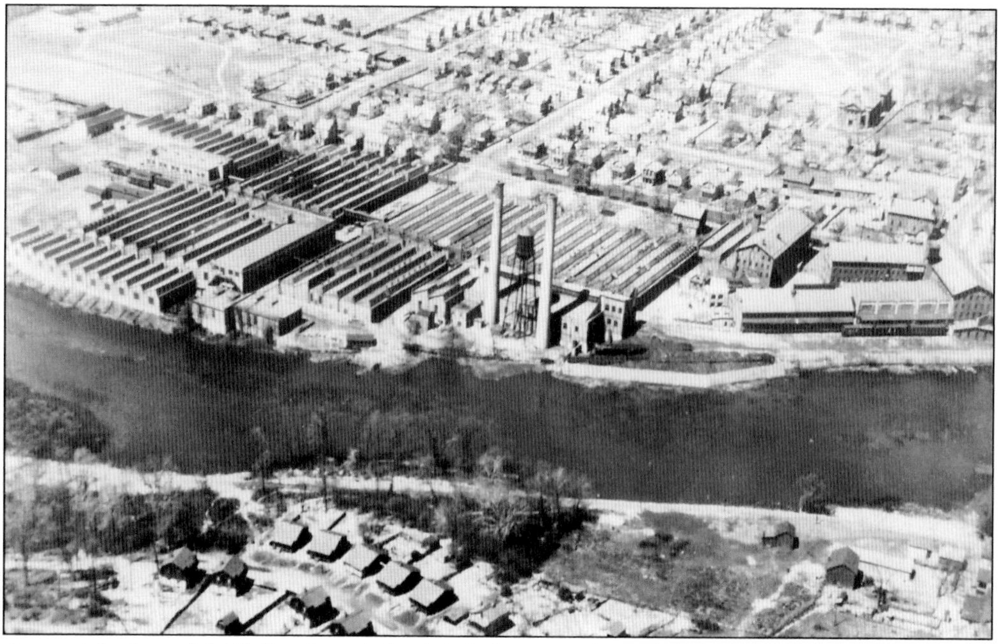

An aerial view of Mill Pond and the Michelin complex, *c.* 1940s. (Courtesy of Milltown Historical Society.)

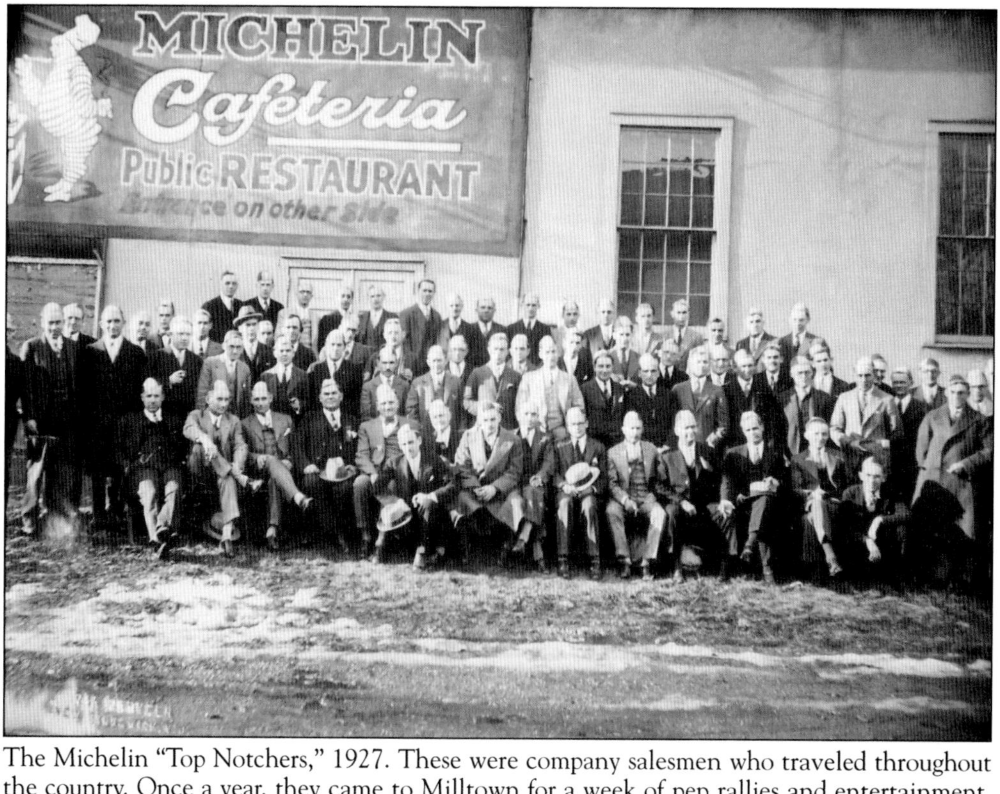

The Michelin "Top Notchers," 1927. These were company salesmen who traveled throughout the country. Once a year, they came to Milltown for a week of pep rallies and entertainment. This photograph was taken by VanDerVeer Studios. (Courtesy of Charlie Nenninger.)

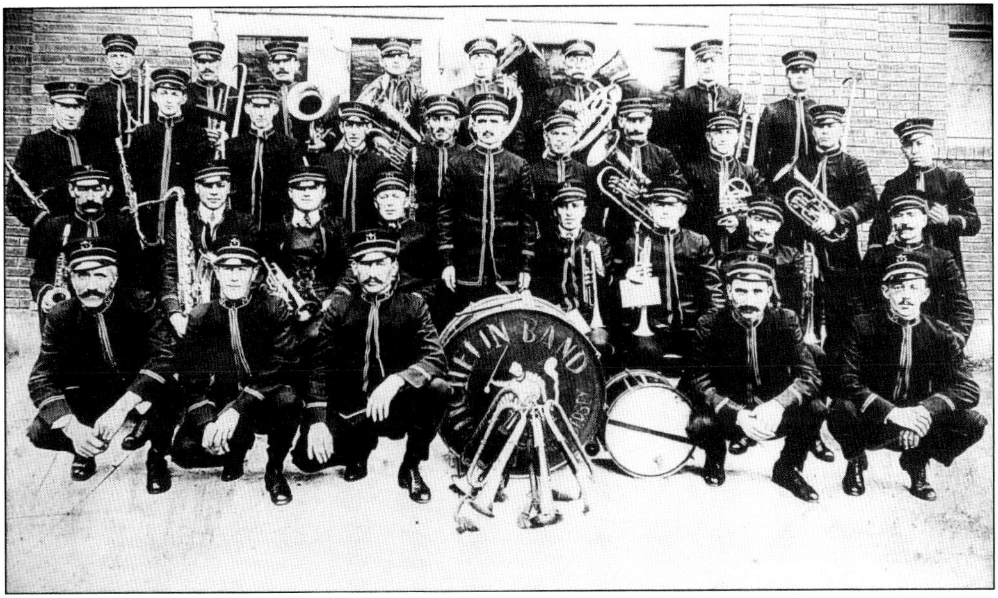

The Michelin Band poses in front of the Community House on North Main Street, in the 1920s. The band leader, Rene Fonteix Sr., is standing behind the drums. (Courtesy of Rita Carina.)

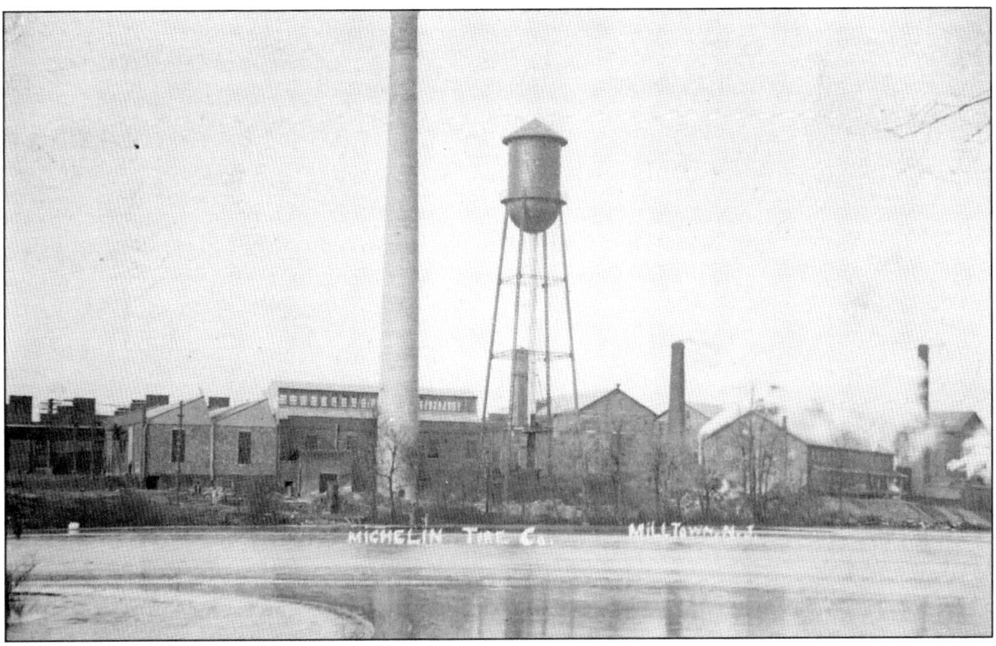

The Michelin Tire Company, seen from across the Mill Pond, *c.* 1910. (Courtesy of Irma Lown.)

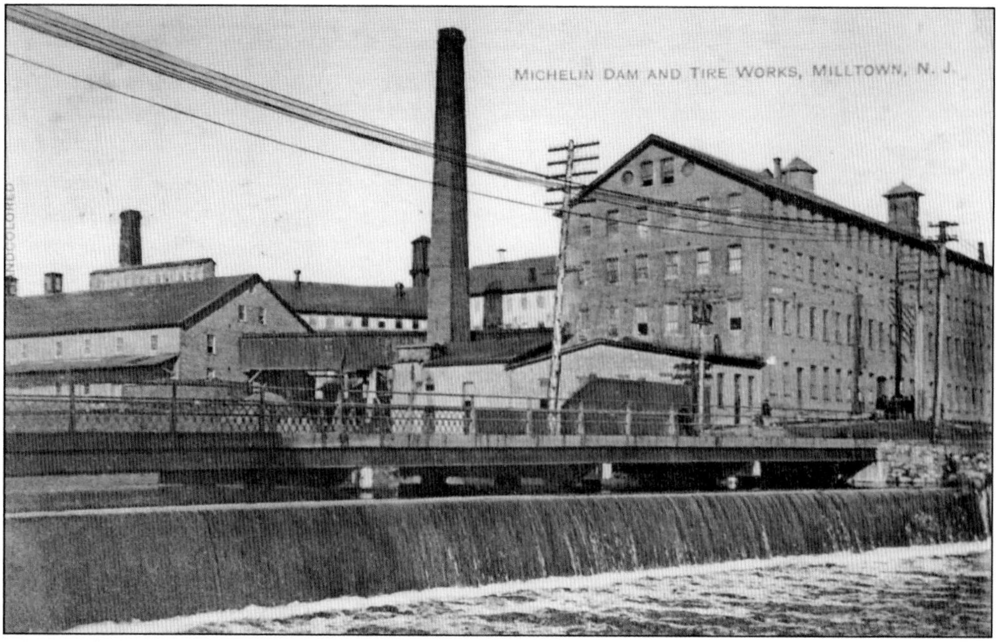

The Michelin complex, bridge, and dam, 1908. (Courtesy of Brian Harto.)

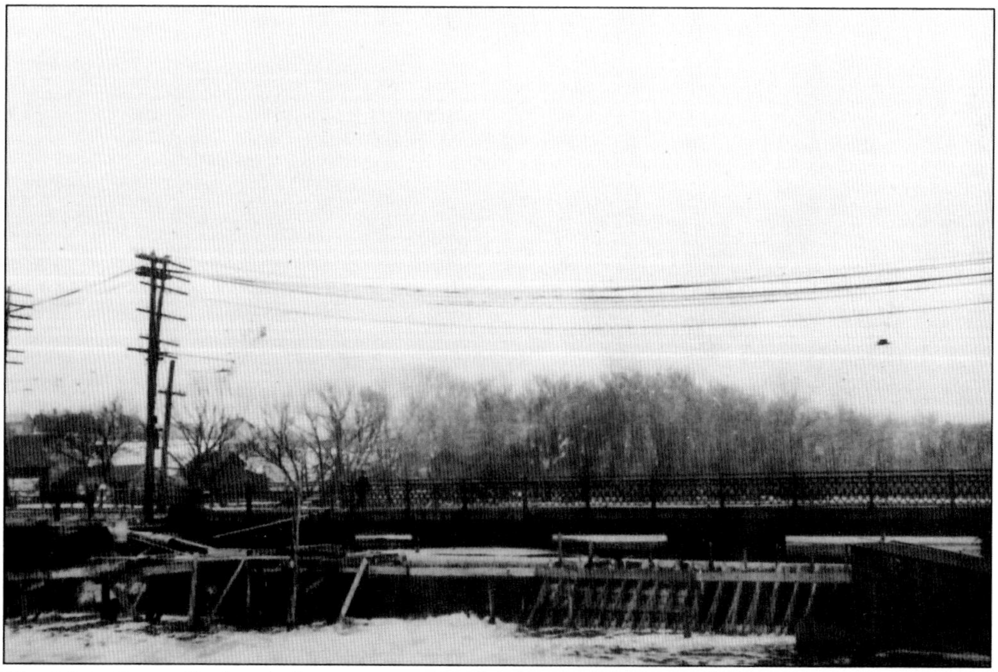

The Main Street Bridge, looking west, *c.* 1917. The new dam is under construction, and it has cost about $50,000. Only a foot wide at the top, it widens to 10 feet at the bottom, with 6 feet of it buried beneath the pond. (Courtesy of Rita Carina.)

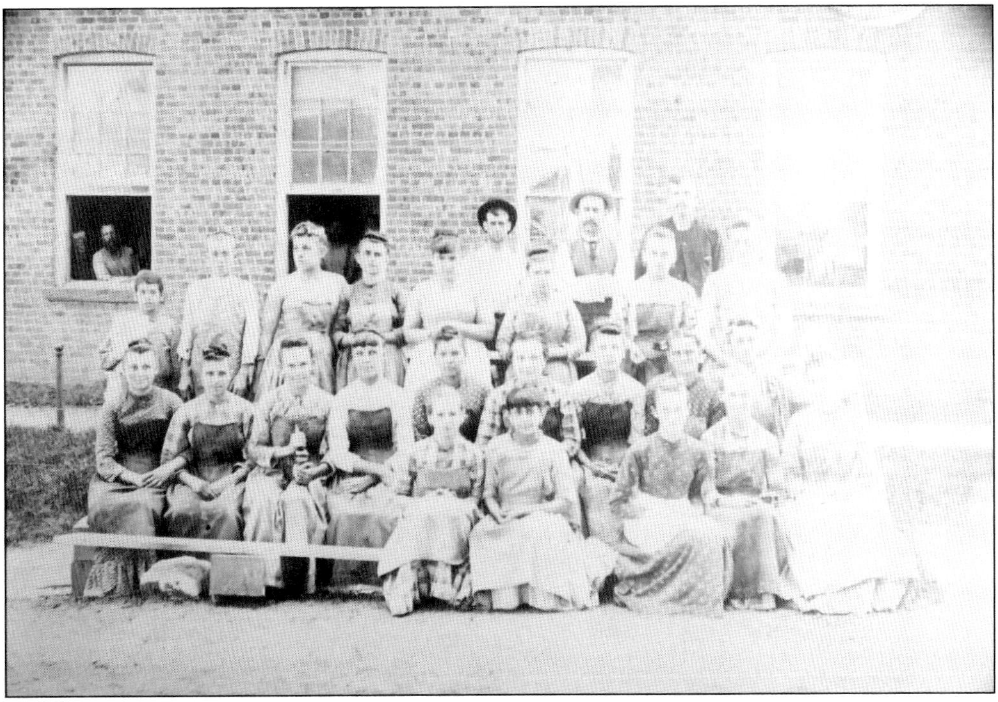

Several rubber companies called Milltown home. Christopher Meyer came to the town in 1843, but his original factory and home burned down in 1845. John Ford supplied Meyer with the finance to rebuild the factory. The employees pictured here worked at the Meyer Rubber Company, c. 1890. (Courtesy of Rita Carina.)

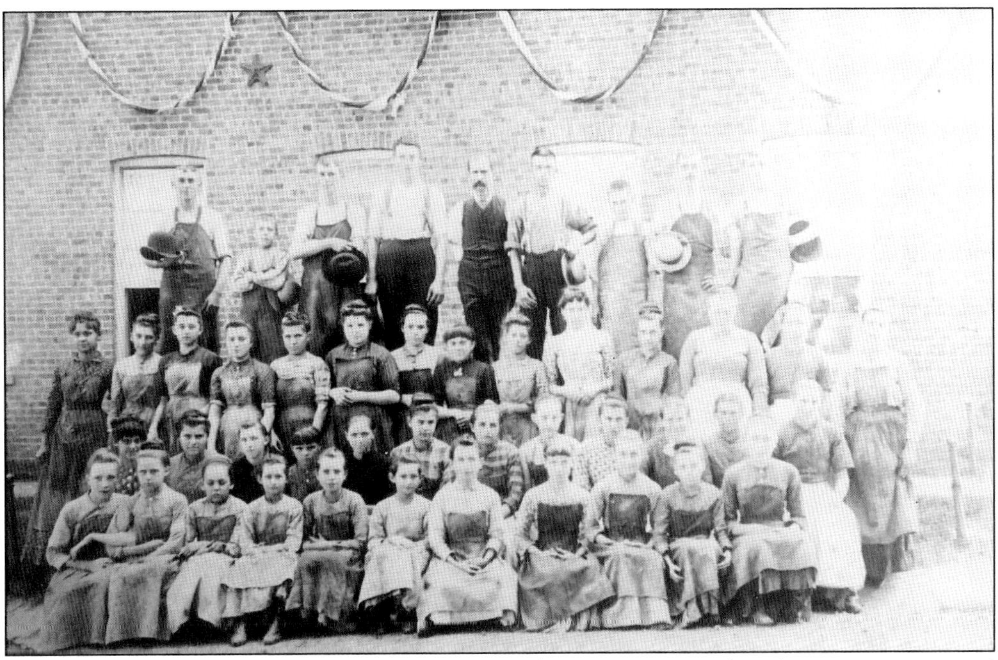

Meyer Rubber Company employees, c. 1845. The company employed men, women, and children. (Courtesy of Rita Carina.)

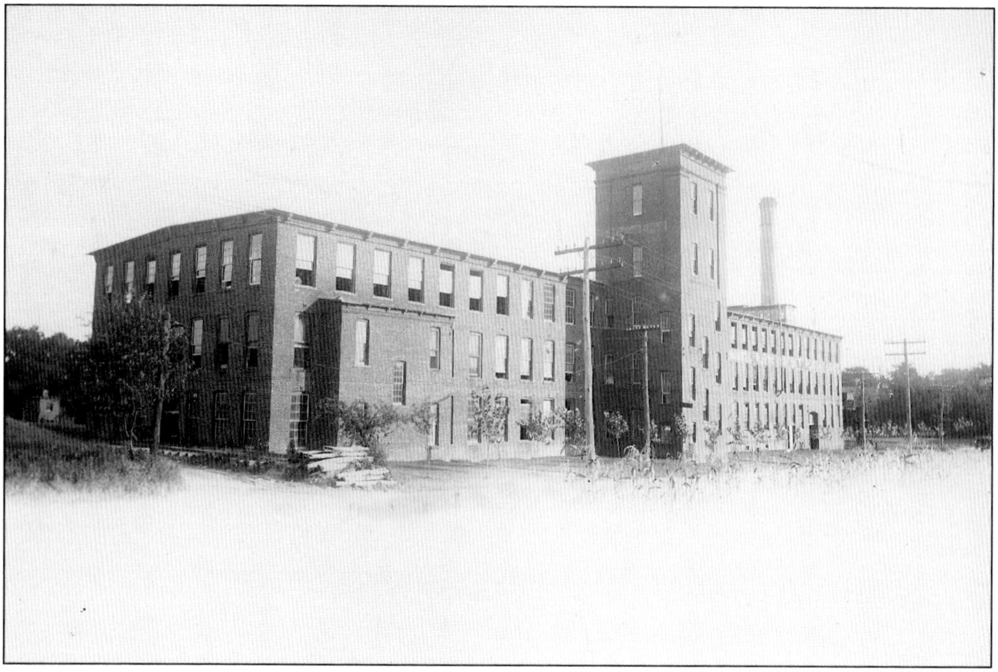

The Russell Playing Card Company on Washington Avenue. Designated a National Historic Site, the building is now "The Mill" condominiums. The building originally housed the India Rubber Company, and was built in 1899 by John C. Evans. It went out of business in 1901. The building was used by the Michelin Tire Company and the United States Rubber Company. The Russell Playing Card Company occupied it from 1912 to 1936. (Courtesy of Milltown Historical Society.)

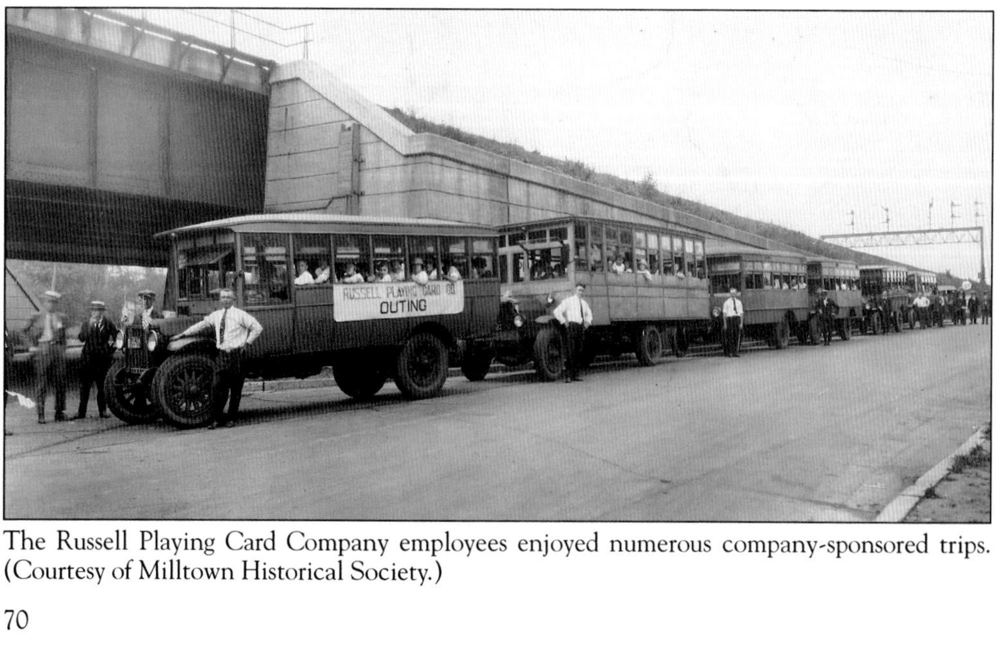

The Russell Playing Card Company employees enjoyed numerous company-sponsored trips. (Courtesy of Milltown Historical Society.)

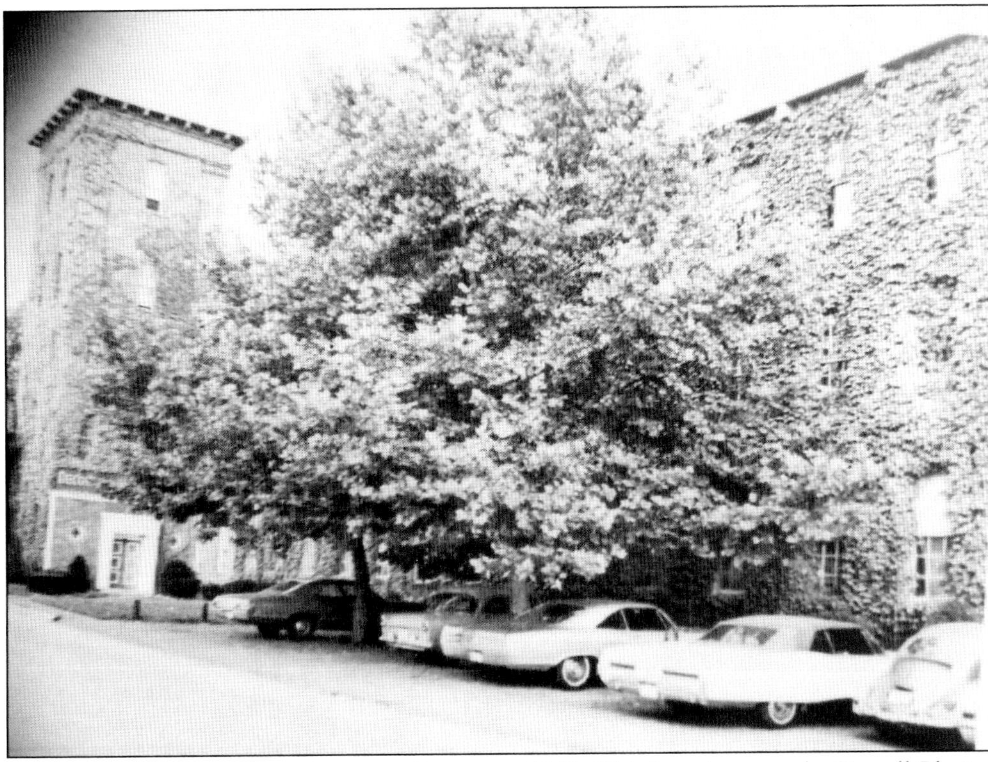

The Decorated Metal Manufacturing Company, 1965. This location was the Russell Playing Card factory. (Courtesy of Charlie Nenninger.)

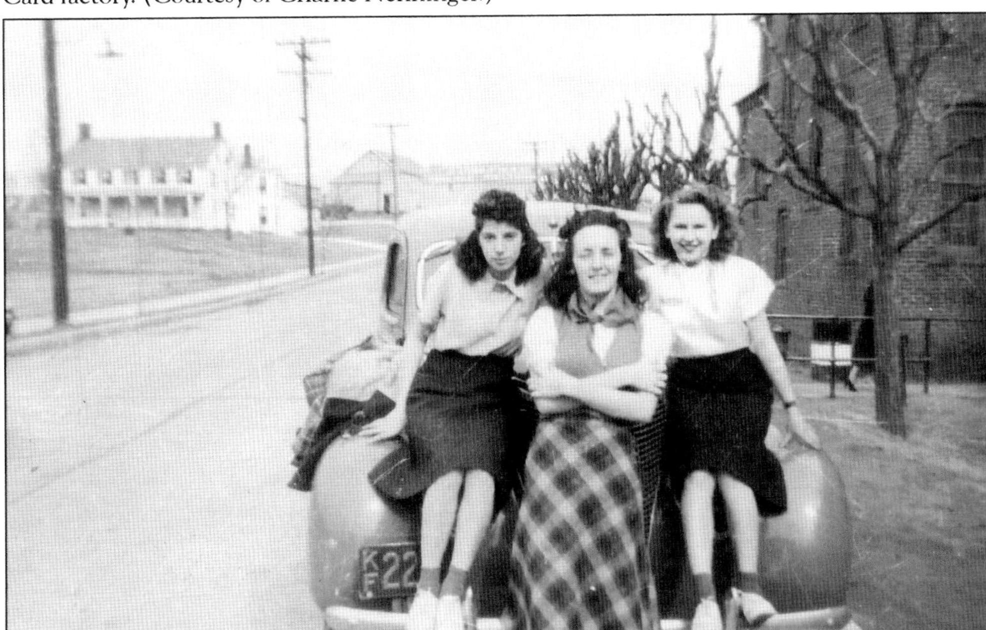

In 1939, Metalfield Inc. occupied the Russell Playing Card Company building. These three young women were taking a lunch break. Pictured here are, from left to right, Helen Barus, Liz Haas, and Olga La Komie. (Courtesy of Helen Barus Moscar.)

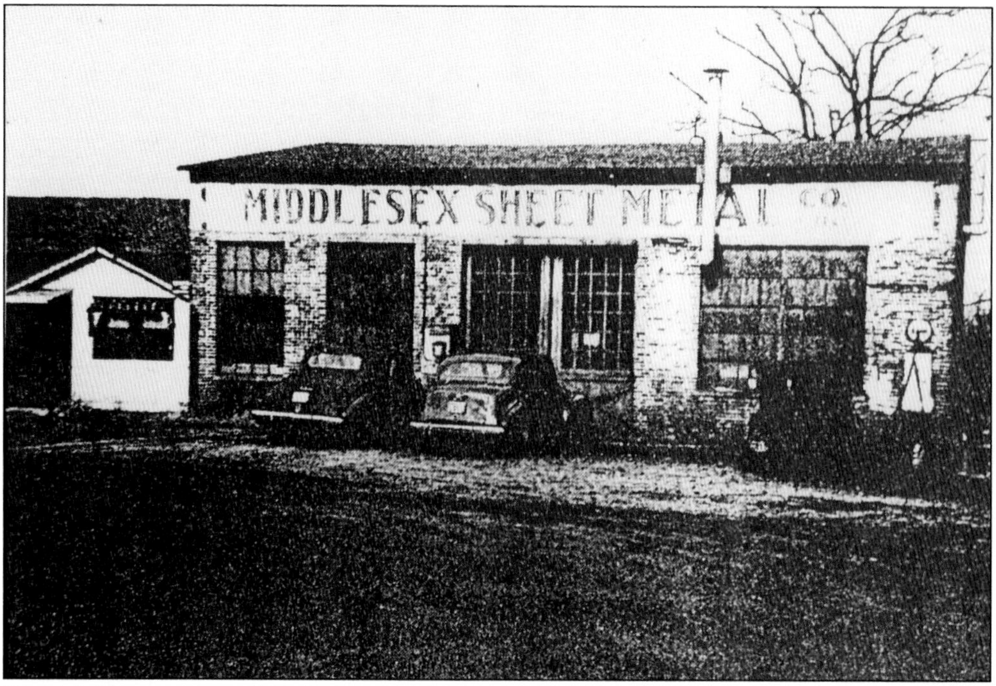

The Middlesex Sheet Metal Company, Inc., was founded in September 1937 by Ralph Quackenbush, Phillip King, and Vincent Vanacore. This building was located behind Henry Christ's Plumbing and Heating Supply Store, on land behind the current Milltown Pharmacy. (Courtesy of Joan Dallas.)

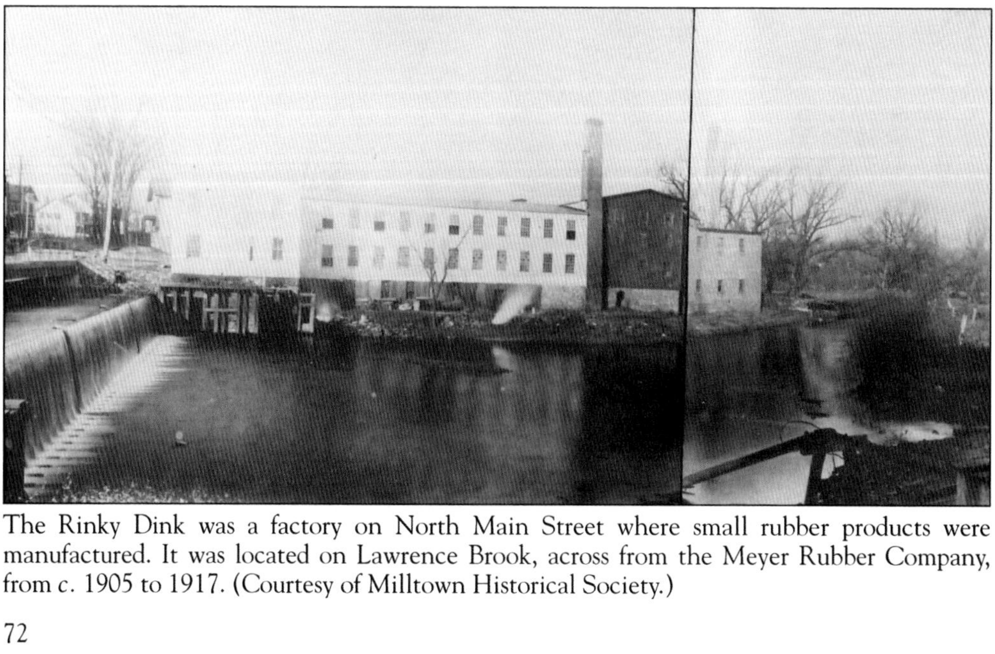

The Rinky Dink was a factory on North Main Street where small rubber products were manufactured. It was located on Lawrence Brook, across from the Meyer Rubber Company, from *c.* 1905 to 1917. (Courtesy of Milltown Historical Society.)

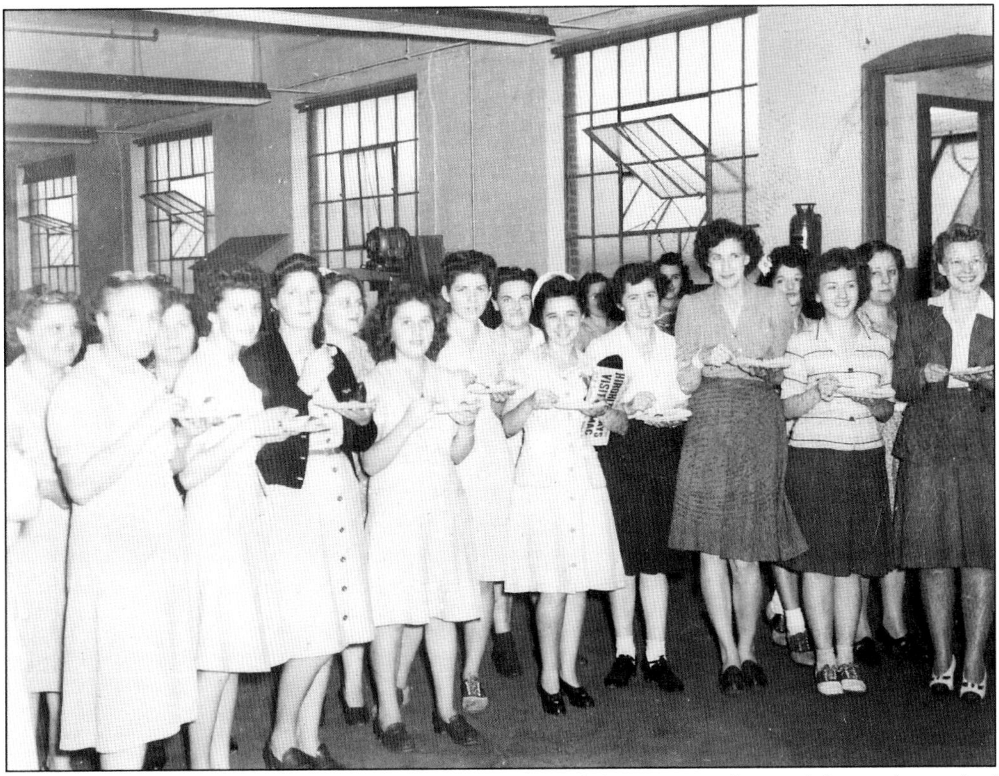

At Johnson & Johnson's elastic goods factory on Ford Avenue, workers celebrate the end of World War II. The woman in the dark sweater is Yolanda Barus Schickner. (Courtesy of Yolanda Barus Schickner.)

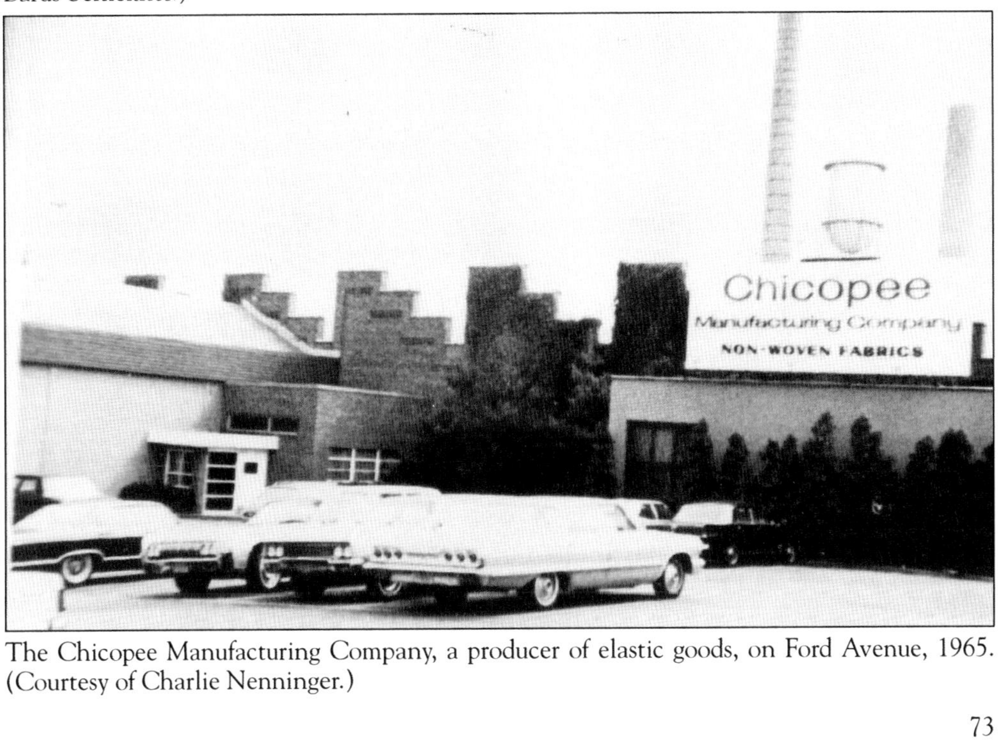

The Chicopee Manufacturing Company, a producer of elastic goods, on Ford Avenue, 1965. (Courtesy of Charlie Nenninger.)

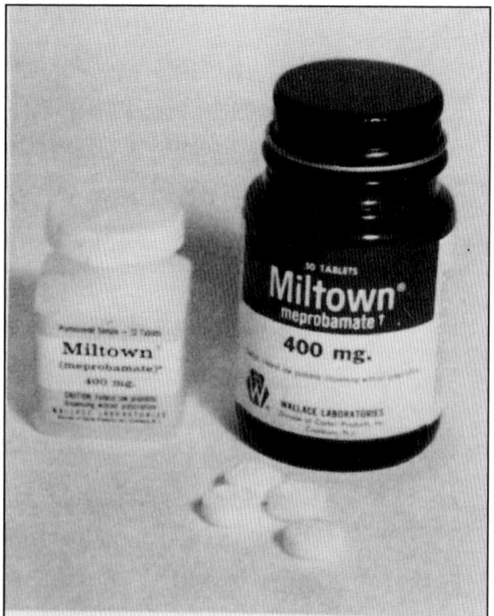

Miltown was a classic example of a superb product—"an entirely new type of tranquilizer with muscle relaxant action."

Because of its reputation as a pleasant, even sleepy, small town, Milltown was chosen, in 1955, as the name of a new tranquilizer produced by the Wallace Laboratories, a division of Carter Products, in nearby North Brunswick. Federal regulations required the name be altered, and "Miltowns" were soon a popular choice. (Courtesy of Julius J. Osowick and James Farrell.)

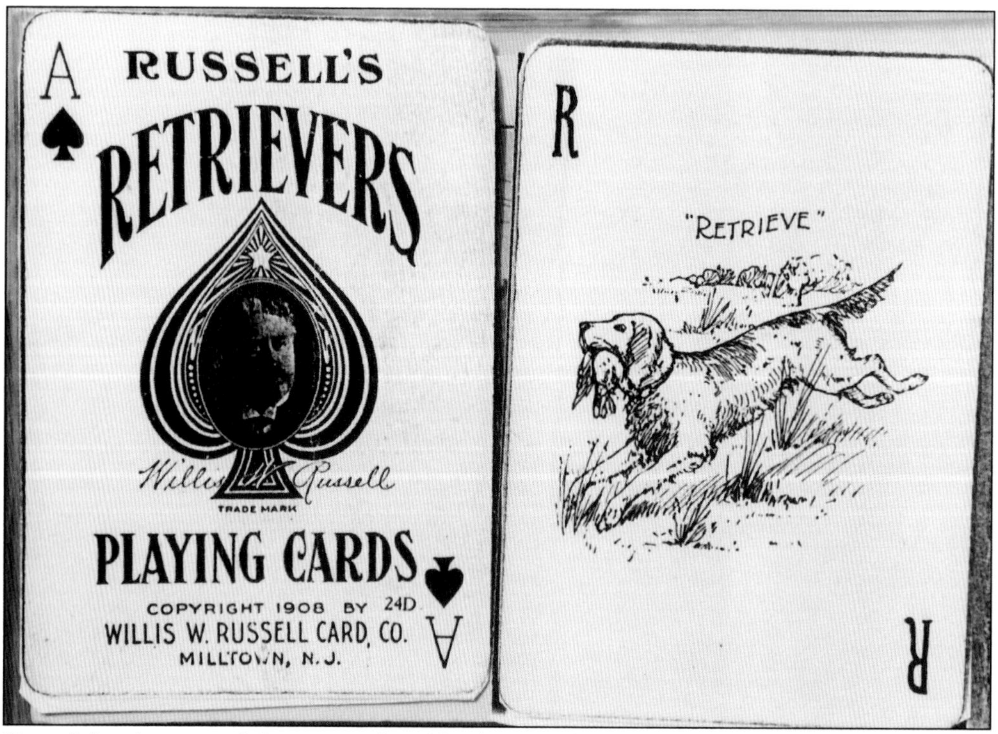

One of the playing card designs produced by the Russell Playing Card Company between 1908 and 1911. (Courtesy of Norm Carina.)

Six

Fireworks!

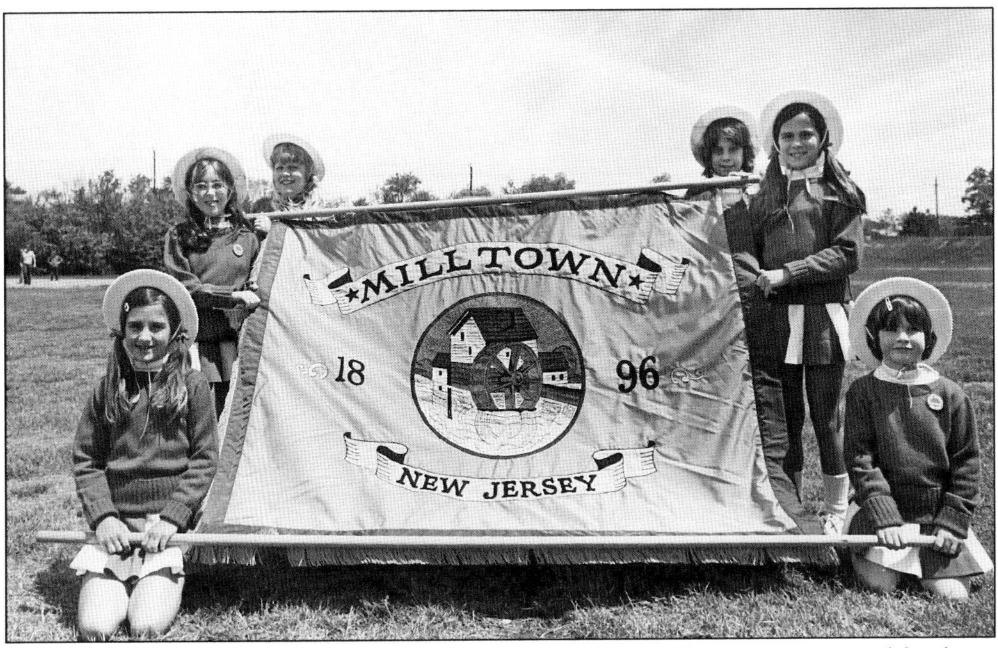

Milltown's official flag, created for the Bicentennial of the United States, was carried for the first time on July 4, 1976. Holding the flag are, from left to right: (front row) Debra Whitman and Erin Gregorowicz; (middle row) Joan Brennan and Sandra Whitman; (back row) Katie Hansen and Paulette Crabiel. (Courtesy of Joan Herbert Whitman.)

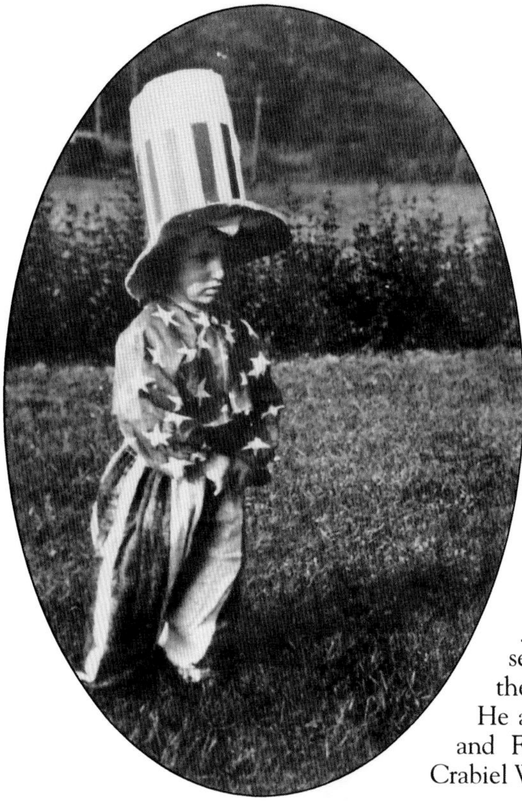

David B. Crabiel, dressed for the Fourth of July, in the 1930s. He would later go on to serve as mayor of Milltown from 1968 to 1979, the longest mayoral term in the town's history. He also served as Middlesex County Freeholder and Freeholder Director. (Courtesy of Paulette Crabiel Wahler.)

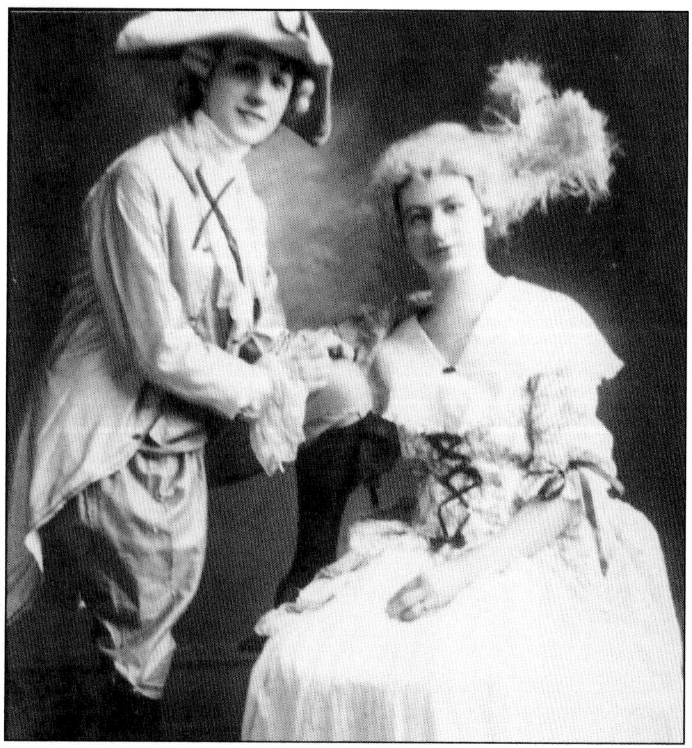

These two women participated in a pageant for the Grand Opening of the Community House, c. 1907. The woman dressed as George Washington is Marie Young. (Courtesy of Brian Harto.)

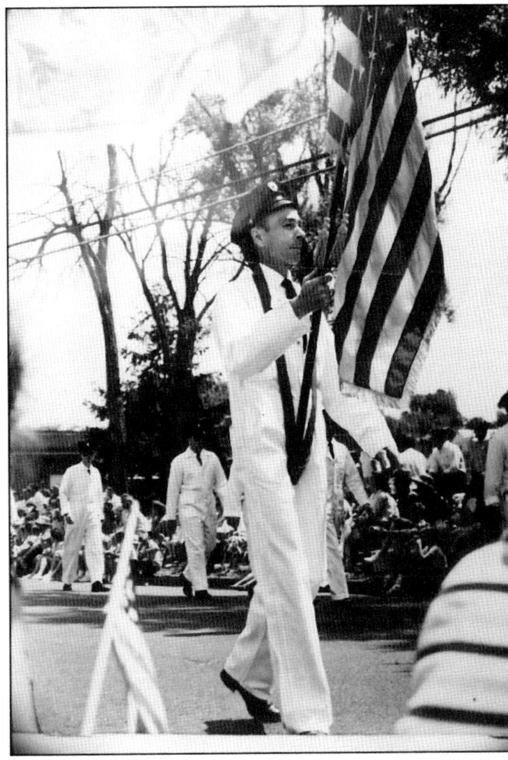

Ken Selover carried the American Flag for the Rescue Squad during this Fourth of July parade in the early 1970s. (Courtesy of Ken Selover.)

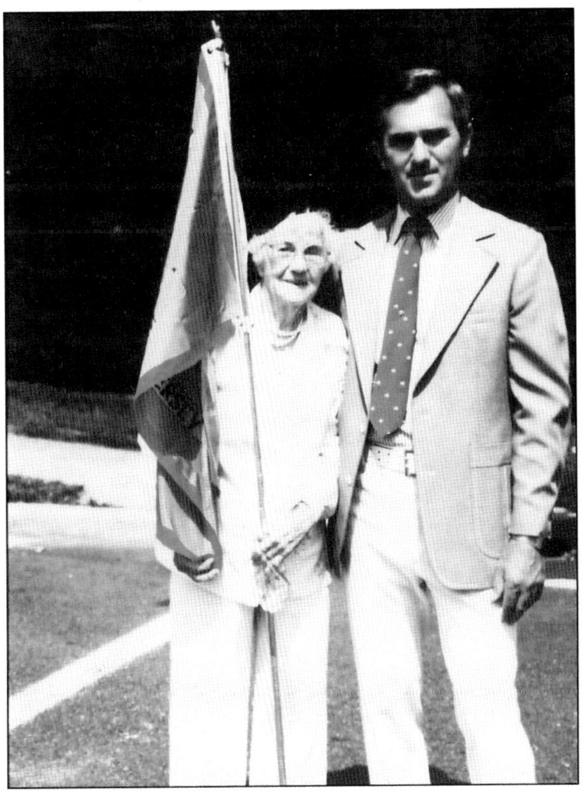

This photograph was taken during the 1980s. Mayor Jack Whitman poses on the Fourth of July with Lilliam Falk Schwendeman, who designed the official flag of Milltown in 1976. (Courtesy of Joan Herbert Whitman.)

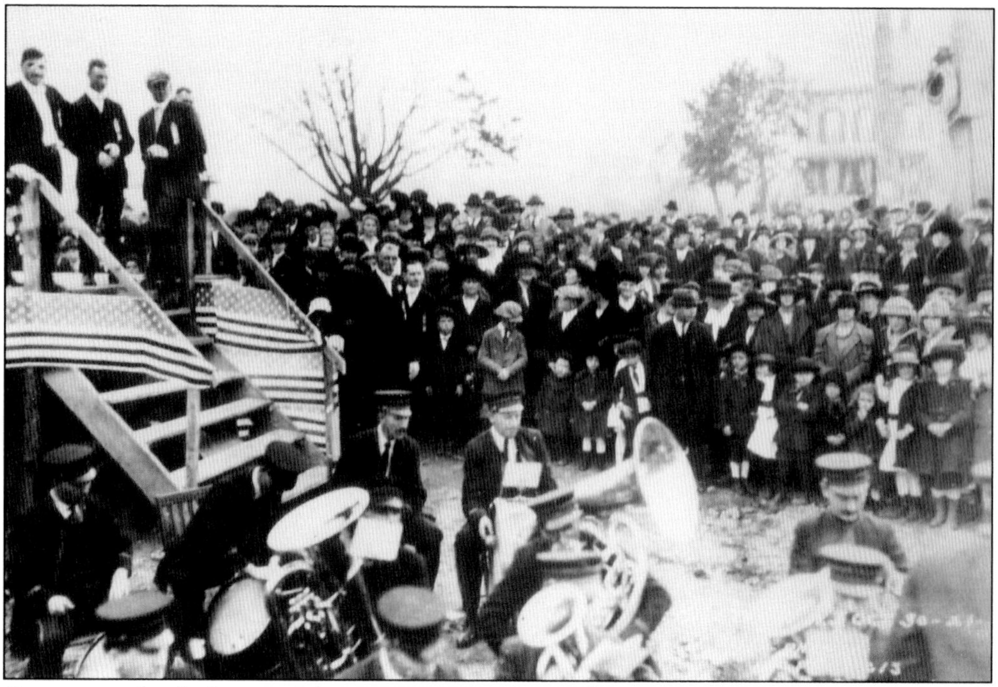

Ceremonies for the laying of the cornerstone at Our Lady of Lourdes Roman Catholic Church attracted large crowds on October 30, 1921. In the background is the Baier farm. (Courtesy of Rita Carina.)

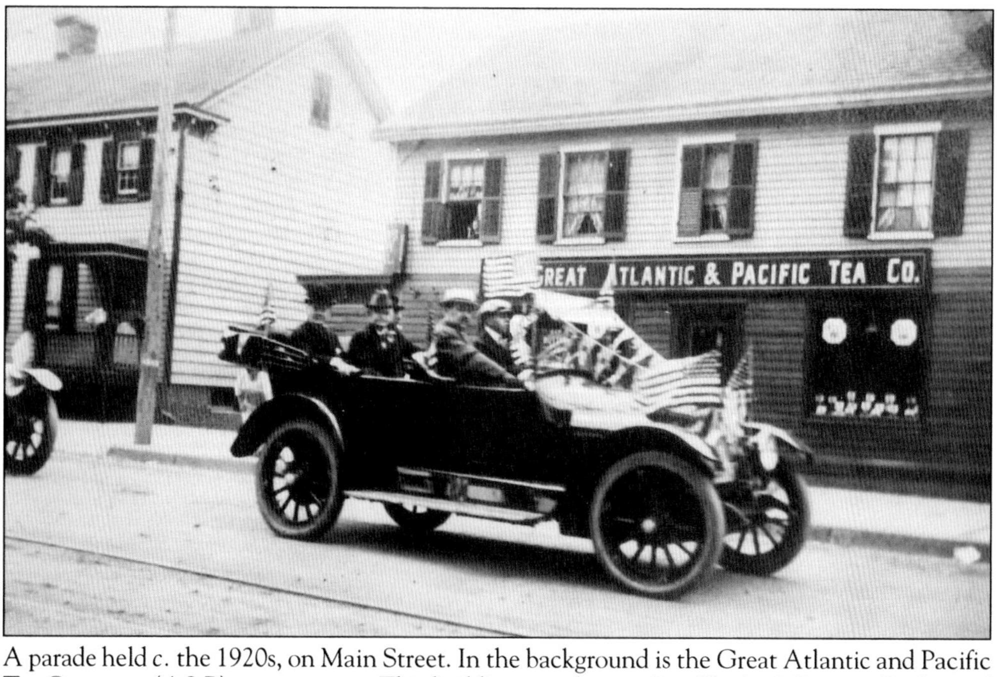

A parade held *c.* the 1920s, on Main Street. In the background is the Great Atlantic and Pacific Tea Company (A&P) grocery store. This building now houses Ray Kimber's Factory Outlet and the Milltown Tavern. (Courtesy of Hazel Jacobsen Denhard.)

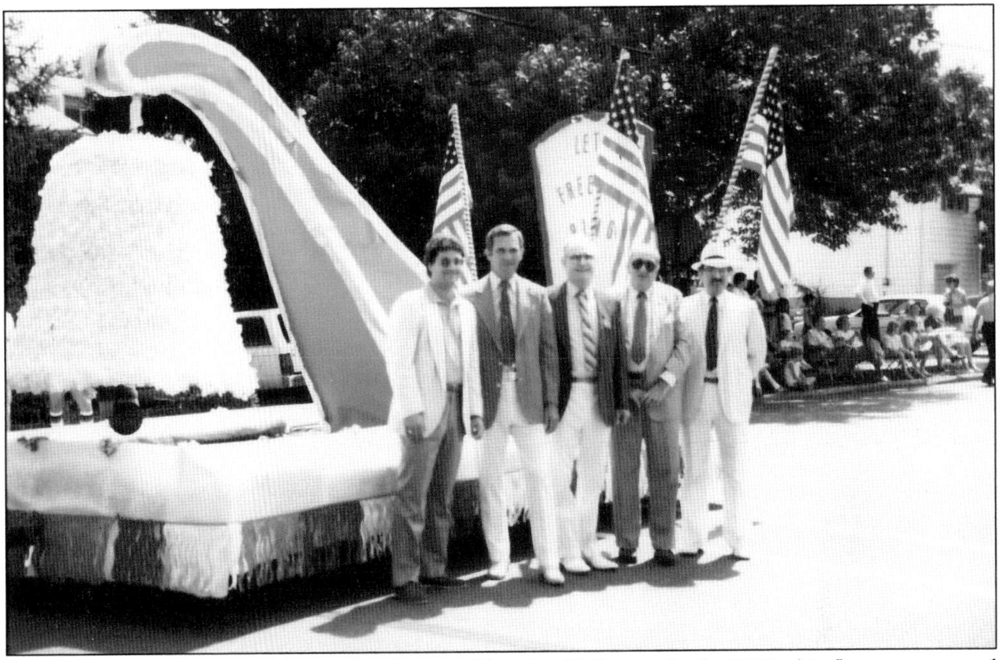

Floats are always an integral part of Milltown's Fourth of July parade. In 1985, this float was created for the "Let Freedom Ring" theme. Pictured with Mayor Jack Whitman are Councilmen Robert Adochio, William Liddy, Milton Cowan, and Peter Fama. (Courtesy of Joan Herbert Whitman.)

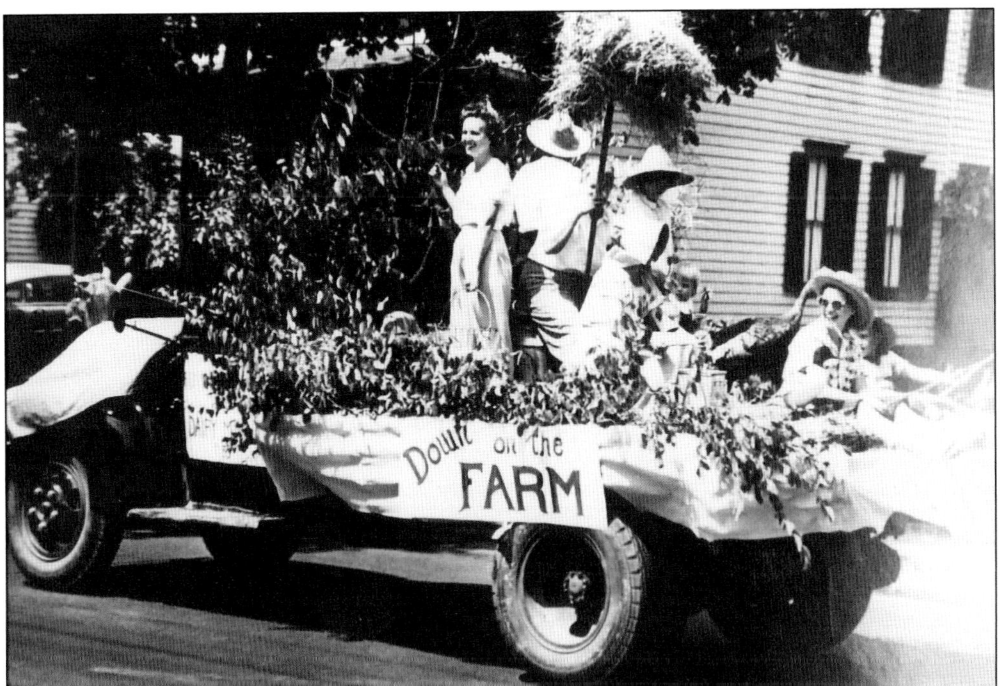

The "dairy maids" ride a float in the 1950s. Holding the tree is Lillian Schwendeman. Betty Martin is seated. (Courtesy of Betty Martin.)

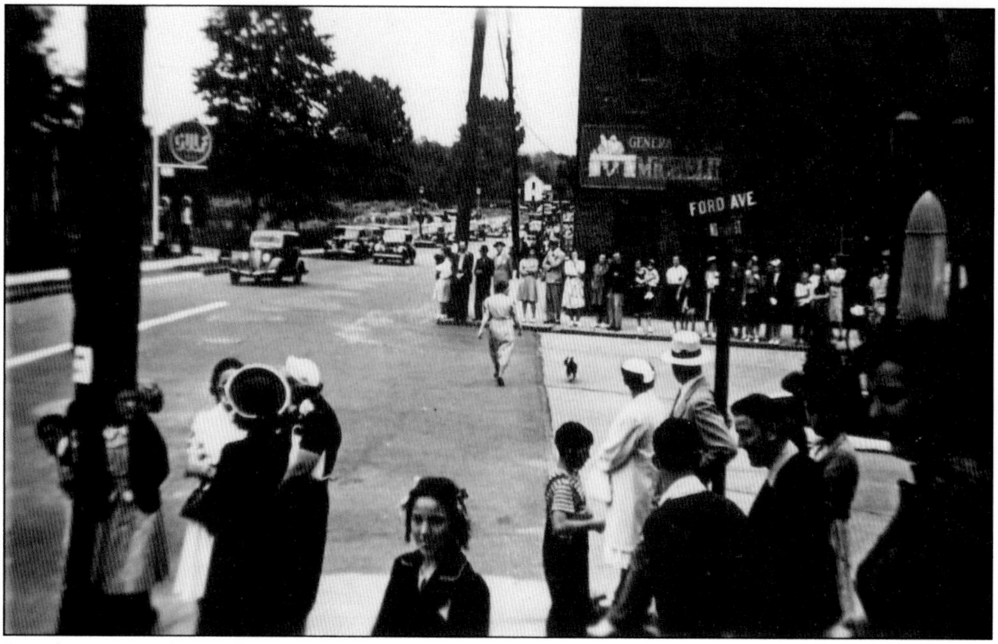

People waiting for Milltown's 1940 Fourth of July Parade, at the corner of North Main Street and Ford Avenue. The photograph was taken by Michael George Ondre, who was manager of the Cleveland Container Corp., building.#14, of the Michelin complex from 1940 to 1945. (Courtesy of Michael George Ondre.)

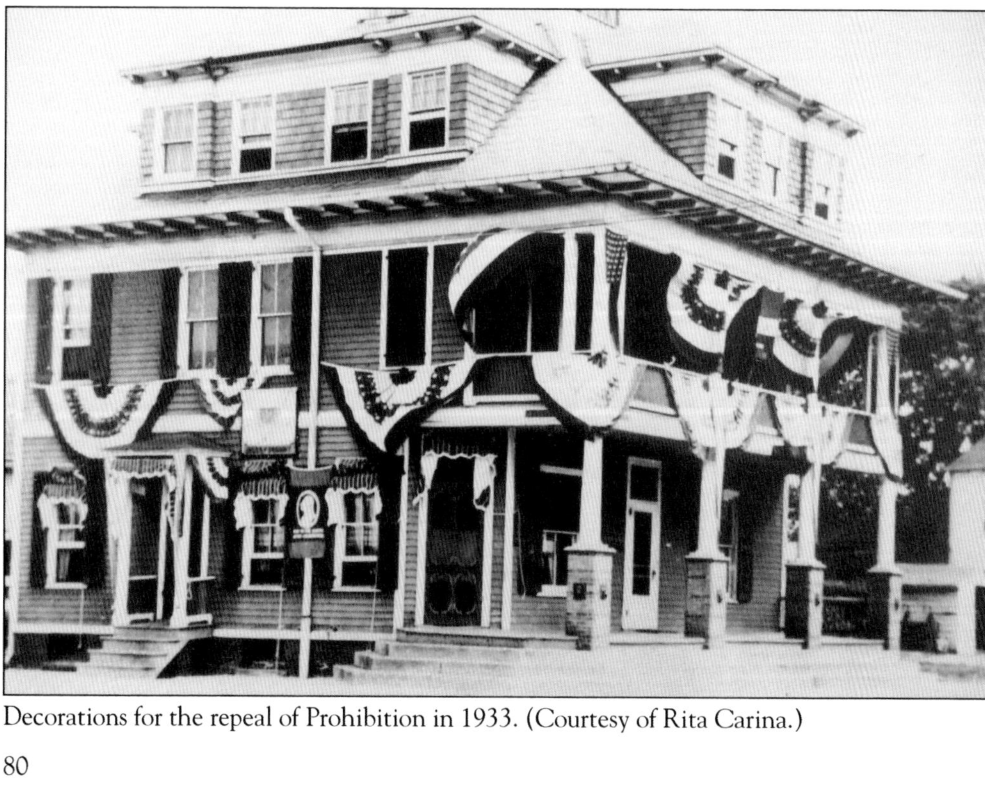

Decorations for the repeal of Prohibition in 1933. (Courtesy of Rita Carina.)

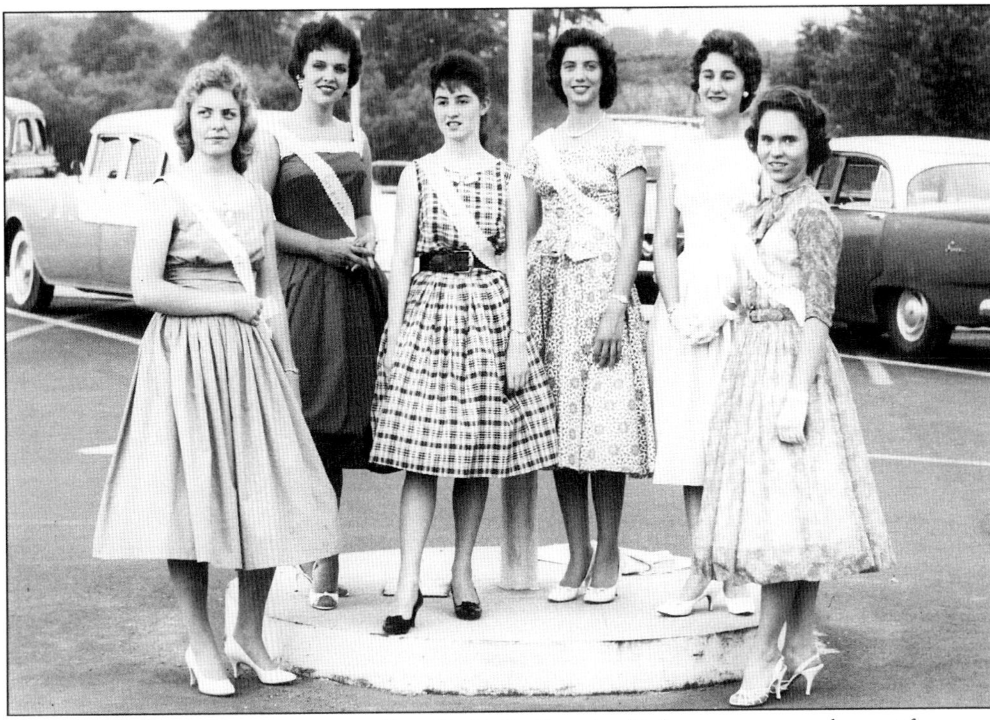

The Miss Milltown Pageant, originally called Miss Fourth of July, was an annual event for many years. The first Miss Milltown was Joan Herbert (to the right of the pole), pictured here posing with the other contestants in 1959. They are, from left to right, Carol Wolff, Carol Gebhardt, Joan Barbely, Carol Findon, and Barbara Holzapfel. (Courtesy of Joan Herbert Whitman.)

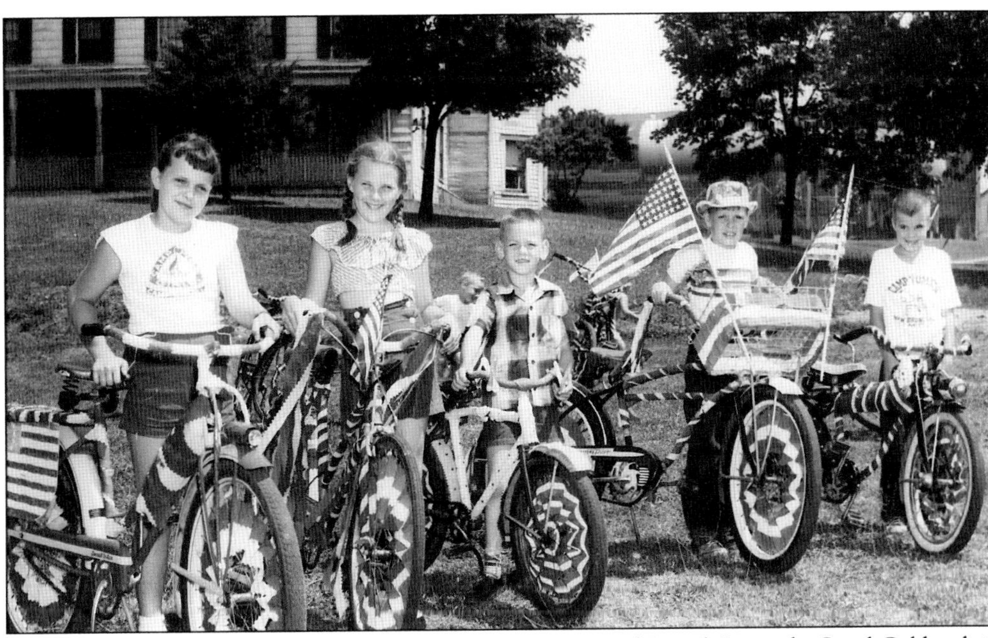

On July Fourth, 1953, these children won the "Best Decorated Bicycle" awards. Carol Gebhardt is the child standing on the left and Joe Moscar is on the far right. (Courtesy of Helen Barus Moscar.)

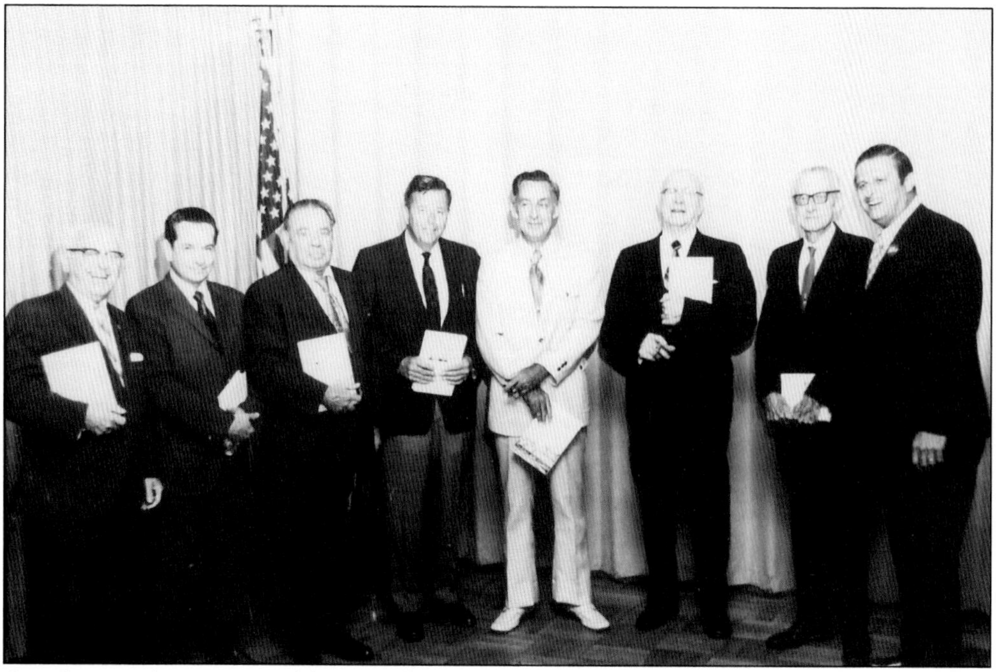

A gathering of mayors to celebrate Milltown's 75th anniversary, in 1971. Posing here are, from left to right, Art Sterner (1952–53), John Vandeputte (1960–67), Joseph DeHart (1940–42), J. Edward Crabiel (1948–51), Charles V. Booream (1956–59), Harry Meyers (1922–23), C.V.L. Booream (1932–33), and David B. Crabiel (1968–79). (Courtesy of Lynda Crabiel Cummings.)

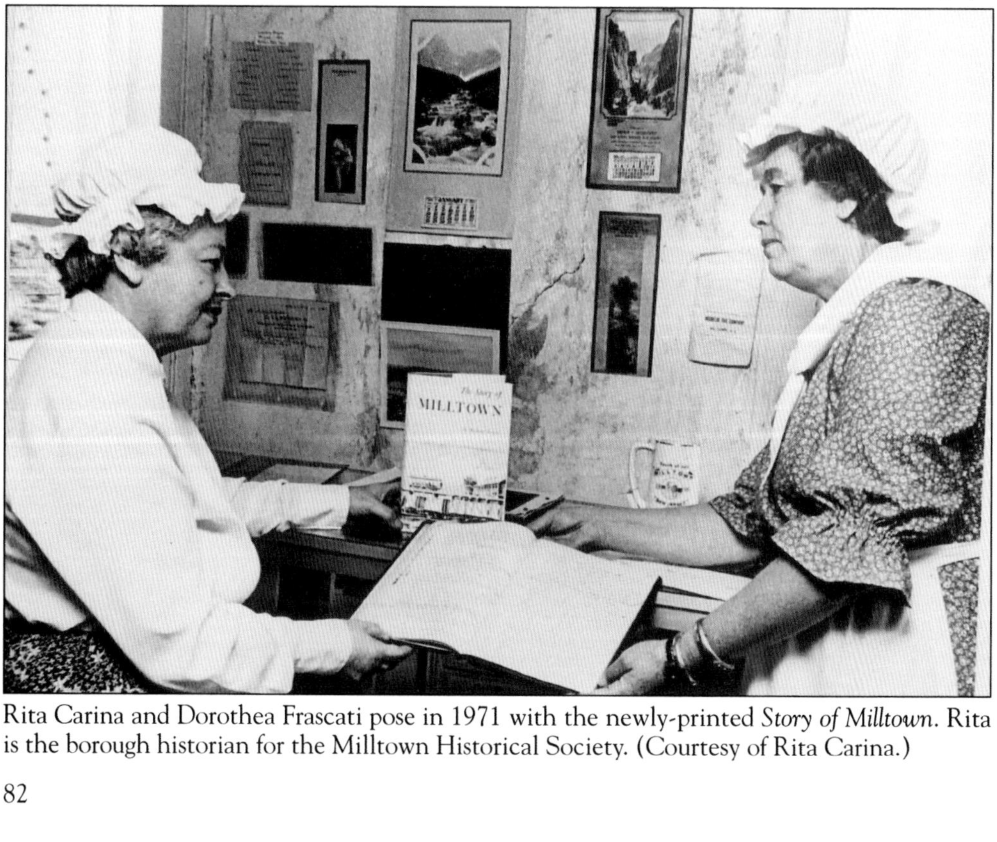

Rita Carina and Dorothea Frascati pose in 1971 with the newly-printed *Story of Milltown*. Rita is the borough historian for the Milltown Historical Society. (Courtesy of Rita Carina.)

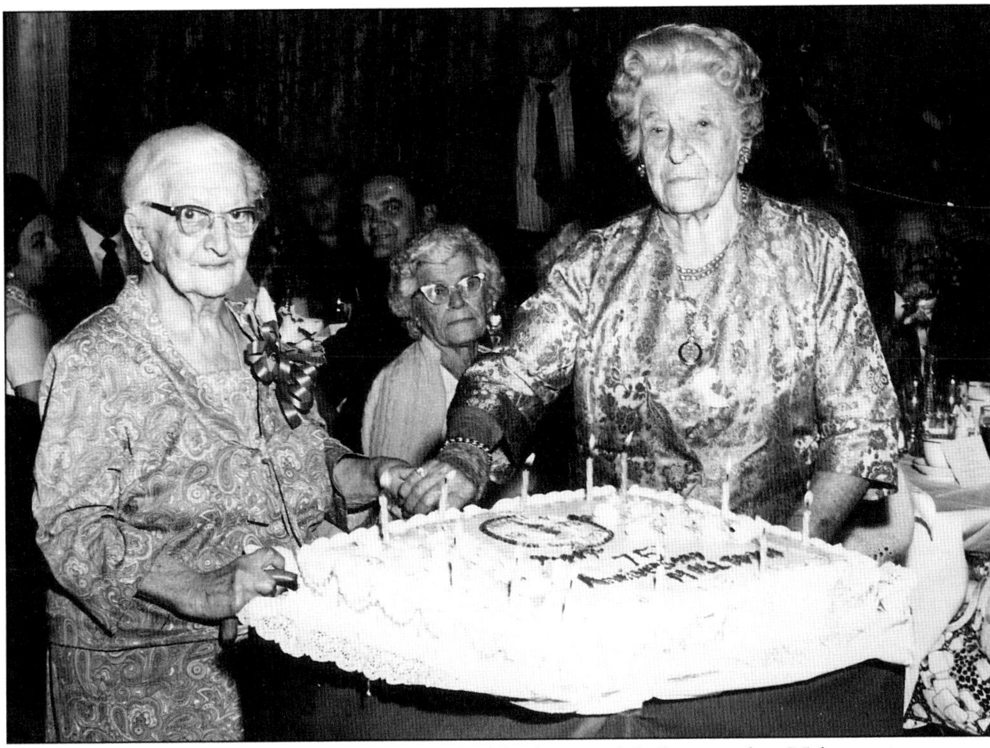

Mrs. Maria DeCarlo and Mrs. Margaret Buhl—honored ladies at the 75th anniversary of Milltown. (Courtesy of Rita Carina.)

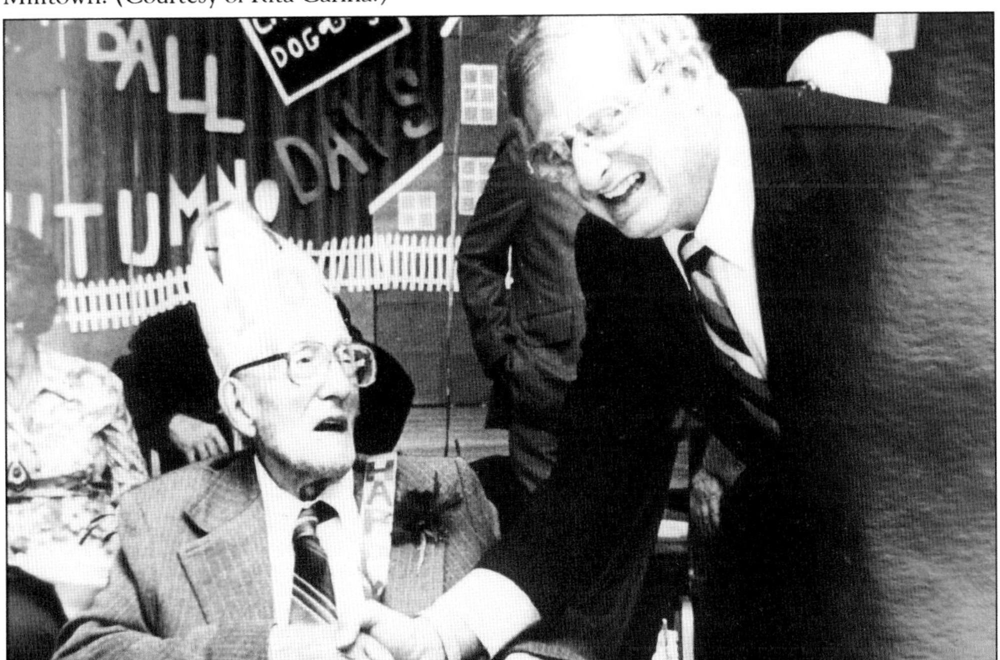

Mayor David B. Crabiel congratulates John Kemp on his 100th birthday, c. 1970s. (Courtesy of Paulette Crabiel Wahler.)

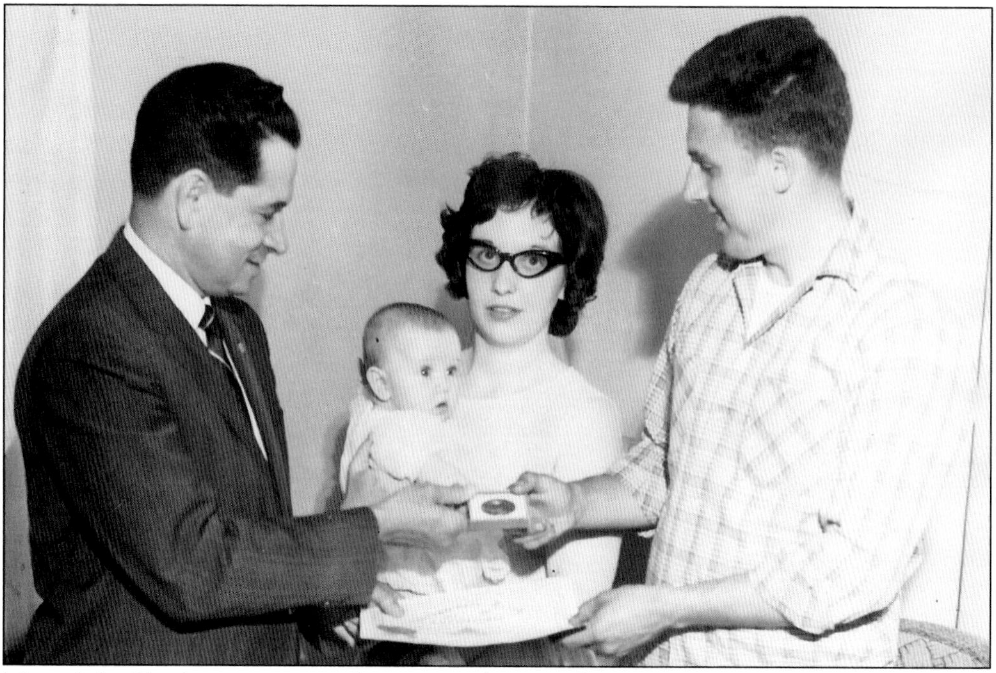

Mayor John Vandeputte congratulates Mr. and Mrs. Jefferson Lee Wilson on being the parents of the first baby born to a Milltown family in 1964, the Tercentenary of New Jersey. All babies born that year had their pictures taken and placed in a permanent record at the Milltown Public Library. The practice was repeated in 1976 for America's Bicentennial. That year's baby, Danny Pintauro, went on to Hollywood and is best know for appearing in "Who's The Boss?" Centennial babies will be likewise honored in 1996. (Courtesy of Edward V. Vetter Sr.)

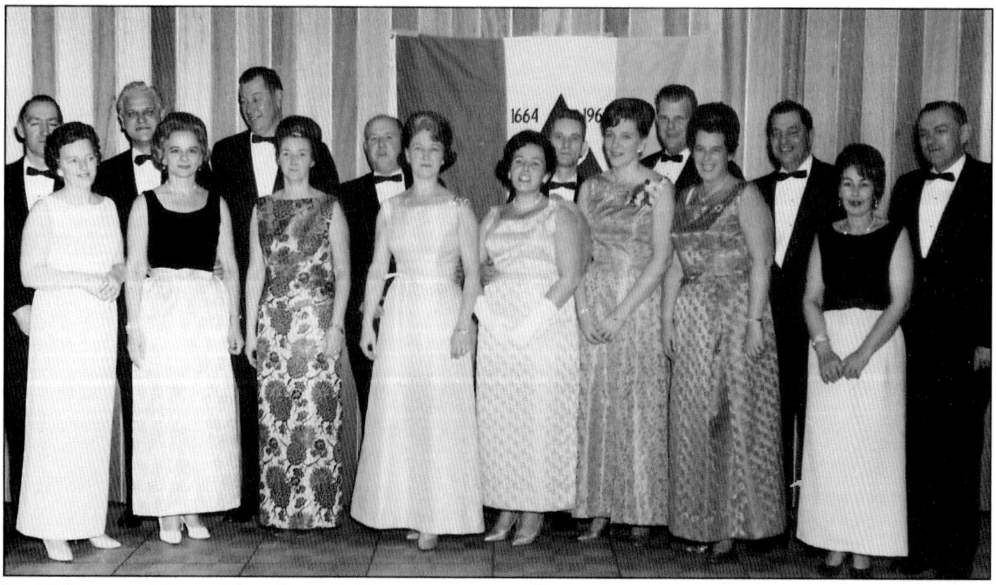

In 1964, to celebrate New Jersey's Tercentenary, Milltown's Tercentenary Committee organized many commemorative events, including a gala ball. The couples pictured here are, from left to right, the Baileys, unknown, the Pawlowskis, unknown, the Bradfords, the Hermanns, the Pondls, and unknown. (Courtesy of Edward V. Vetter Sr.)

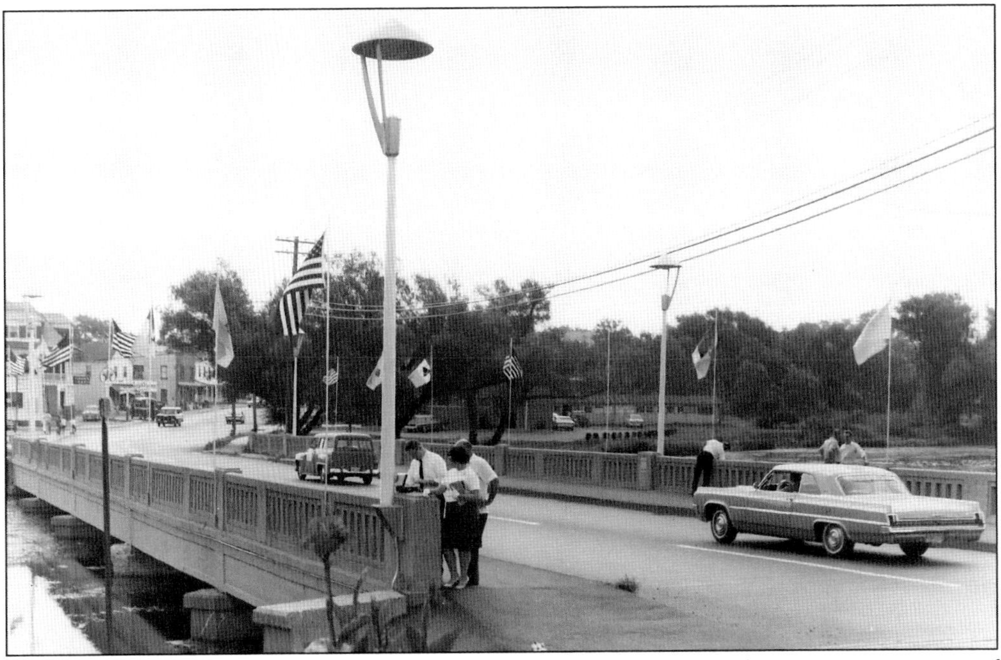

The Milltown Bridge (demolished in 1995) is seen here decorated for the 1964 Tercentenary of New Jersey. (Courtesy of Edward V. Vetter Sr.)

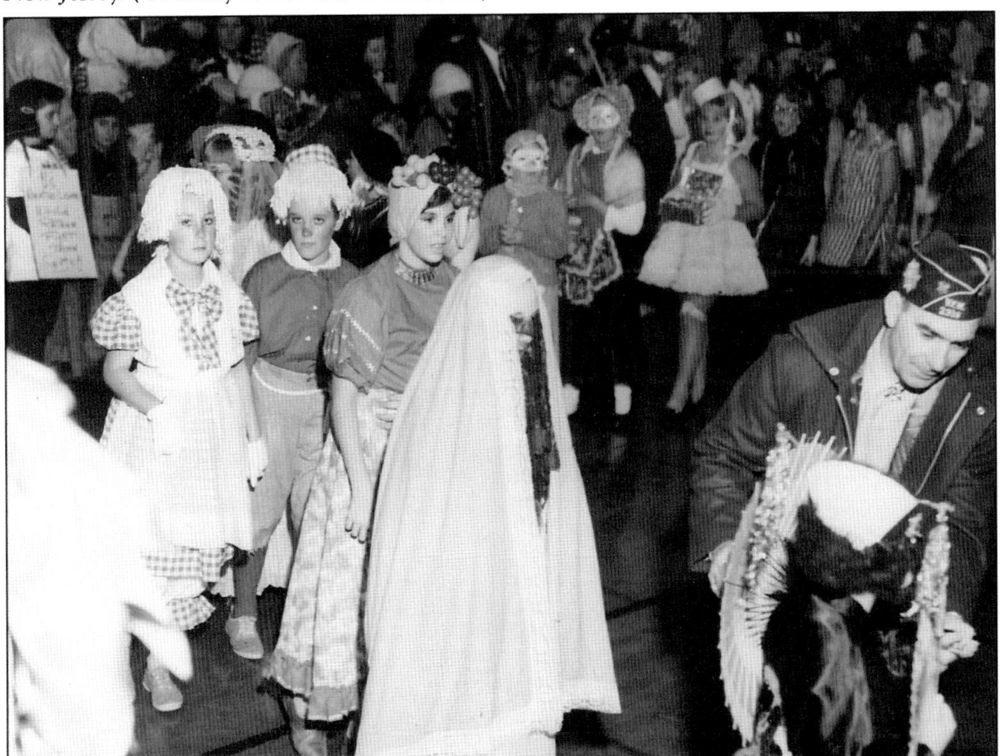

Milltown's annual Halloween Costume parade, sponsored by the Clark-Moetz Post 2319 of the VFW. This picture was taken in the 1960s. (Courtesy of Edward V. Vetter Sr.)

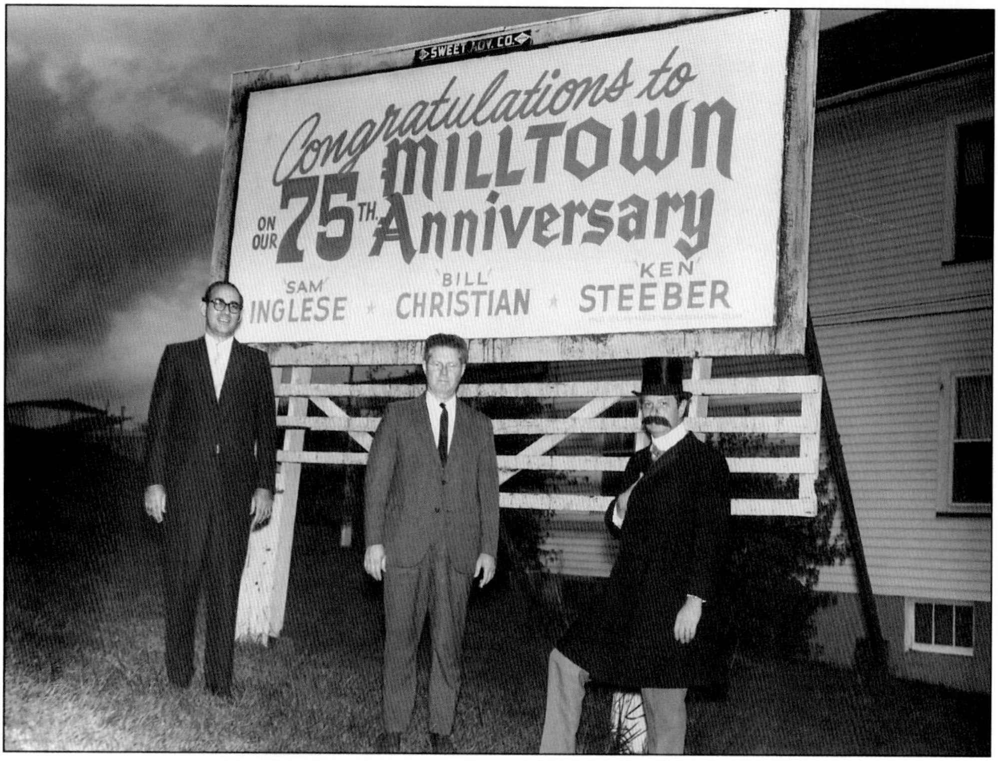

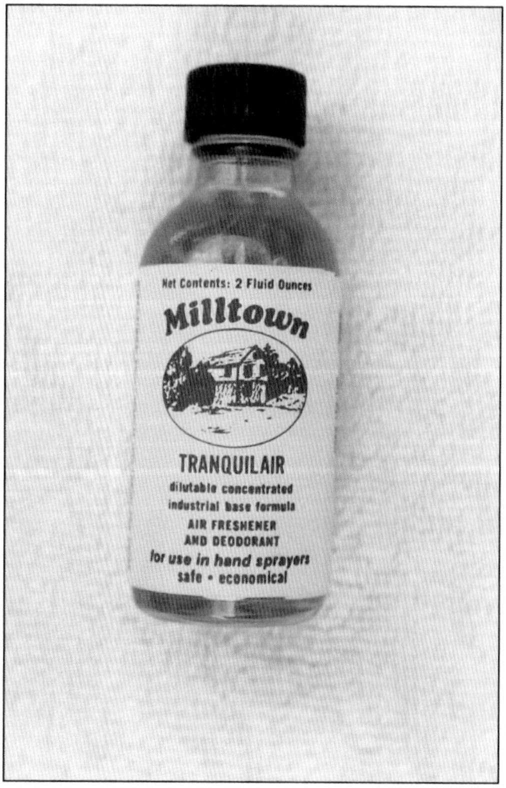

In 1971, Milltown celebrated its 75th anniversary. Pictured here with their billboard are, from left to right, Sam Inglese, Bill Christian, and Ken Steeber. (Courtesy of Eric Steeber.)

Freid Industries, located just over the Milltown border on Fresh Ponds Road in East Brunswick, produced chemicals such as the "Milltown Tranquilair" pictured here. (Courtesy of Drew Harto.)

Seven

Taking Care of Business

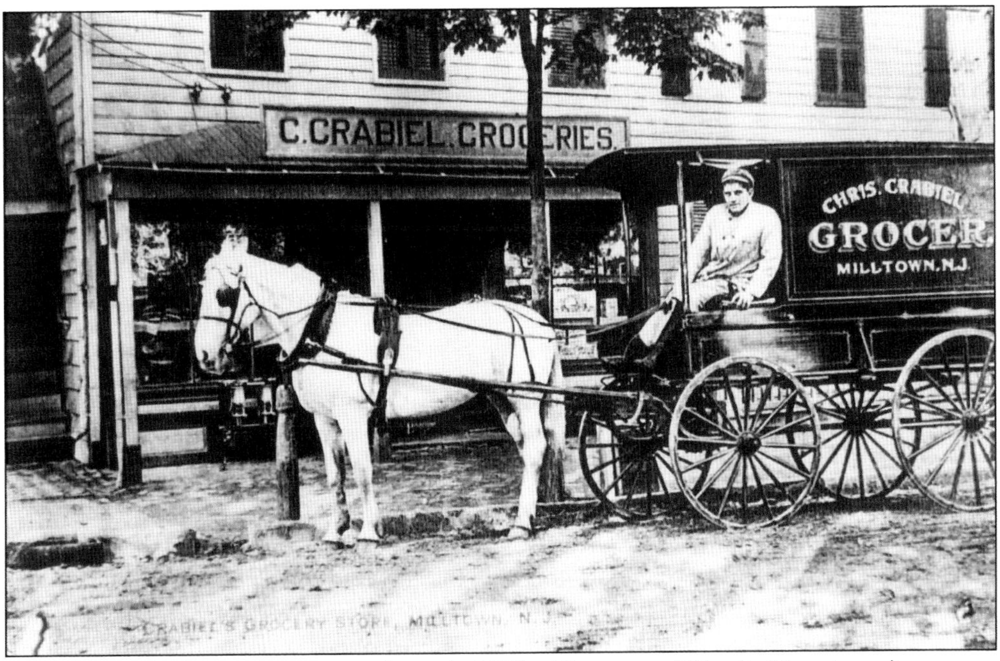

Christian Crabiel's grocery store in the early 1900s. (Courtesy of Charlie Nenninger.)

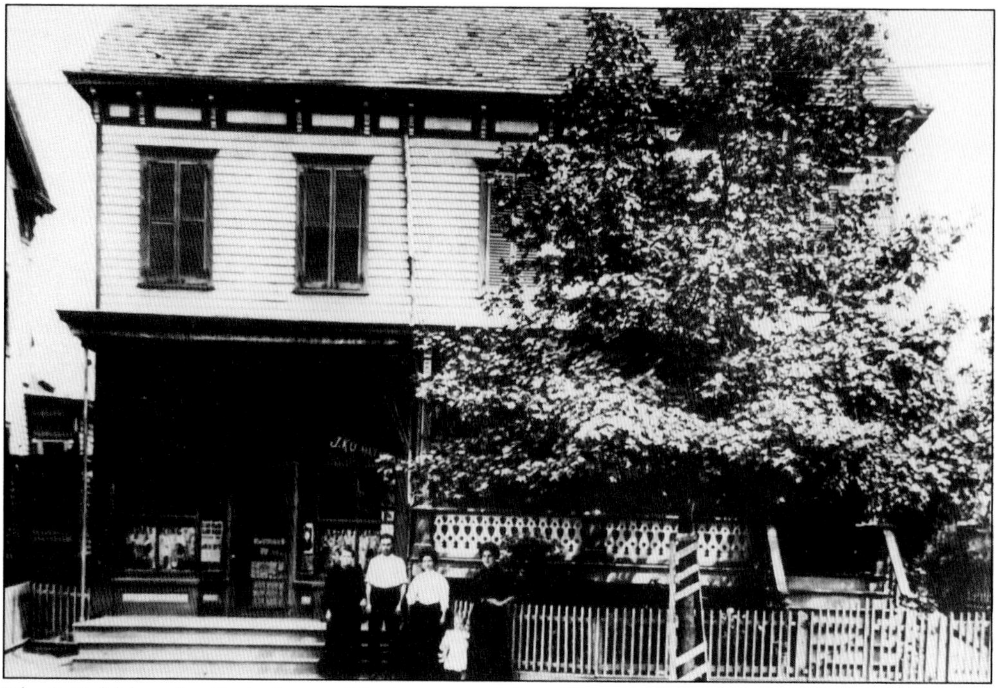

The J. Kuhlthau family, in front of their store on Main Street, c. 1908. Pictured here are, from left to right, Margaret Schudig Kuhlthau, Fred Kuhlthau, Marie Armstrong Kuhlthau, Margaret "Baby" Woerner Johnson, and Barbara Kuhlthau Waters. (Courtesy of Milltown Historical Society.)

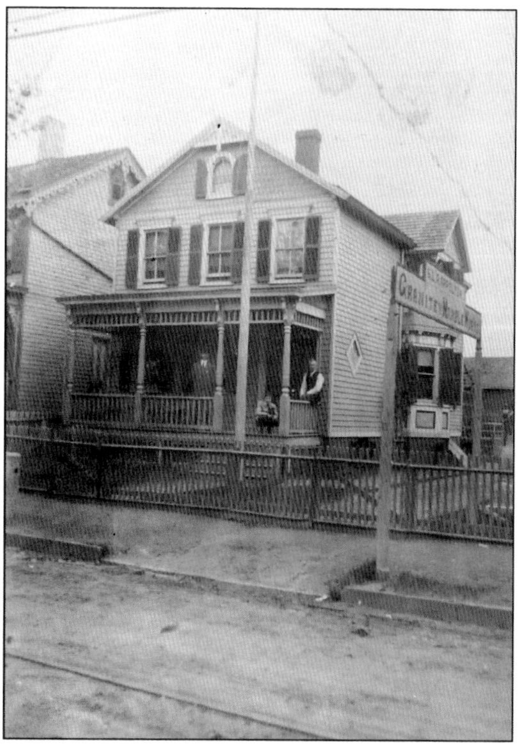

The Rappelyea Granite and Marble Works was located on Main Street in the early 1900s. The company created "Monumental and Cemetery Work of Every Description." Stafford Rappelyea was the second mayor of Milltown, from 1901 to 1902. (Courtesy of Milltown Historical Society.)

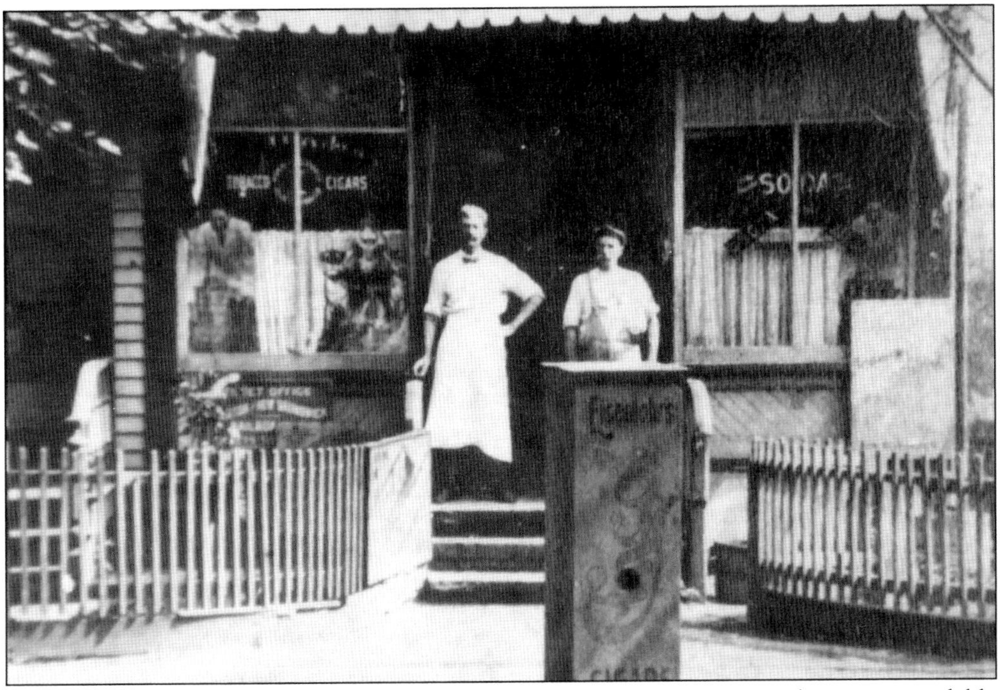

Charles Hodapp's Confectionary Store, on Main Street, *c.* 1900. Train tickets were available here. The store was later owned by Hodapp's son Frank. Other owners of the store included Fred Brunning, Miles Kuhlthau, Harold Schlosser, and Frank Wagner. The store was torn down to make way for the parking lot of the Methodist church. (Courtesy of Rita Carina.)

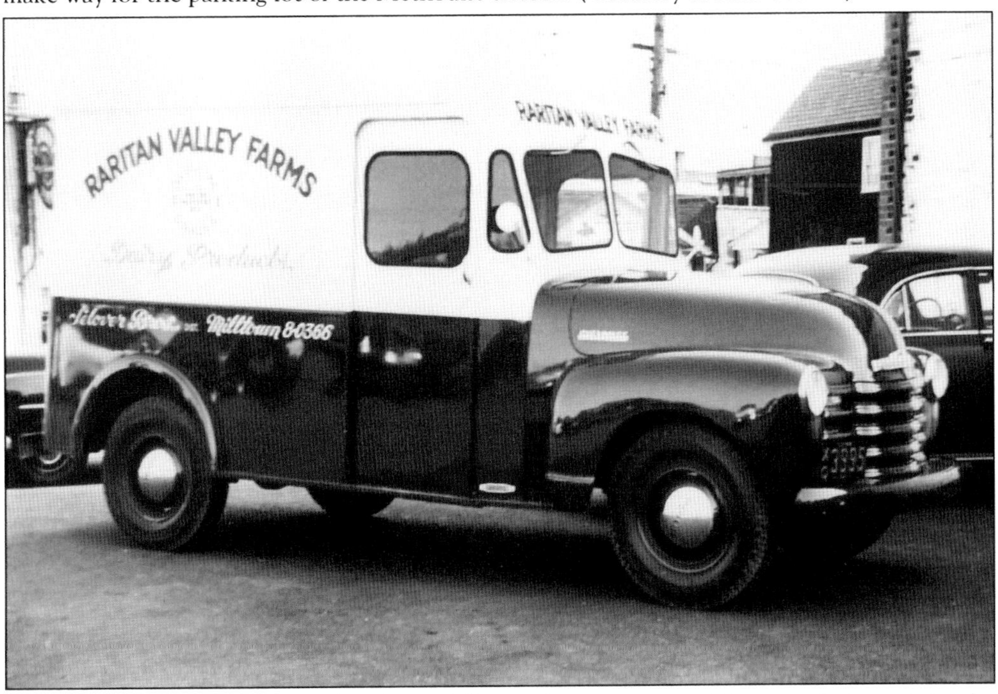

The Selover Brothers delivered milk to Milltown for many years. This was their truck in the 1940s. (Courtesy of Ken Selover.)

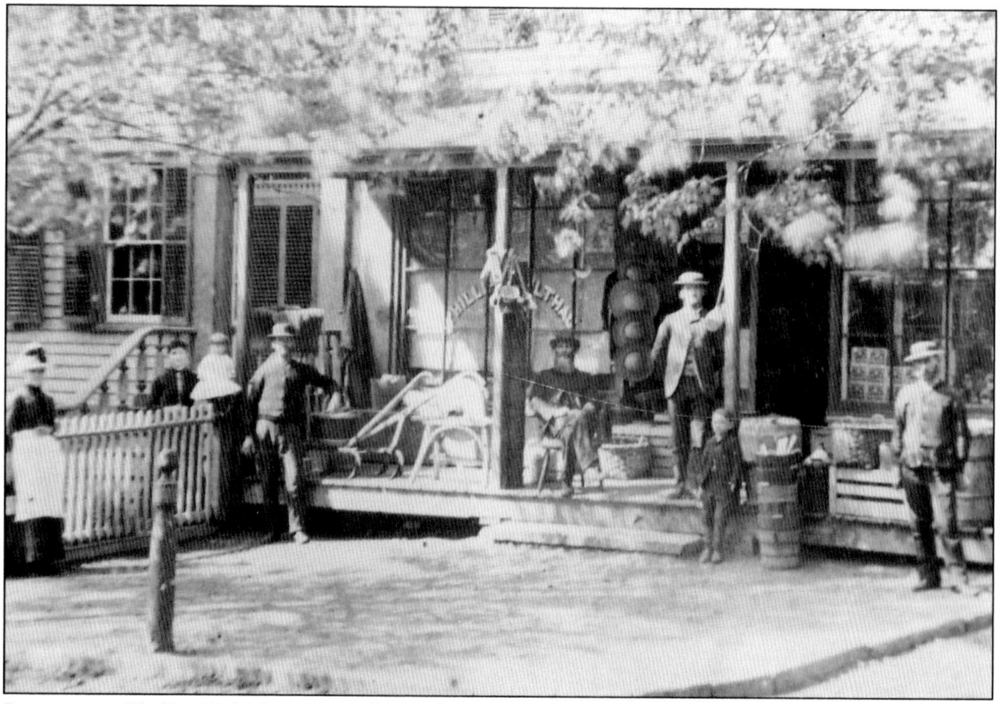

Postmaster Phillip Kuhlthau gazes from the porch of his home, general store, and post office, c. 1886. This is now Milltown General Hardware, at 66 North Main Street. (Courtesy of Milltown Historical Society.)

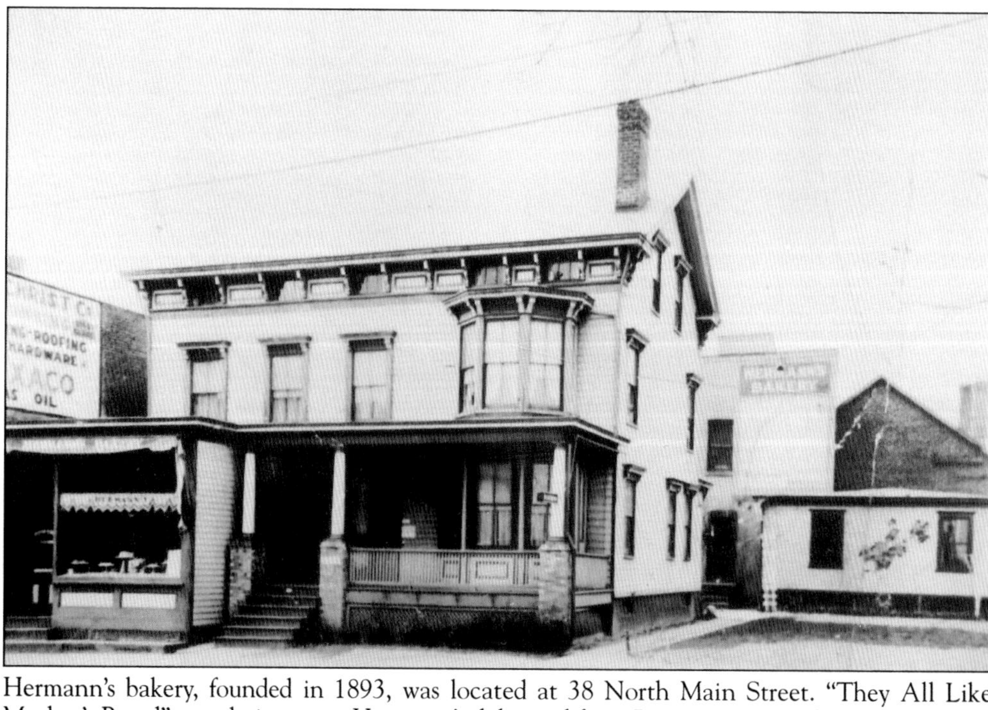

Hermann's bakery, founded in 1893, was located at 38 North Main Street. "They All Like Mother's Bread" was their motto. Hermann's delivered from Piscataway to Helmetta with their horse-drawn wagon. (Courtesy of Rita Carina.)

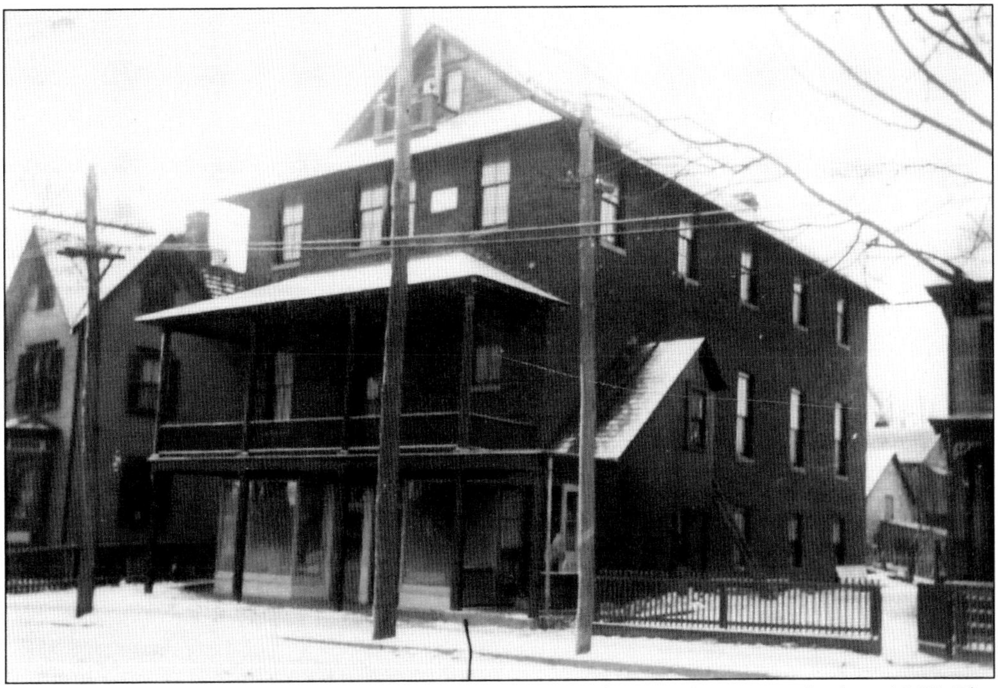

Red Man's Hall, currently the Masonic Lodge, at 30 North Main Street, was built in 1907. The Milltown chapter of the nationwide Red Men organization once had five hundred members. (Courtesy of Rita Carina.)

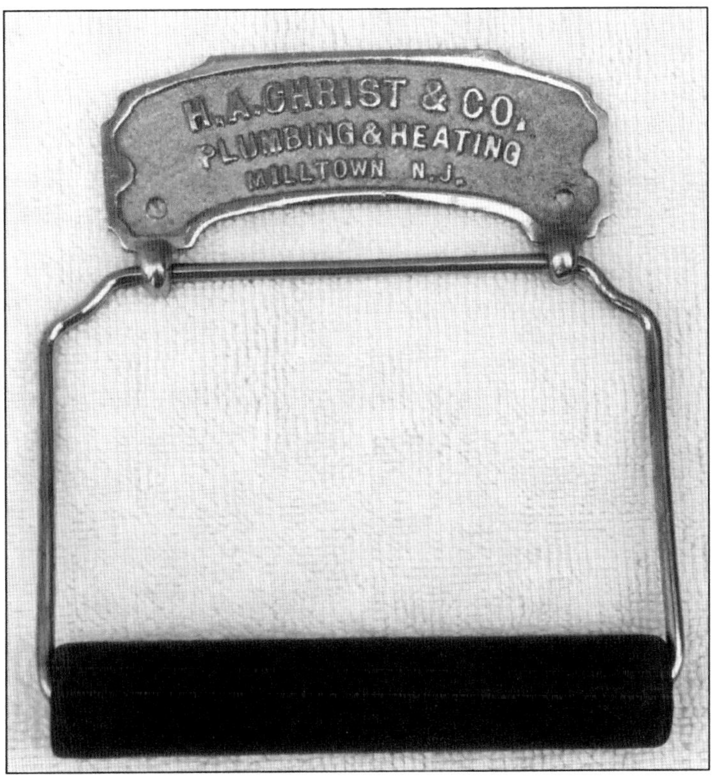

Henry Christ operated a Plumbing and Heating Supply business in Milltown for over thirty years. The item pictured was a promotional giveaway. (Courtesy of George Guise.)

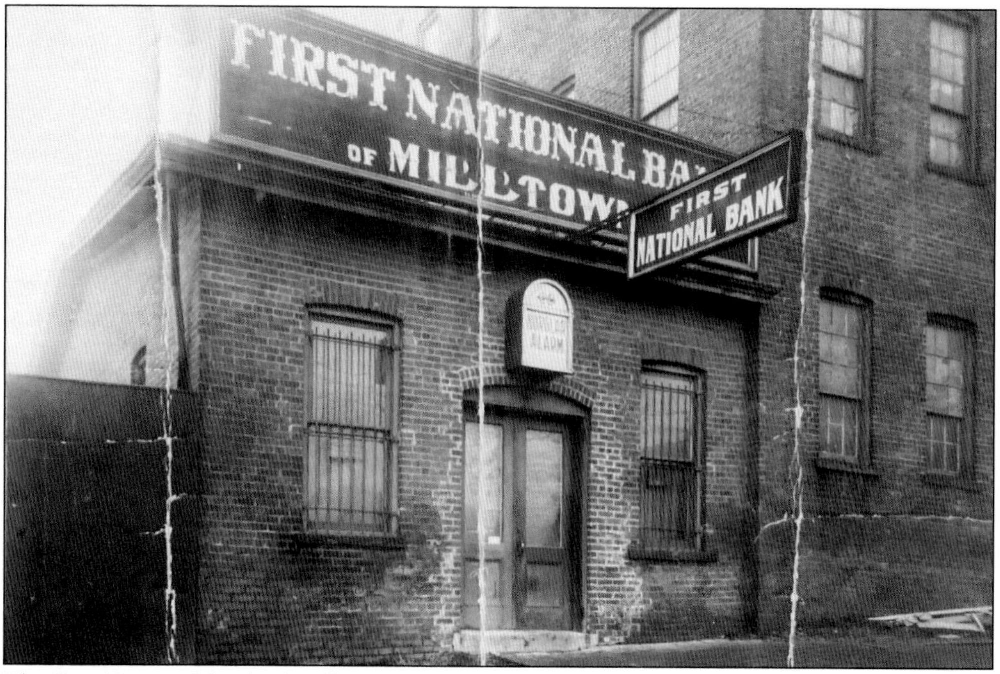

The First National Bank of Milltown was originally attached to the back of Michelin Building #1 on North Main Street, and is seen here *c.* 1917. (Courtesy of Milltown Historical Society.)

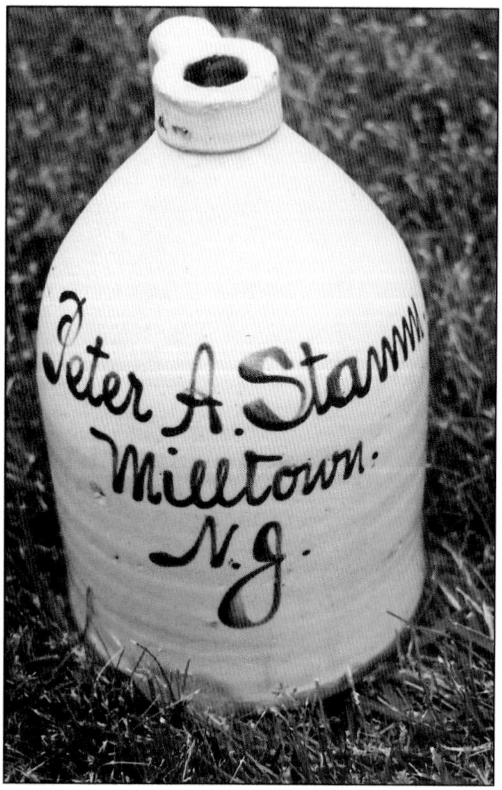

In the 1880s, Peter A. Stamm had a bottling house on Ryders Lane. He purchased beer and whiskey in barrels, then sold it in these jugs. (Courtesy of Brian Harto.)

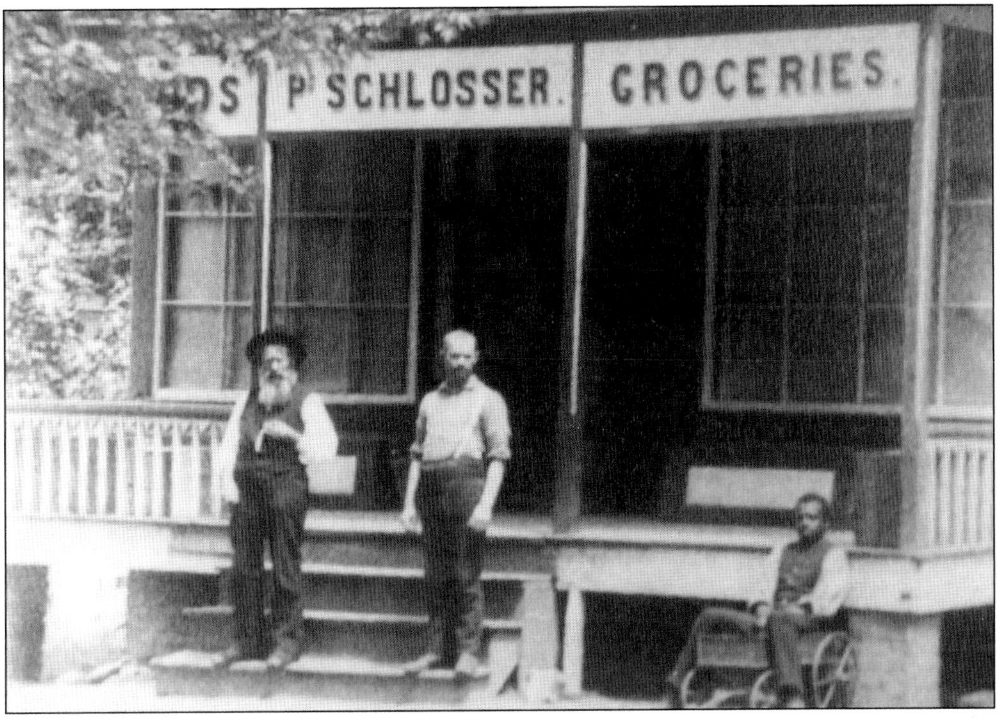

Phillip Schlosser Sr. and Phillip Schlosser Jr. stand in front of their grocery store in 1890. The Milltown Amoco is now located at this site. (Courtesy of Rita Carina.)

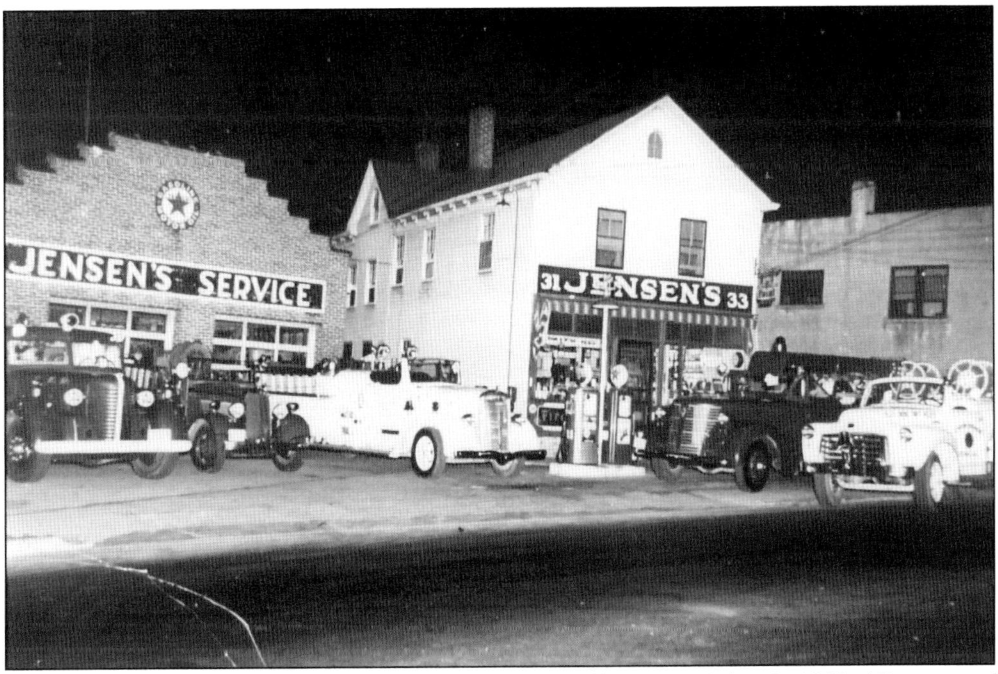

Firemen's Night at the Firemen's Carnival, held in Milltown on July 19, 1950. (Courtesy of Milltown Historical Society.)

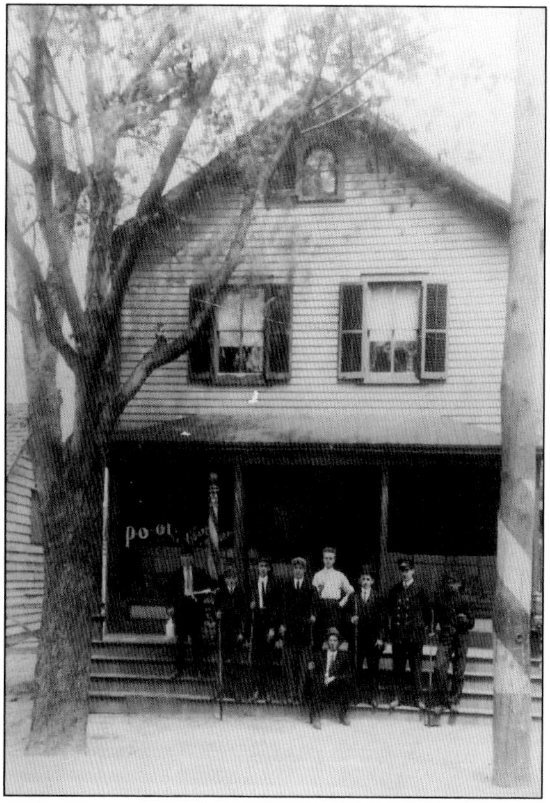

Christian Jensen's Barbershop and Pool Hall, c. 1920s. Pictured here, from left to right are Art Beecher, Charles Sevenhair, John Dorn, Conrad Geer, Chris Jensen, George Schaeffer, John MacKinsey, and Mr. Arvie. Ed Geer is seated. (Courtesy of Ken Selover.)

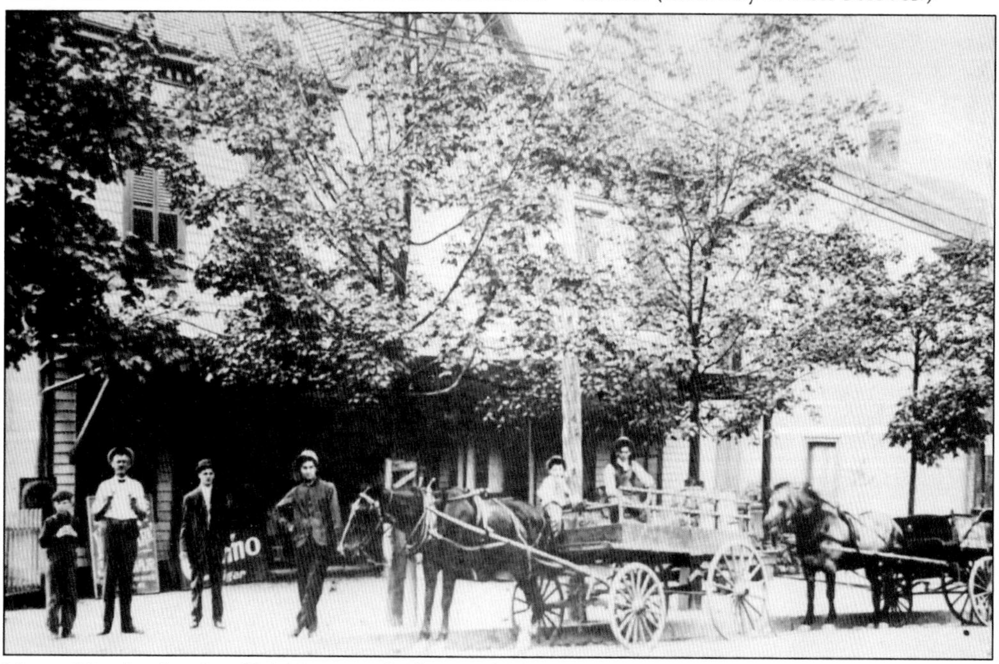

Henry Hartlander, Jim Kuhlthau, and Chris Kuhlthau, in front of 80 South Main Street, which was William Kuhlthau's store and a post office. "The Banana Man" and his son are in the wagon. Chris Kuhlthau's wagon follows, pulled by "Flick" the horse. (Courtesy of Irma Lown.)

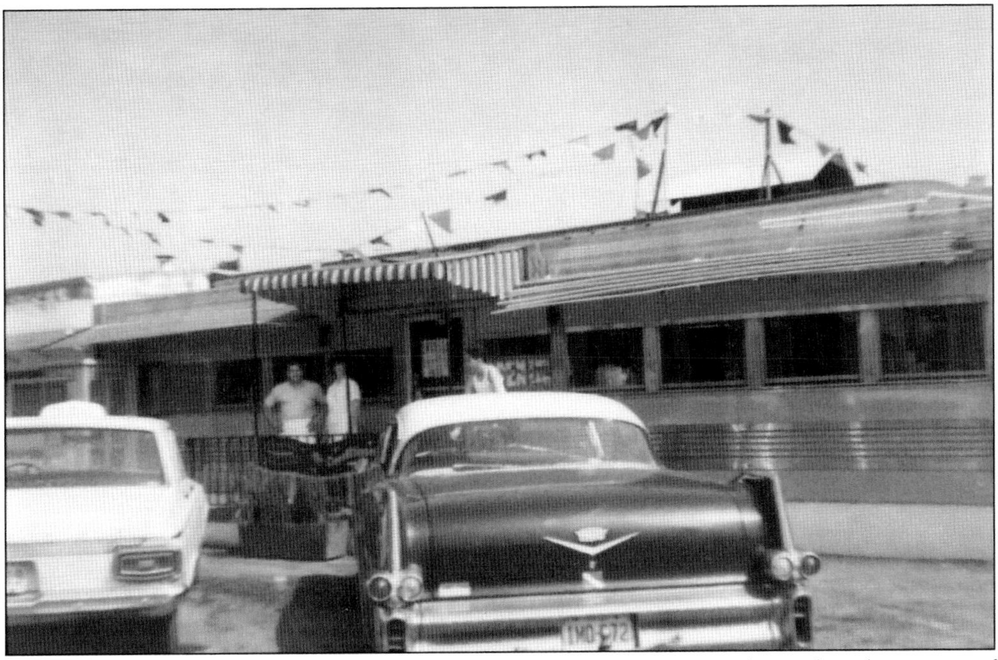

This is a rare picture, *c.* early 1960s, of the Milltown diner that was located at the corner of South Main Street and Washington Avenue, now the Hess Gas Station. Standing on the porch are Richie Mascarelli and Sally Fuchs. (Courtesy of Richie Williams.)

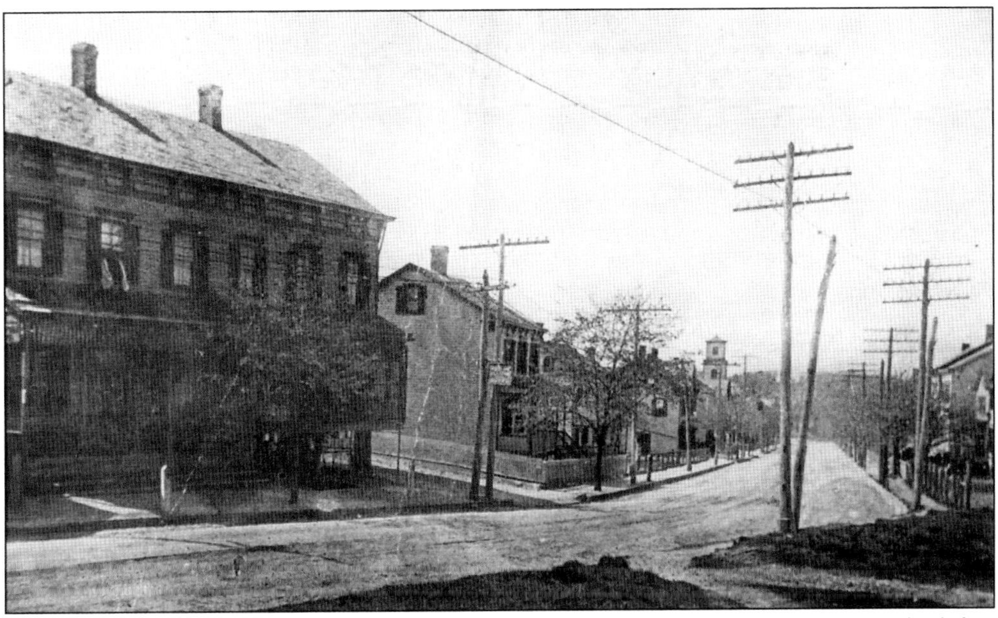

South Main Street, at Violet Terrace, looking north, *c.* early 1900s. The building on the left is the Milltown Hotel, currently Van's Tobacco Shop. (Courtesy of Rita Carina.)

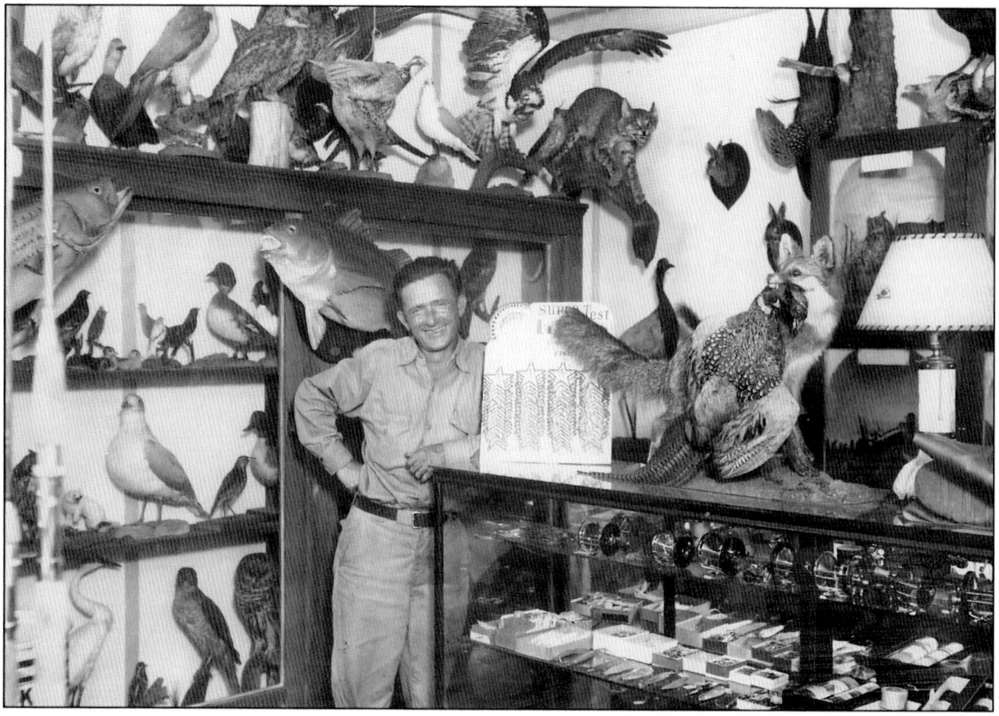

Arthur J. Schwendeman, proprietor, inside the showroom of his new taxidermy store building at 119 South Main Street, *c.* 1940s. (Courtesy of the Schwendeman family.)

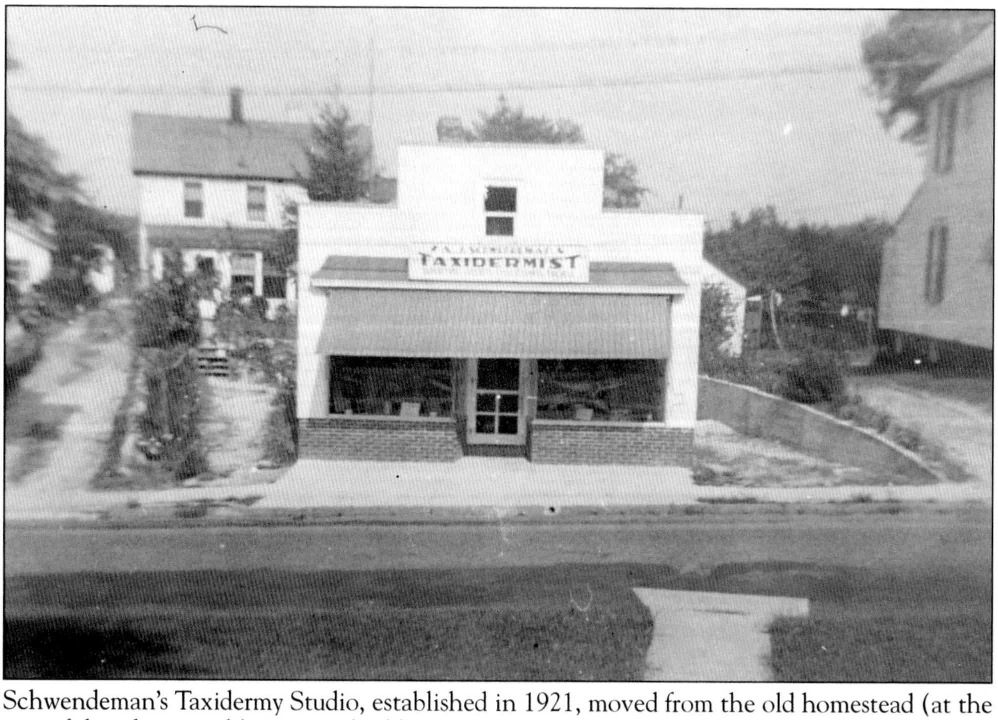

Schwendeman's Taxidermy Studio, established in 1921, moved from the old homestead (at the rear of this photograph) to a new building, in 1939. (Courtesy of the Schwendeman family.)

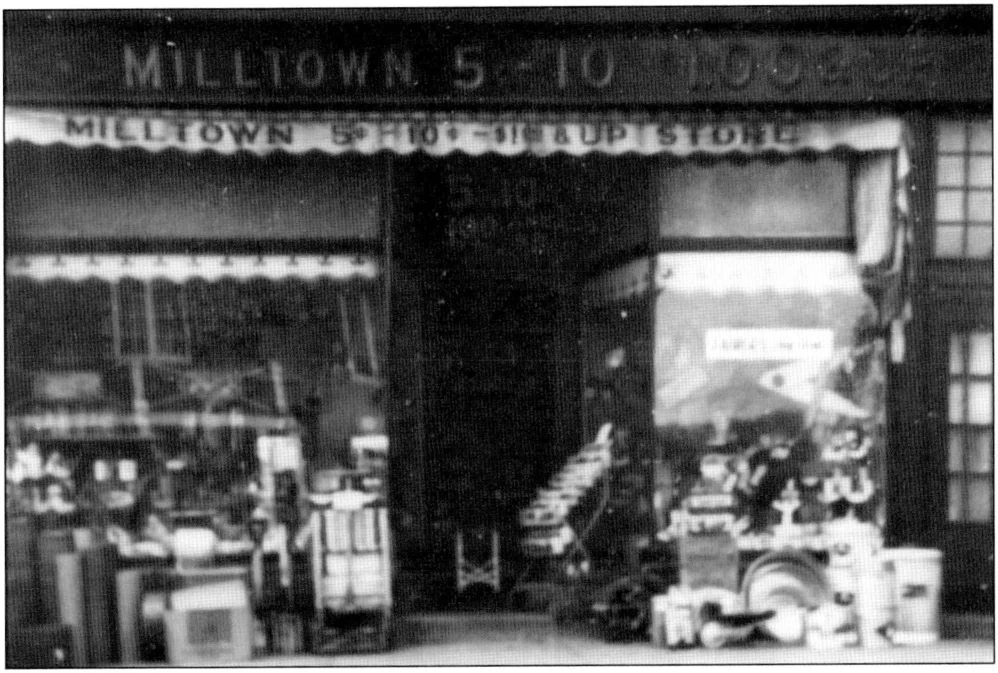

The Milltown Five and Ten Cent Store, at 36 North Main Street, currently housing Rocco's Barber Shop and Dr. Kelleman, O.D. (Courtesy of Rita Carina.)

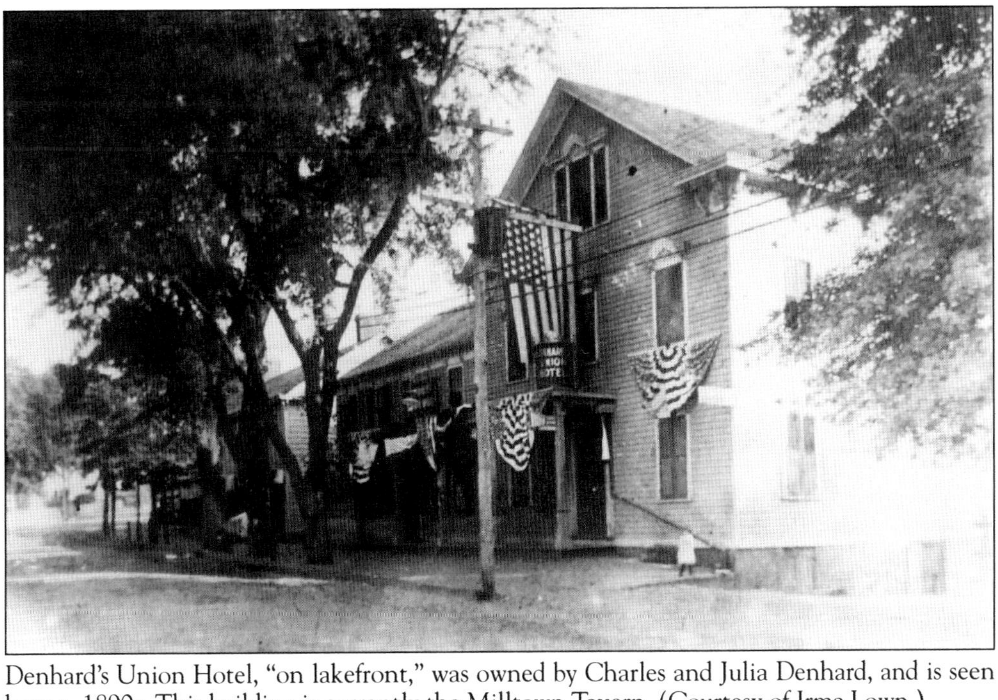

Denhard's Union Hotel, "on lakefront," was owned by Charles and Julia Denhard, and is seen here *c*. 1890s. This building is currently the Milltown Tavern. (Courtesy of Irma Lown.)

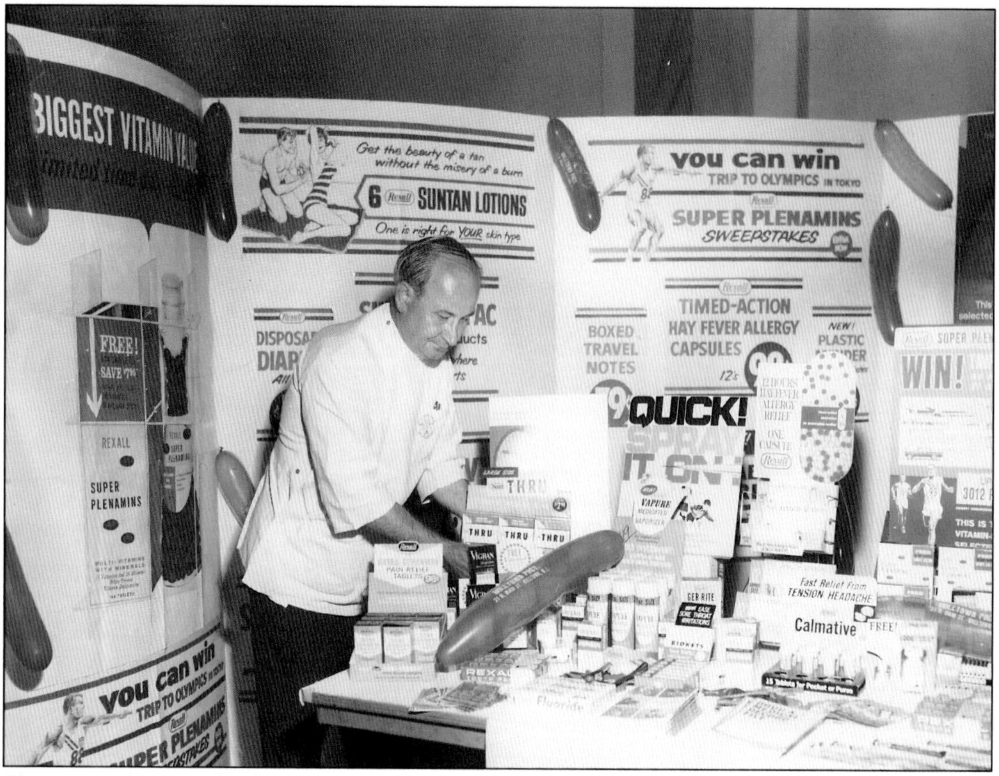

Pharmacist Louis Lukach sets up his display for a town business show held in 1964. (Courtesy of Edward V. Vetter Sr.)

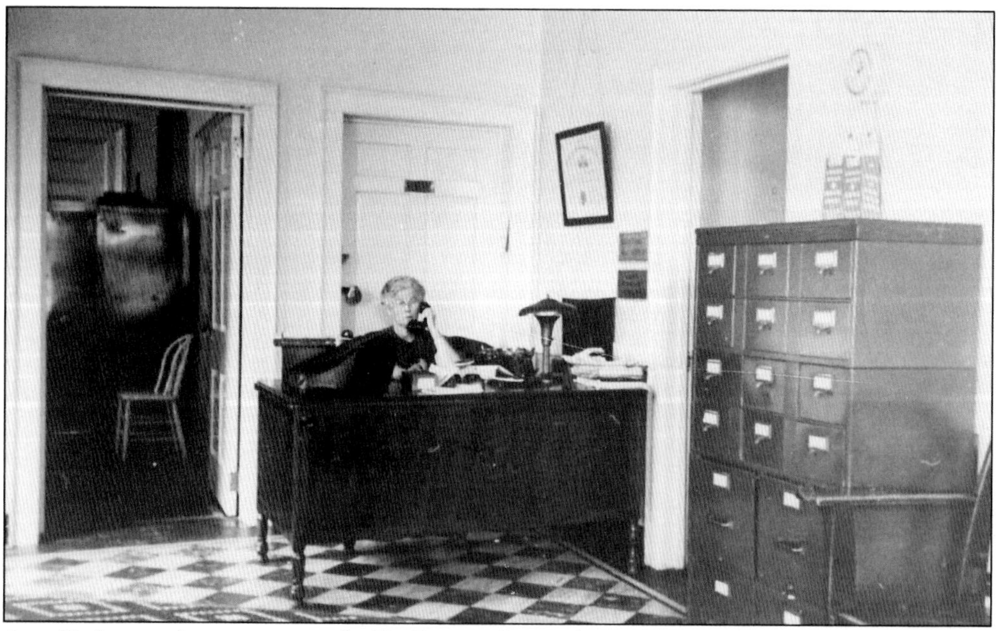

Ann Hofer was the receptionist for Dr. Forney during the 1940s. The home, which still houses a doctor's office, is one of the few remaining Victorian buildings in Milltown, and is located at 96 North Main Street. (Courtesy of Irma Lown.)

Eight

Honor and Glory

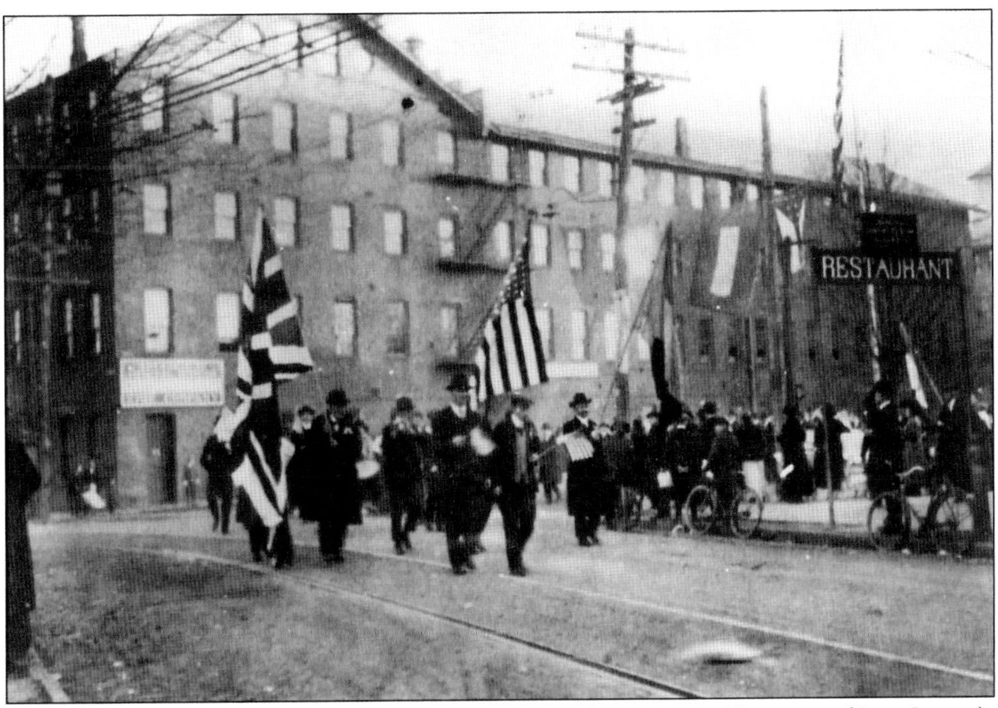

A military parade marches past Ford Avenue on November 7, 1918. (Courtesy of Irma Lown.)

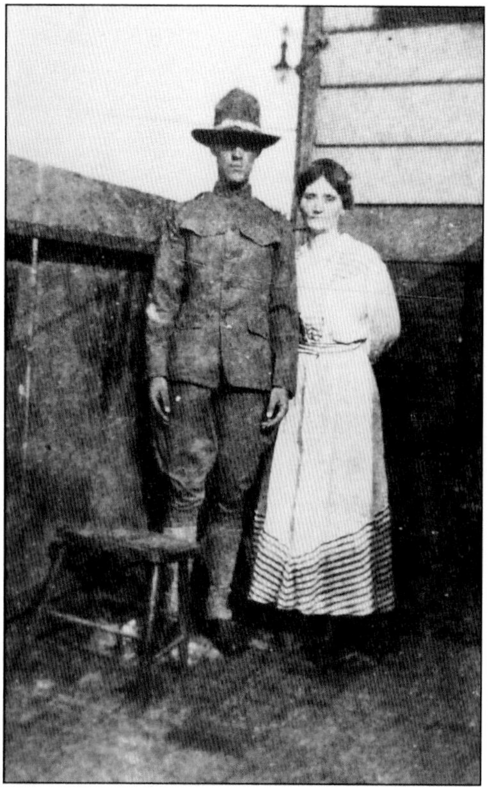

George H. Stilwell Sr. and his mother, before he left for war in 1917. (Courtesy of George H. Stilwell Jr.)

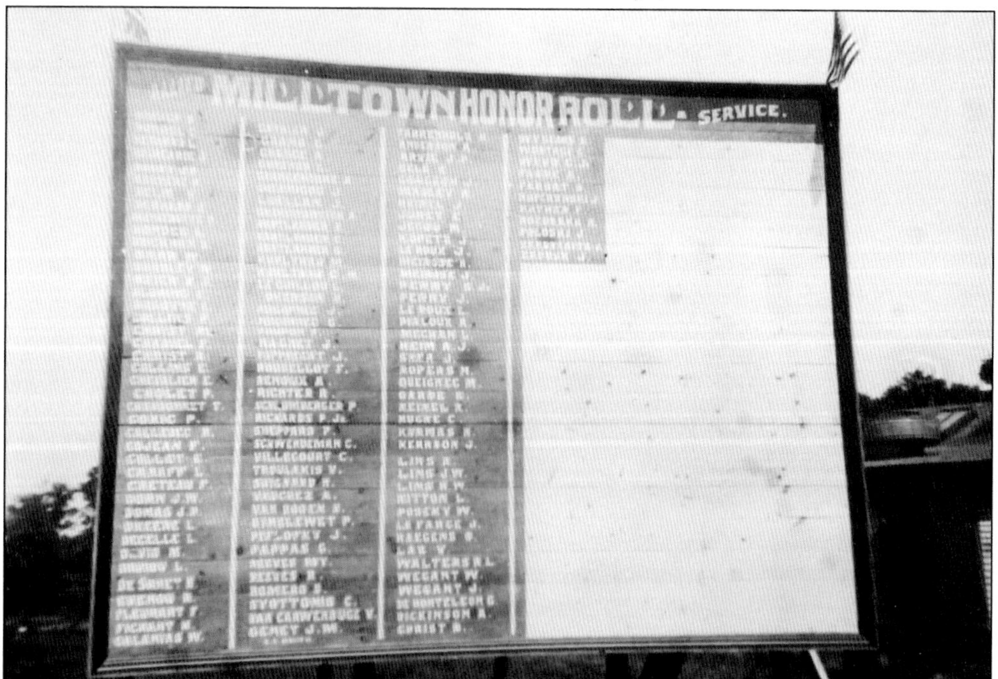

This Milltown Honor Roll listed Milltown residents who were serving in World War I at that time. (Courtesy of the Donald Hermann family.)

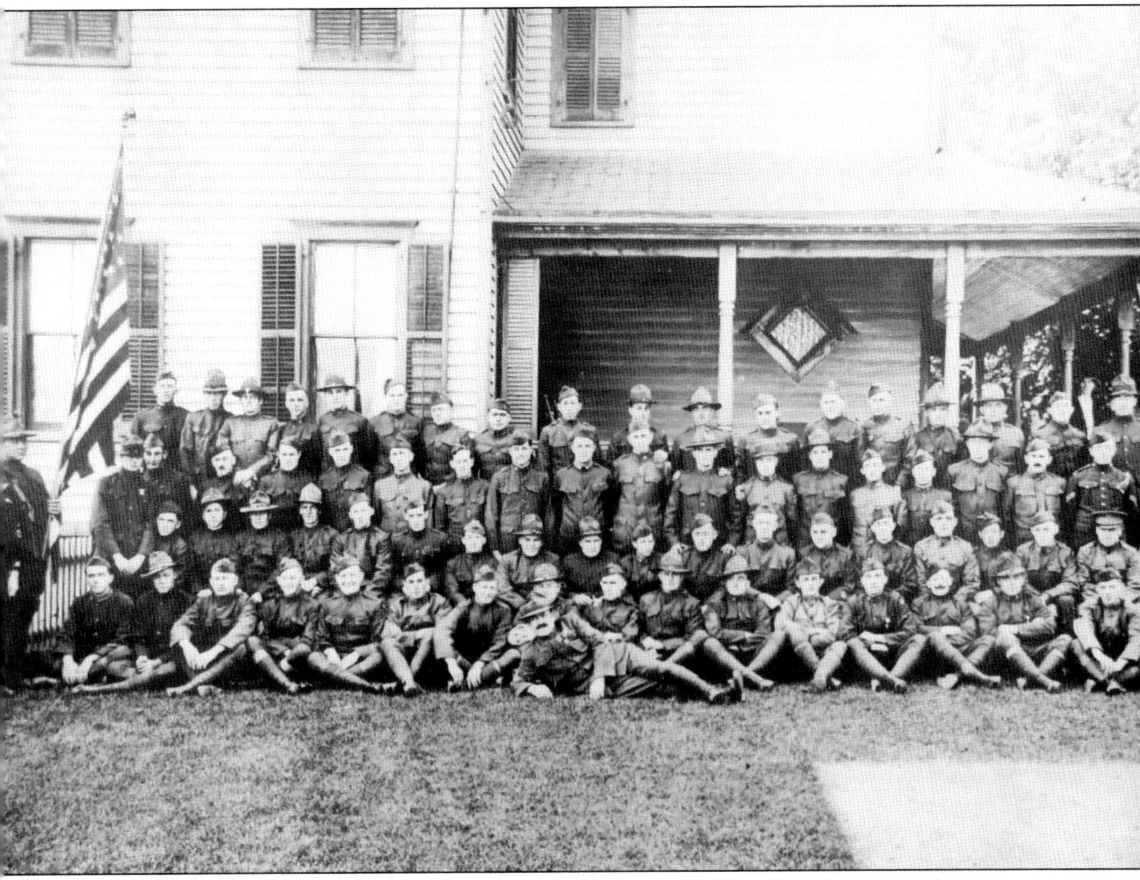

Milltown area veterans of World War I pose in front of the French School on Main Street in 1919. Pictured here are, from left to right: (front row) Charles Weyd (the sailor), Robert Headley, William Haefner, unknown, Charles Hartlander, John Lins, unknown, unknown, Al Christ, John Dorn, unknown, Conrad Green, George Schork, unknown, unknown, unknown, and unknown (one of the unknowns is Charles Wolff); (second row) Joseph Haefner (holding the flag), unknown, Miles Kuhlthau, unknown, unknown, Joseph Schwendeman, John Heinz, Edgar Collins, Henry Hartlander, Arthur Holz, Edmund Brown, Dan Crabiel, Robert Heimel, Lou Jensen, Henry Baier, unknown, unknown, John Meirose, Art Lins, and Howard (Bruno) Moore; (third row) George Warnsdorfer, Walt Theurich, Henry Smith, Jesse Perry, ? Ochs, Ferdinand Crabiel, unknown, John Heimel, William Schwendeman, John Christ, Irv Crabiel, Leroy Reeves, unknown, unknown, unknown, and Bill Bradley; (back row) unknown, George Hofer, unknown, unknown, Henry Lins, Charles Farenholz, William Sevenhair, Steve Berish, unknown, unknown, Howard Reeves, Bob Walters?, Sheepy Falk, Charles Schwendeman, Ralph Reeves, unknown, Charles Kuhlthau, and unknown. (Courtesy of Charlie Nenninger.)

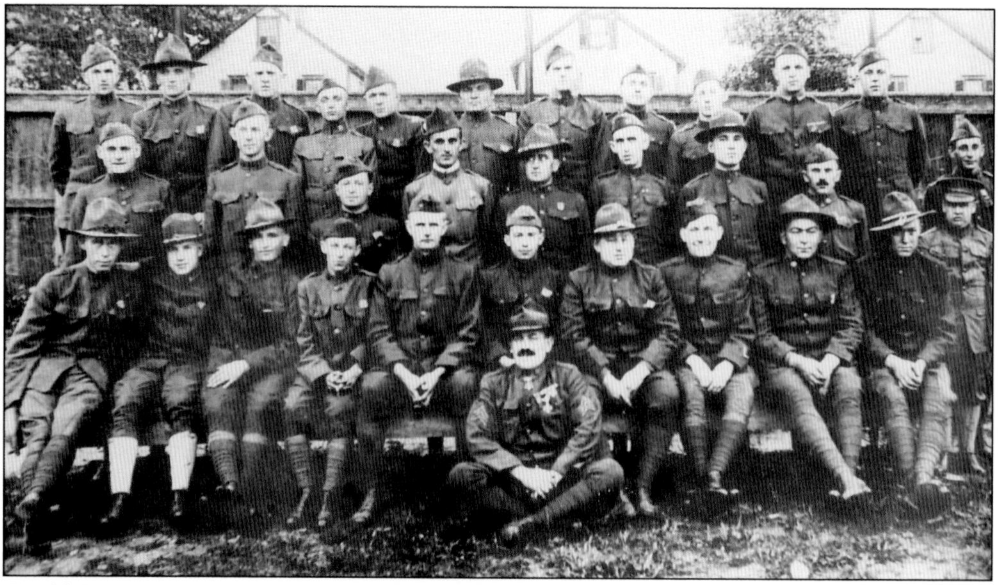

World War I veterans pose at Michelin Athletic Field. These men were also members of the Red Men club. Seen here are, from left to right: (front row) George Hofer, John Christ, Bill Schwendeman, Emil Gruber, Lou Jensen, Henry Hartlander, Charles Woolf (on the ground), Al Christ, John Lins, Joe Haefner, Bill Haefner, and Bruno Moore; (middle row) Henry Bair, Charles Hartlander, Joe Hartlander, George Schork, Conrad Carina, John Dorn, Henry Lins, Mike Nickola, and George Warnsdorfer; (back row) Miles Kuhlthau, Ralph Reeves, Sheepy Falk, Roy Reeves, William Sevenhair, Art Hoelzer, Charles Farenholz, Mickey Kuhlthau, John Heinz, John Heimel, and Robert Heimel. (Courtesy of Ken Selover.)

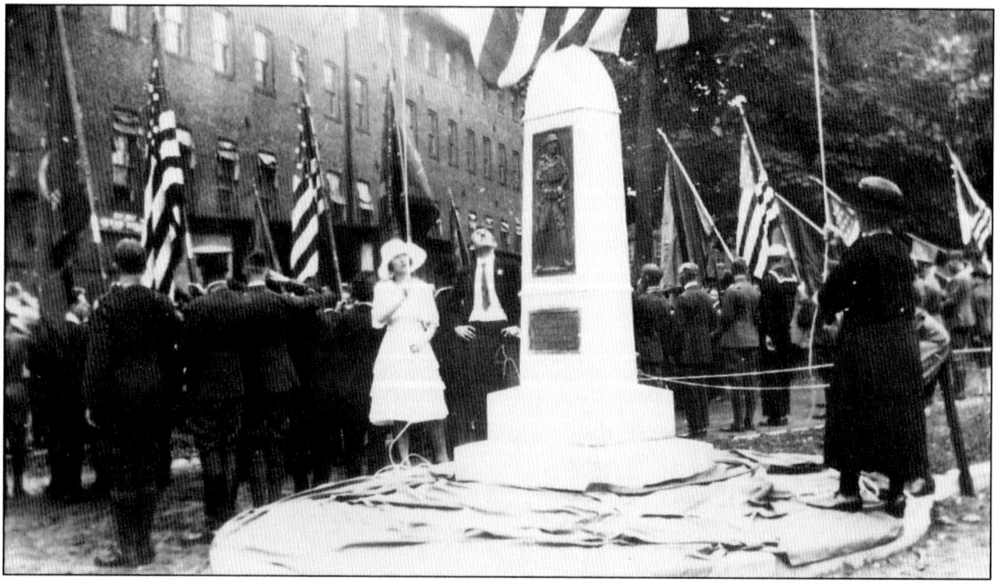

This monument was erected in 1921, to honor World War I soldiers. An elaborate unveiling ceremony was held, during which a huge American flag was draped over the monument and then removed with a rope and pulley. A lone trumpet player played "Taps" from further down Ford Avenue. (Courtesy of the Donald Hermann family.)

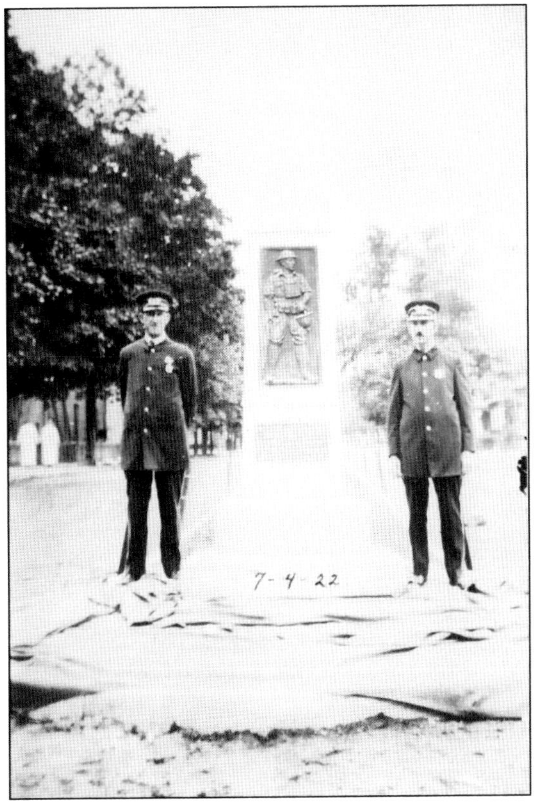

Nicholas Young and George Lins pose at the World War I Monument, located, until the 1990s, in the center of the intersection of Ford Avenue and North Main Street. The date is July Fourth, 1922. (Courtesy of the Donald Hermann family.)

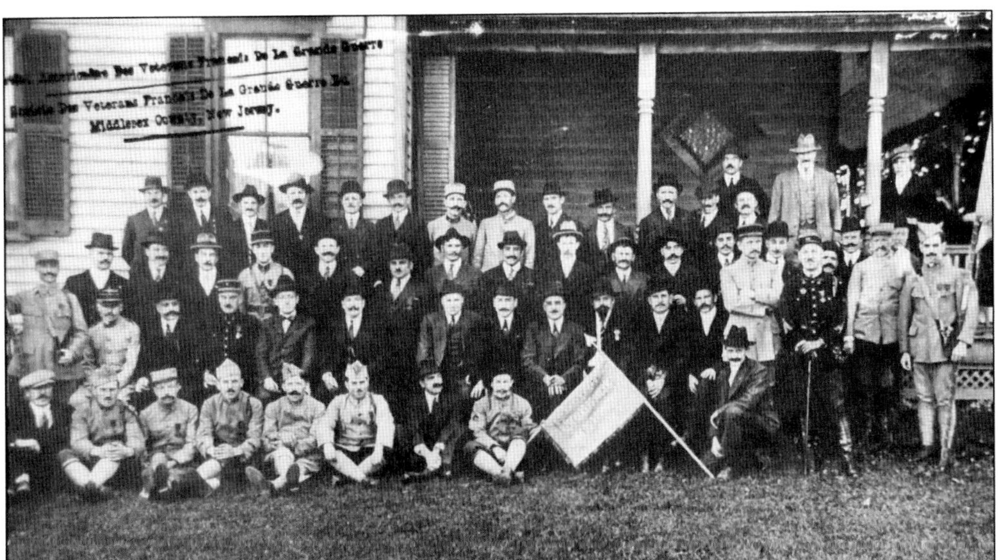

Middlesex County veterans of World War I pose in front of the French School on North Main Street. Most of these men worked at the Michelin factory. (Courtesy of Rita Carina.)

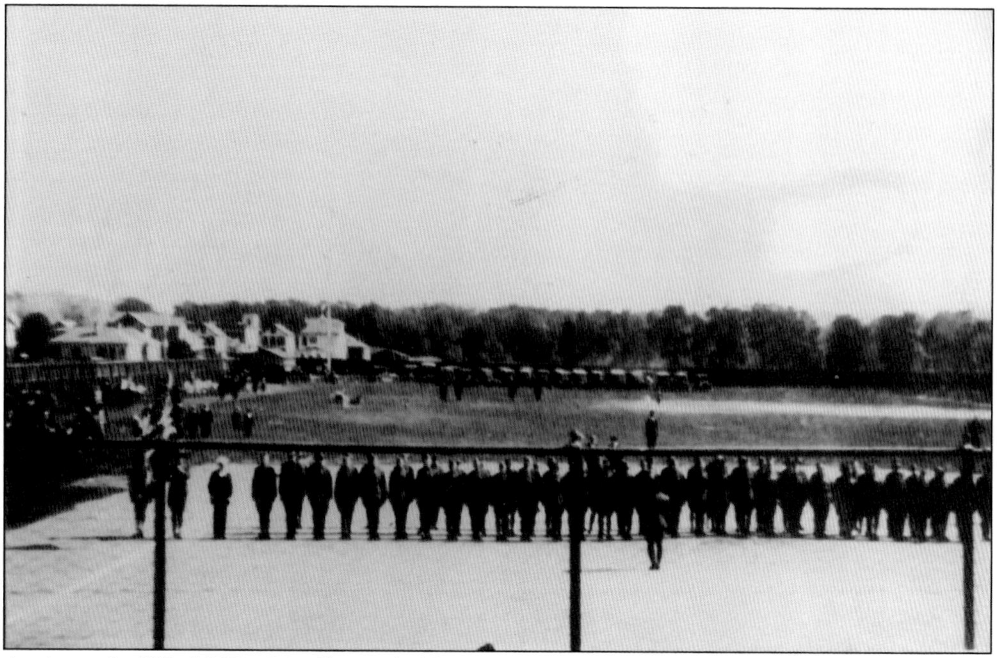

At the end of World War I, Milltown held a Welcome Home ceremony and parade for veterans. This ceremony pictured was held on September 27, 1919, at the Michelin Athletic Field. (Courtesy of Rita Carina.)

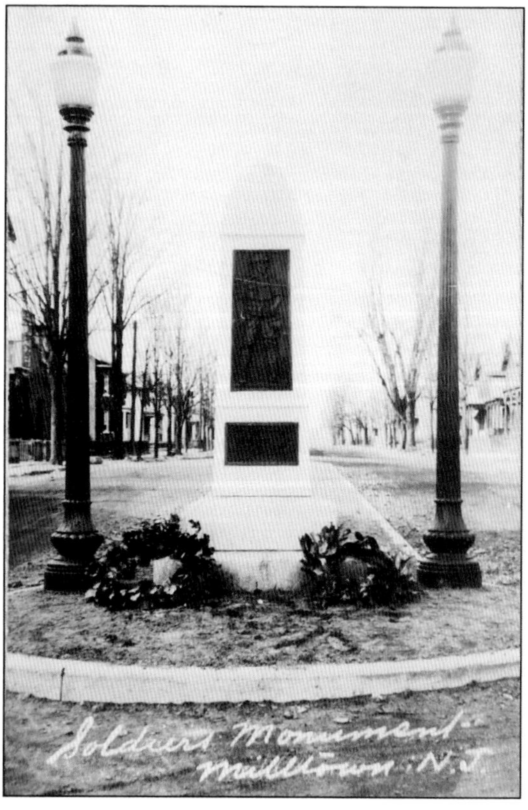

The World War I Monument on Ford Avenue. This monument was knocked over by a truck in 1993, and has not been reinstalled in this or any other location. (Courtesy of the Donald Hermann family.)

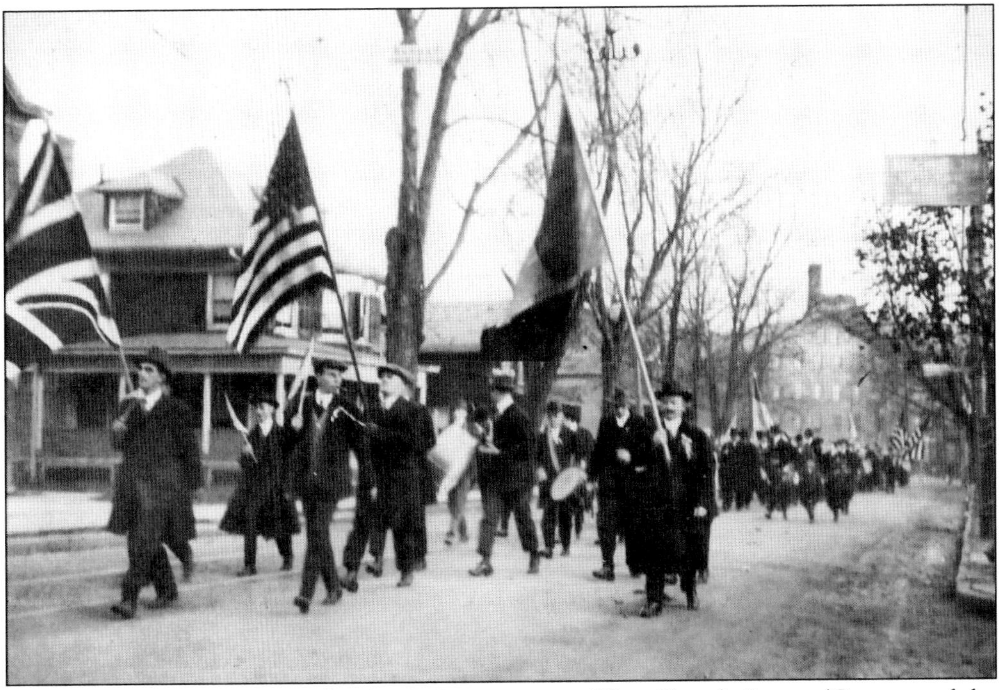

A military parade, on November 7, 1918, as it passes West Church Street. (Courtesy of the Schwendeman family.)

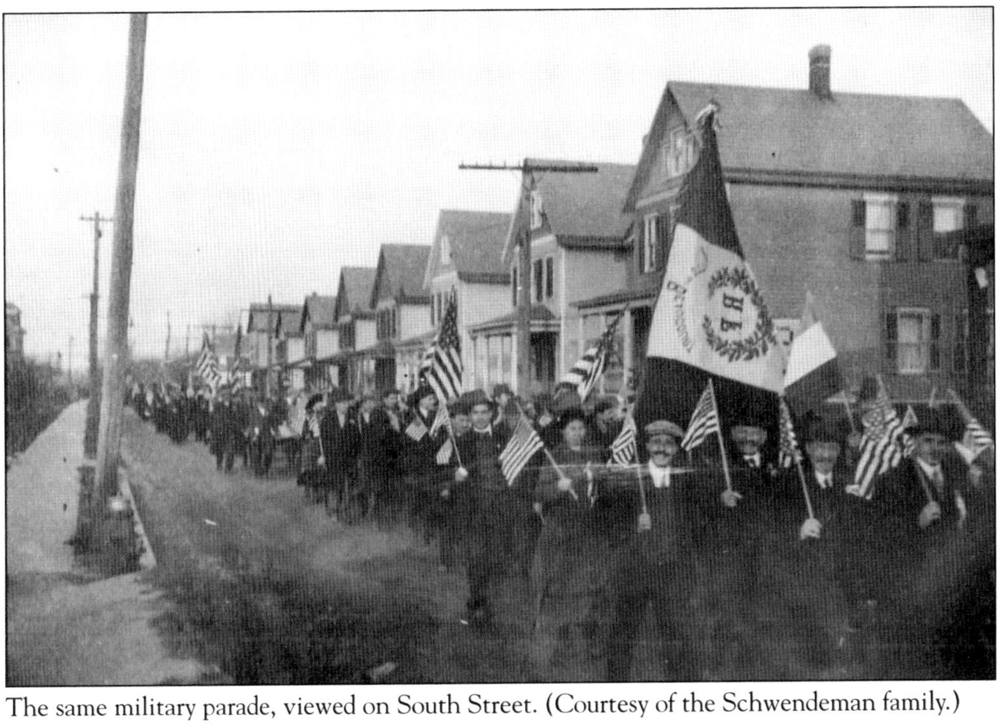

The same military parade, viewed on South Street. (Courtesy of the Schwendeman family.)

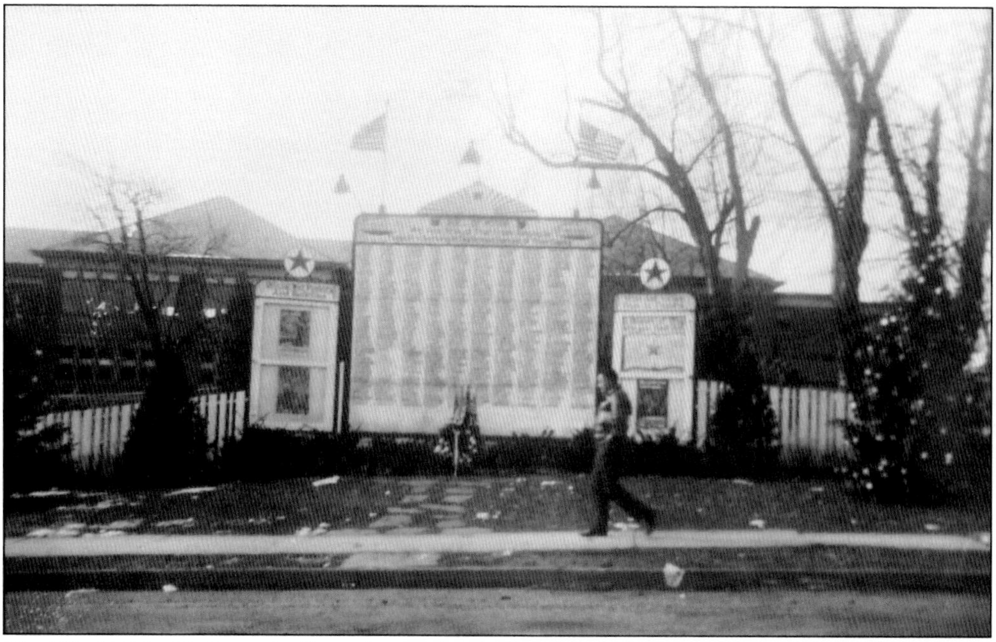

The World War II Honor Roll was located at 74 North Main Street, the current location of the Middlesex Academy of Dance. (Courtesy of Rita Carina.)

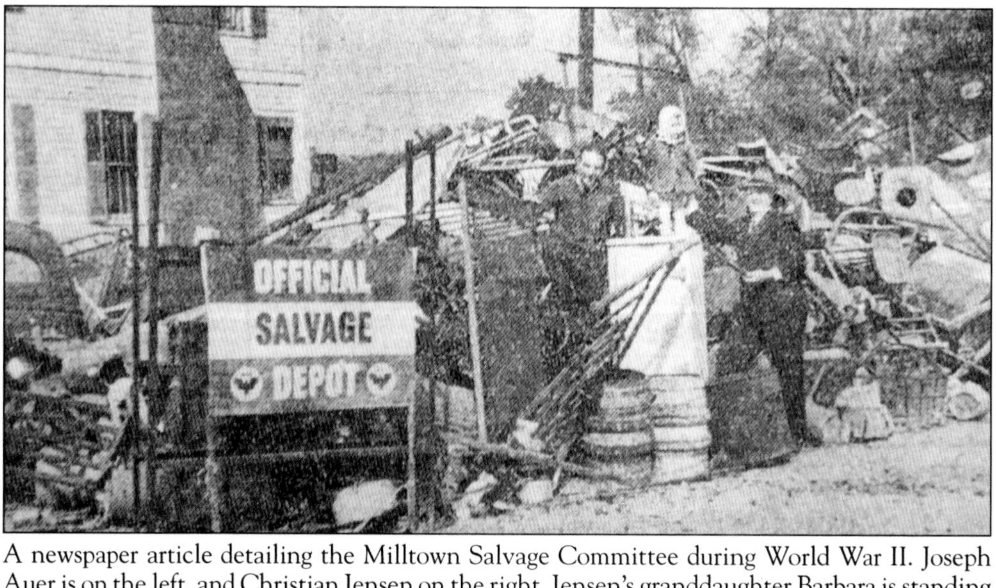

A newspaper article detailing the Milltown Salvage Committee during World War II. Joseph Auer is on the left, and Christian Jensen on the right. Jensen's granddaughter Barbara is standing on the scrap heap. (Courtesy of Barbara Petry.)

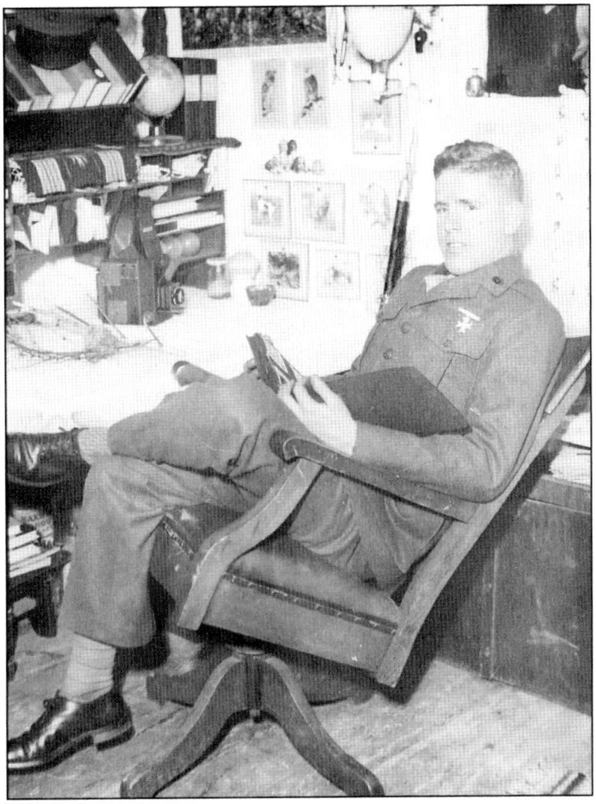

David J. Schwendeman, after Marine Corp boot camp, 1945. (Courtesy of the Schwendeman family.)

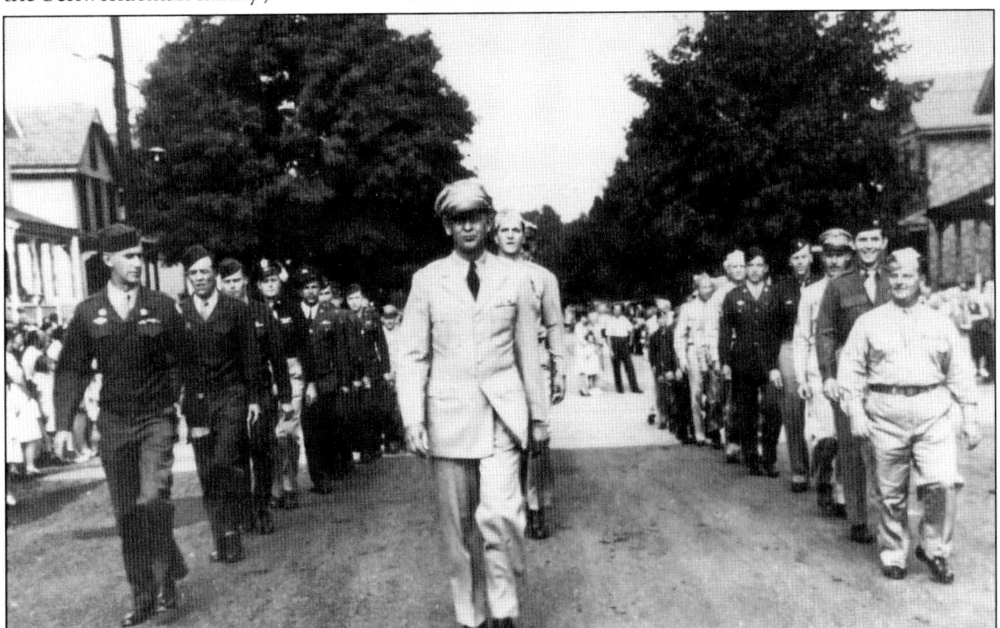

The highest-ranking Milltown serviceman, Leland Rule (center), and Valentine Harto lead other World War II veterans to the Welcome Home ceremonies at Michelin Field in 1946. (Courtesy of Rita Carina.)

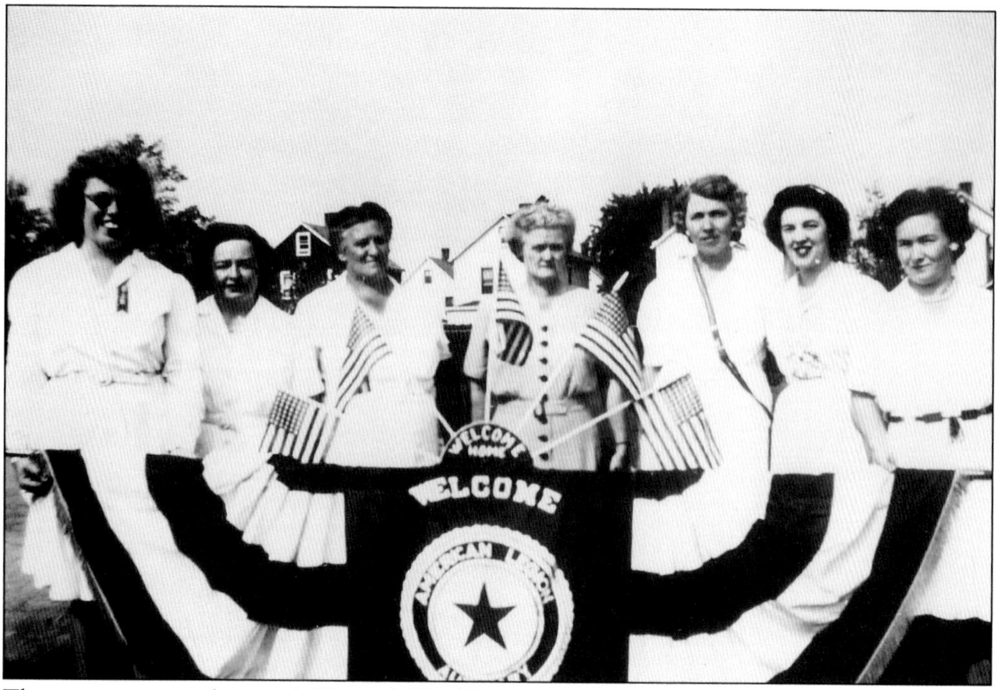

These women, marching in Milltown's World War II Welcome Home parade, were members of the American Legion Perry-Worth Unit #175. They are, from left to right, Marilyn Cockerill, Rita Carina, Grace Krause, Mary Goodman, Katherine Cockerill, Marie Conover, and Jean Bogoney. (Courtesy of Rita Carina.)

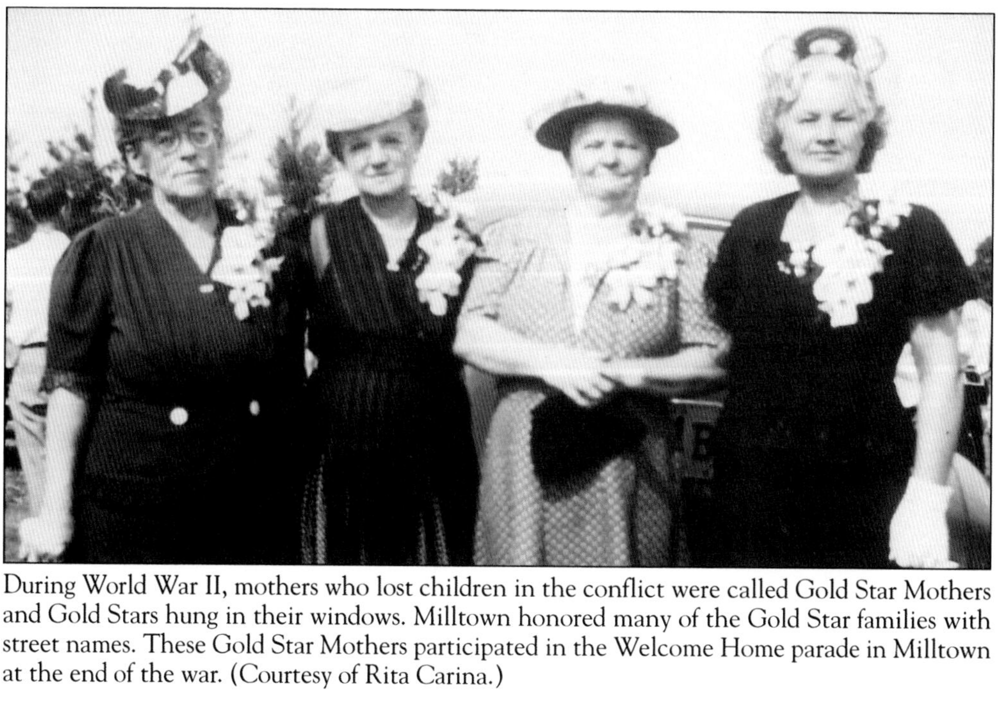

During World War II, mothers who lost children in the conflict were called Gold Star Mothers and Gold Stars hung in their windows. Milltown honored many of the Gold Star families with street names. These Gold Star Mothers participated in the Welcome Home parade in Milltown at the end of the war. (Courtesy of Rita Carina.)

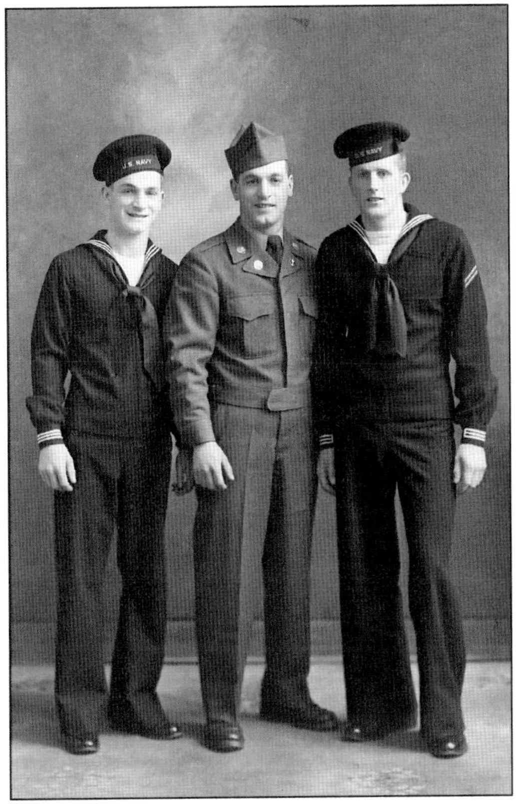

Milltown brothers James Adochio and John "Spike" Adochio, with brother-in-law Victor Barus, pose for this family portrait in 1946. (Courtesy of Helen Barus Moscar.)

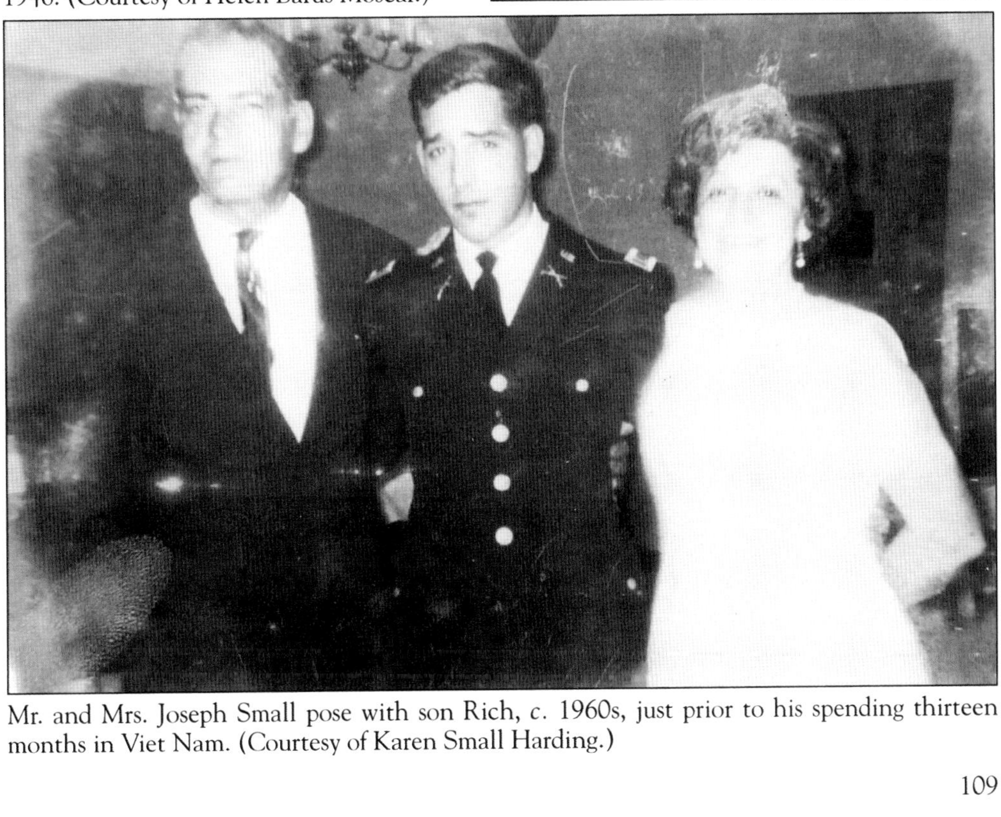

Mr. and Mrs. Joseph Small pose with son Rich, *c.* 1960s, just prior to his spending thirteen months in Viet Nam. (Courtesy of Karen Small Harding.)

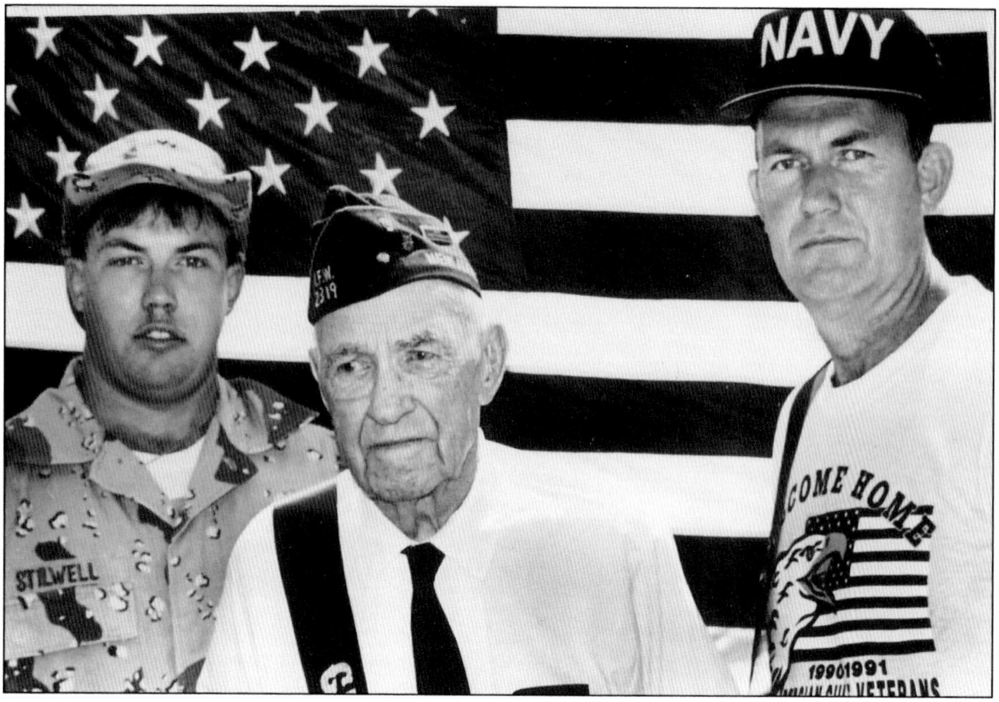

In 1991, the Fourth of July parade was dedicated to welcoming home Milltown soldiers who had served in the Persian Gulf. Serving as Grand Marshalls of the parade were the Stilwells: George M. (who served in Operation Desert Storm), George H. Sr. (who served in World War I), and George H. Jr. (who served in the Viet Nam era). (Courtesy of George H. Stilwell Jr.)

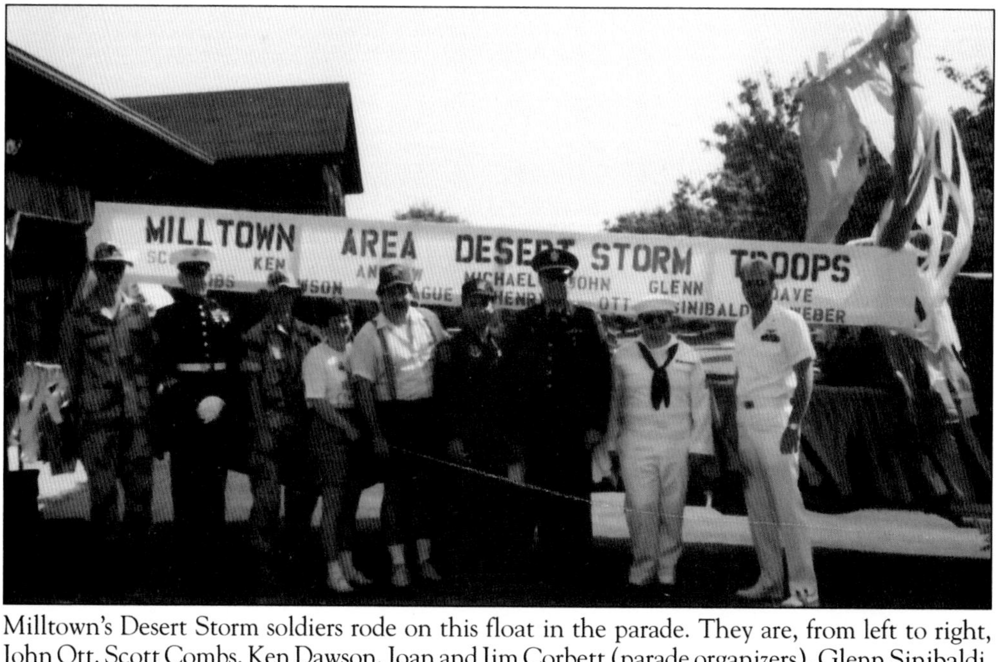

Milltown's Desert Storm soldiers rode on this float in the parade. They are, from left to right, John Ott, Scott Combs, Ken Dawson, Joan and Jim Corbett (parade organizers), Glenn Sinibaldi, Andrew Hague, Michael Henry, and Dave Weber. (Courtesy of Joan and Jim Corbett.)

Nine

To Protect and Serve

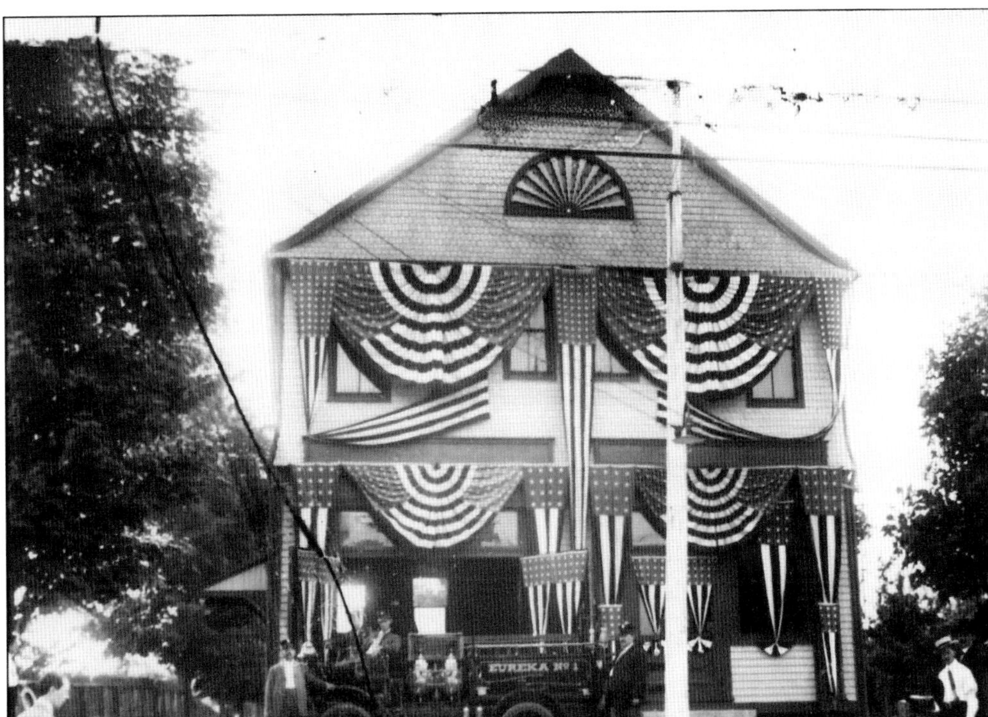

Milltown's first fire engine was also the first motorized fire engine in Middlesex County, arriving in September 1911. The firehouse was decorated for the occasion and firemen celebrated with a clam bake and picnic. (Courtesy of Bruce Bronson.)

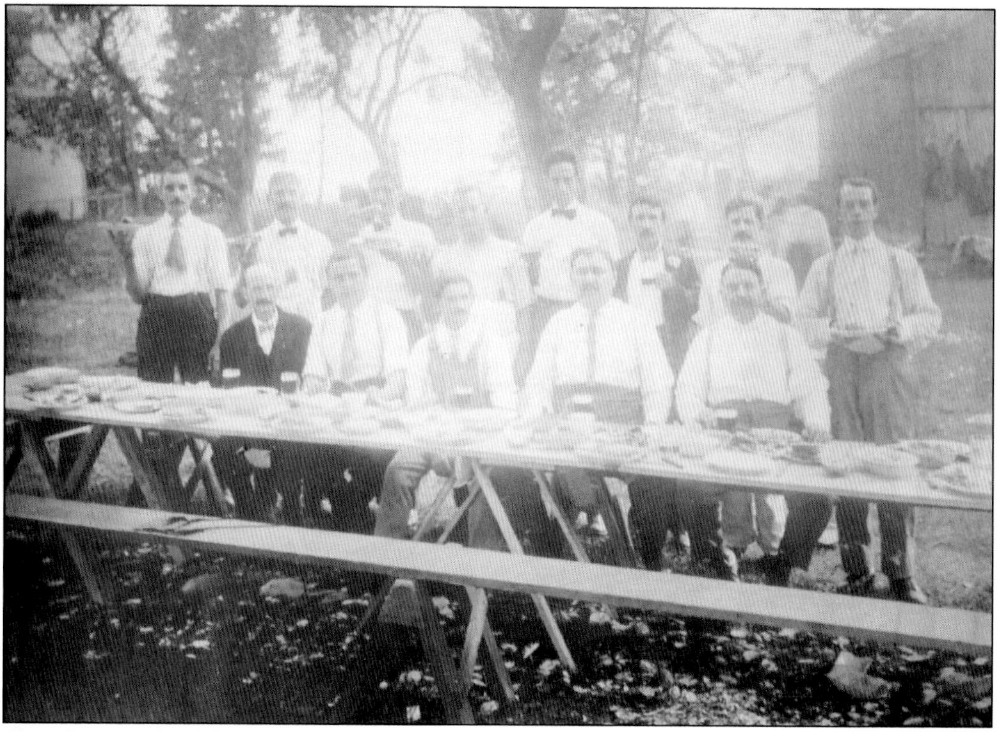

This photograph of the Firemen's Picnic and Clam Bake Committee was taken on September 11, 1911. Mayor Conrad "Dutch" Richter is seated at the right. (Courtesy of Eureka Fire Museum.)

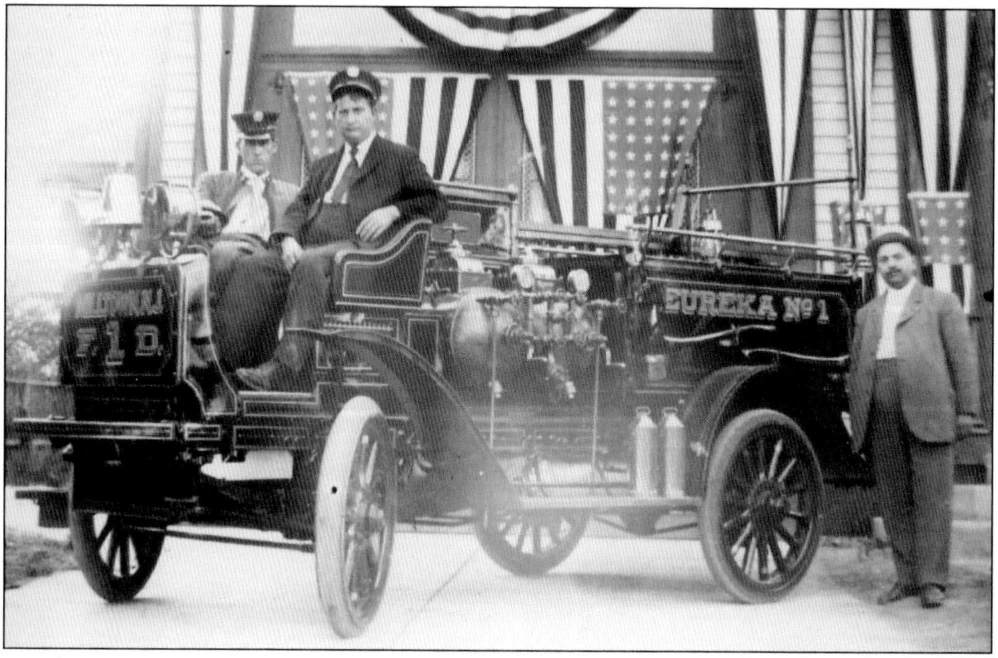

O. Christian Kuhlthau, Addison Thompson, and Mayor Conrad "Dutch" Richter pose at the South Main Street Firehouse, in September 1911. (Courtesy of Eureka Fire Museum.)

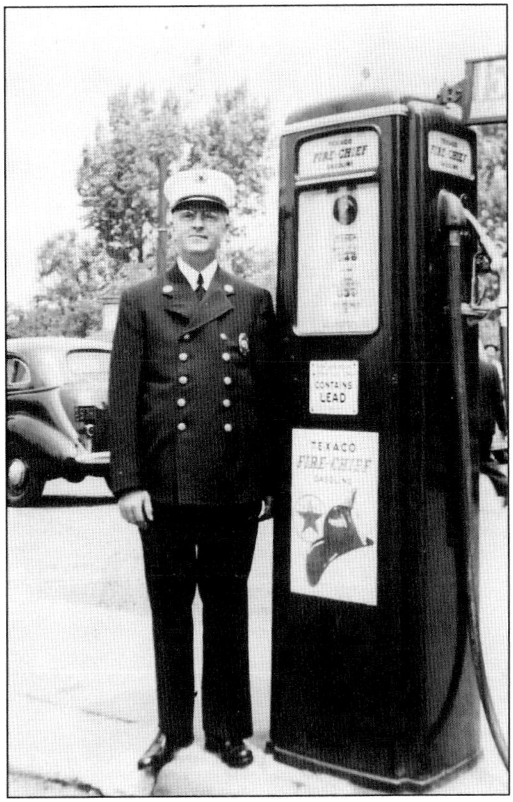

Fire chief Christian Jensen poses in front of his Texaco Fire Chief pump in 1938. (Courtesy of Barbara Petry.)

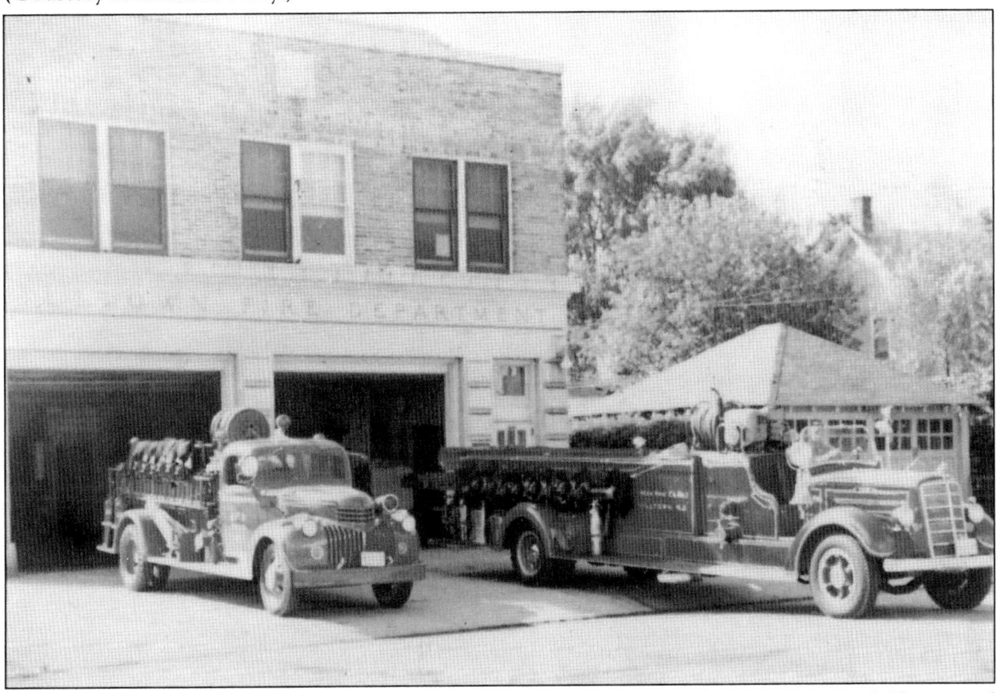

Parked in front of the Eureka Hose Company No. 1, on Cottage Avenue, are a 1945 Chevy and a 1939 Mack, *c.* 1960. (Courtesy of Norm Carina.)

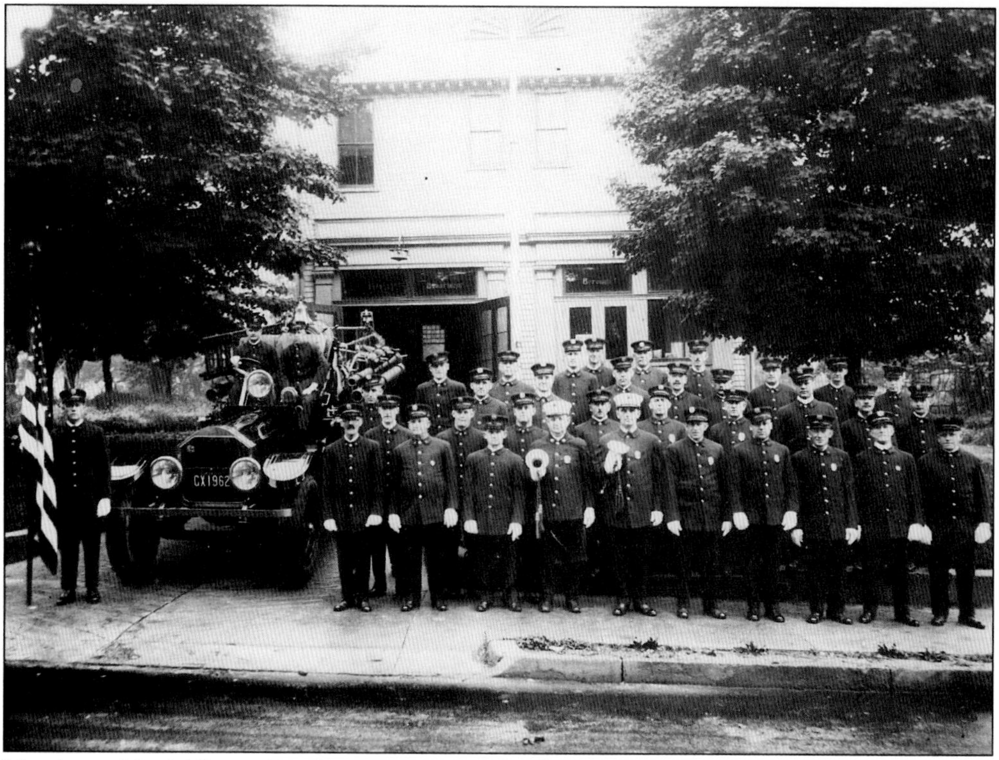

Members of the Milltown Fire Department pose for this picture in 1925, prior to a parade in New Brunswick. Edgar Waters is holding the flag. The photograph was taken by I.S. VanDerveer. Recently, the Milltown Fire Department took an updated version of this picture, using the same 1921 LaFrance fire truck, with Fred Waters (son of Edgar) holding the flag. (Courtesy of Eureka Engine Company No. 1.)

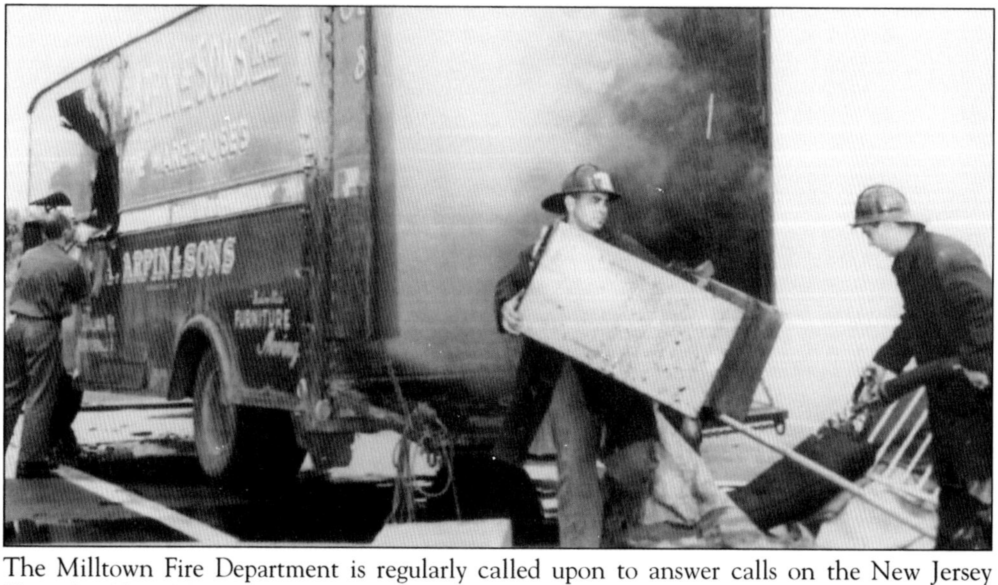

The Milltown Fire Department is regularly called upon to answer calls on the New Jersey Turnpike. Here, Norm Carina, Steve Shalayda, and John "Bud" Haefner respond to a truck fire in the late 1950s. (Courtesy of Norm Carina.)

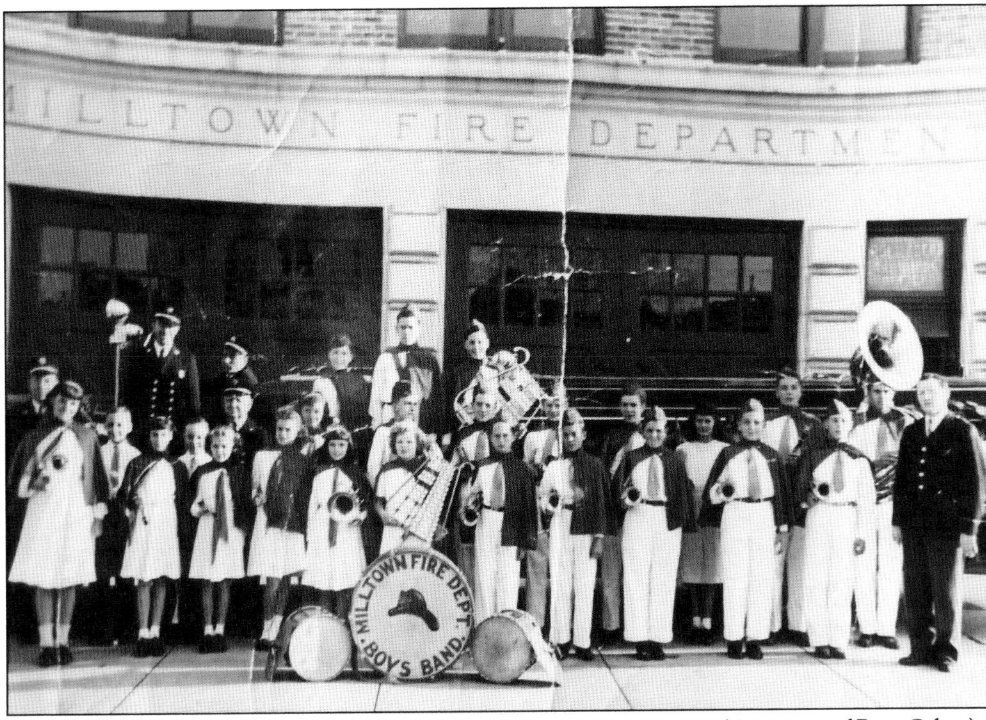

The Milltown Fire Department Boy's Band, with girls, in the 1940s. (Courtesy of Ron Giles.)

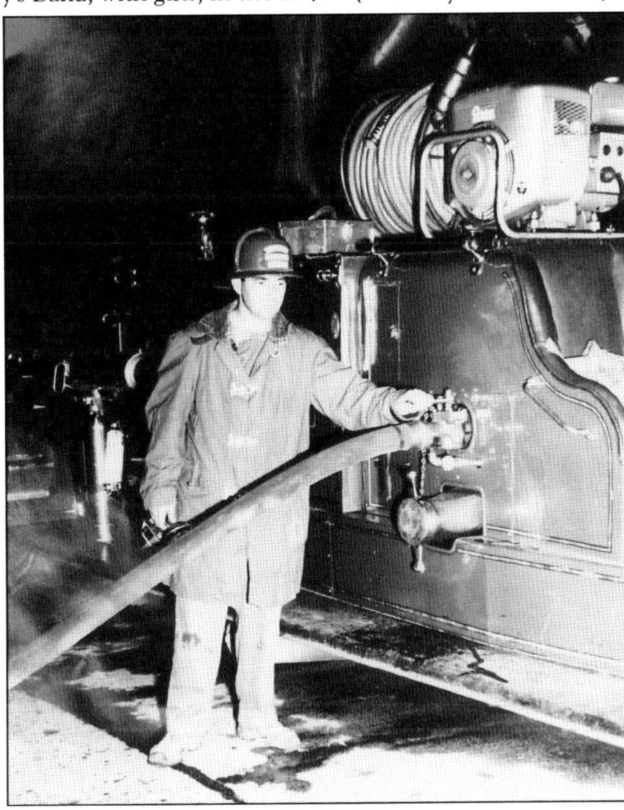

Norm Carina, operating the pump on Milltown's 1939 Mack Firetruck. (Courtesy of Norm Carina.)

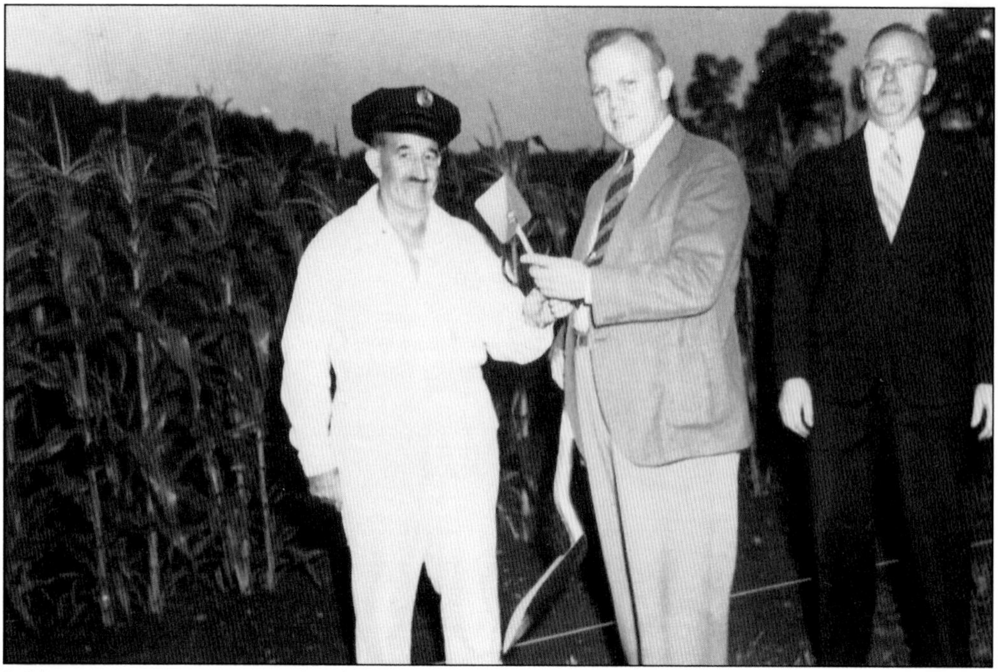

Ribbon-cutting ceremonies for the Milltown Rescue Squad Building on Washington Avenue, 1946. This building was later used as the Municipal Building, and razed in 1994. Pictured here are, from left to right, Captain Valentine, Mayor Walter Richter, and Christian Jensen. (Courtesy of Lloyd Pulda.)

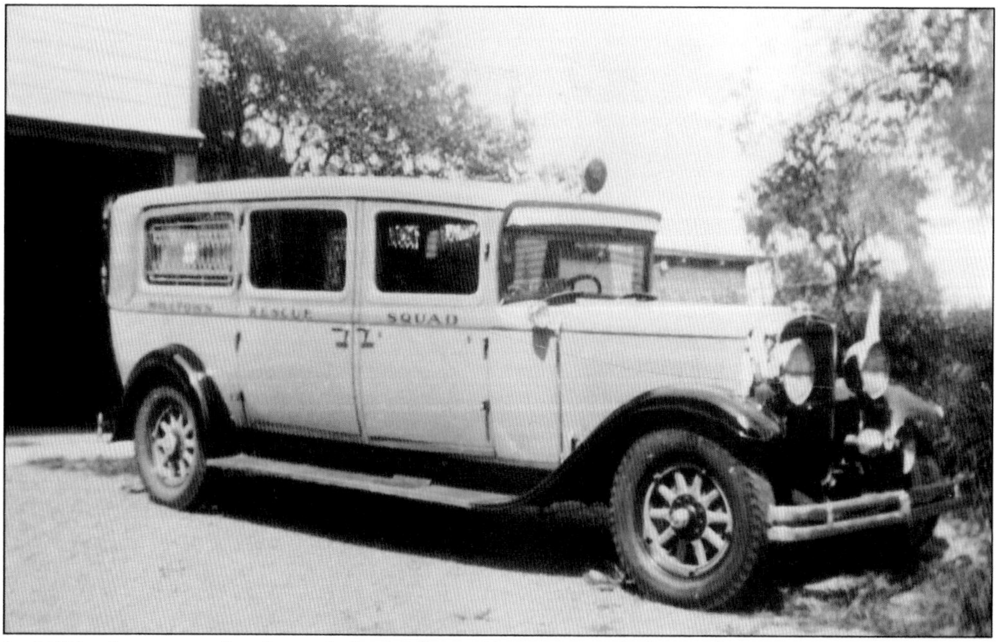

In 1937, when it was first formed, the Milltown Rescue Squad obtained its first ambulance, a 1931 Nash, from the Toms River Fire Department. It was housed for two years in the building that is now the Eureka Fire Museum, behind the Main Street Firehouse. (Courtesy of Charlie Nenninger.)

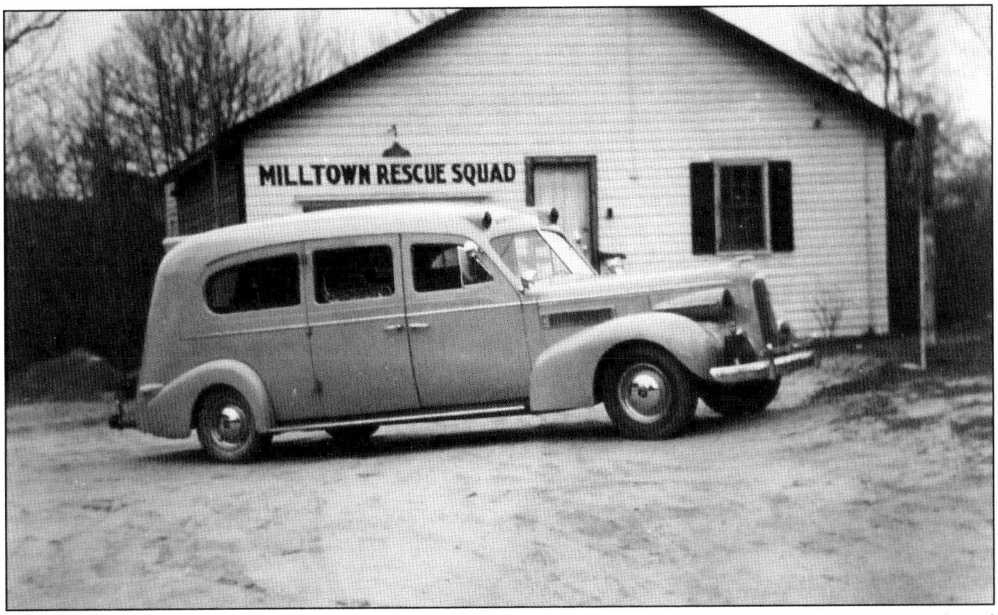

The Milltown Rescue Squad purchased an old freight station from the Raritan River Railroad in 1939. It was placed behind Jensen's Texaco Station, and renovated to house the squad's new 1939 LaSalle ambulance. It was finished in 1940. The rescue squad called this building home until 1947. (Courtesy of Milltown Public Library.)

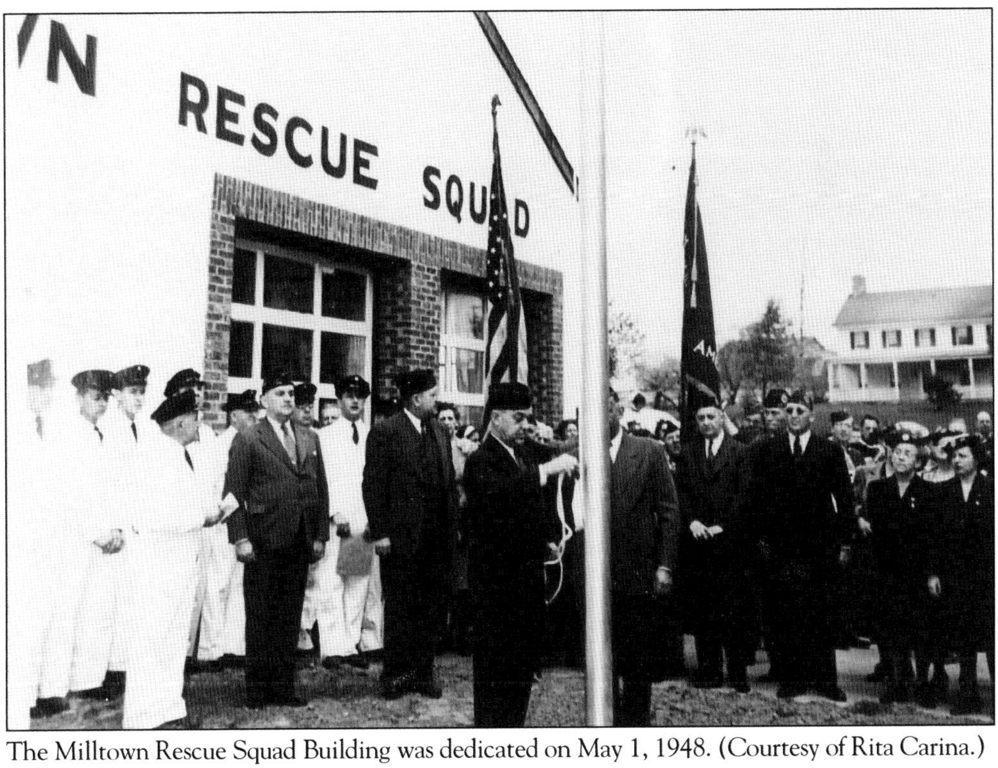

The Milltown Rescue Squad Building was dedicated on May 1, 1948. (Courtesy of Rita Carina.)

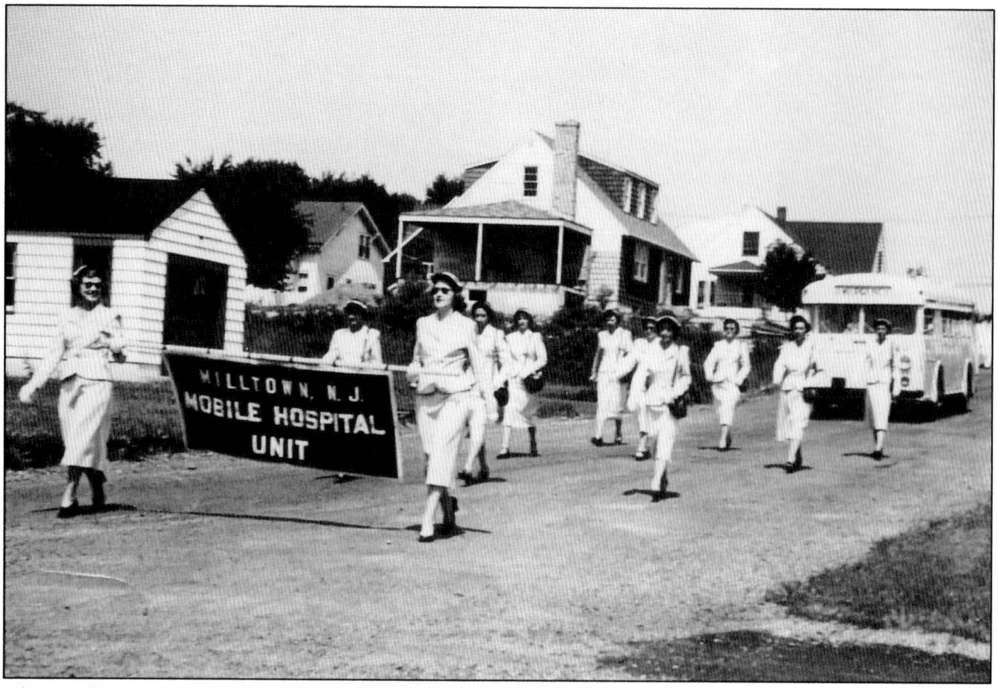

The Milltown Mobile Hospital Unit (not a part of the rescue squad) marches in a parade, *c*. 1953. This group was formed in 1949, during the Cold War. (Courtesy of Ken Selover.)

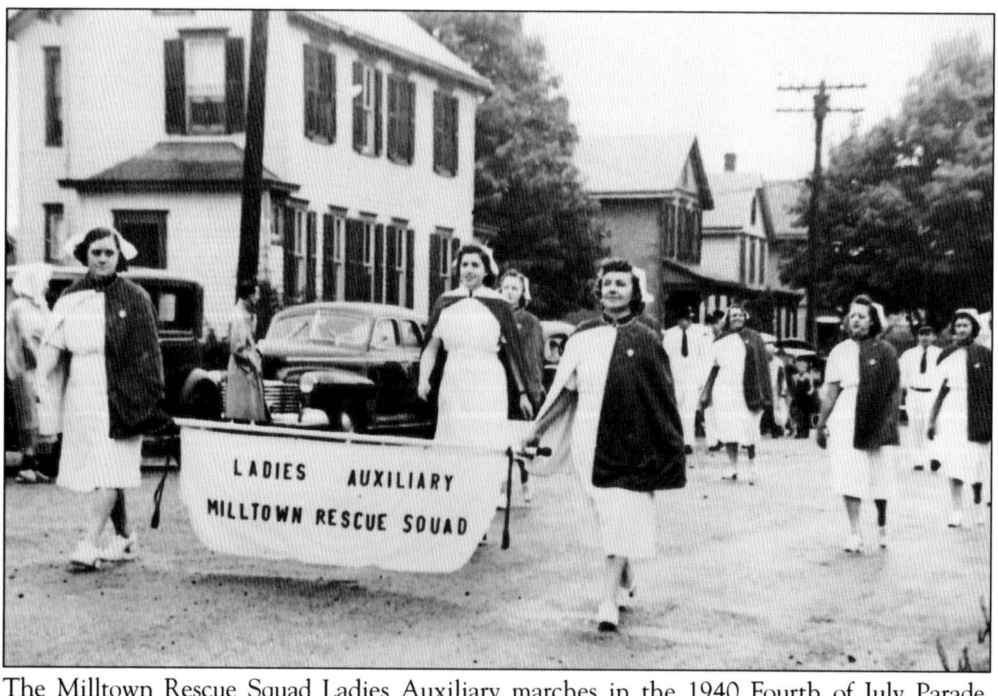

The Milltown Rescue Squad Ladies Auxiliary marches in the 1940 Fourth of July Parade. (Courtesy of Milltown Public Library.)

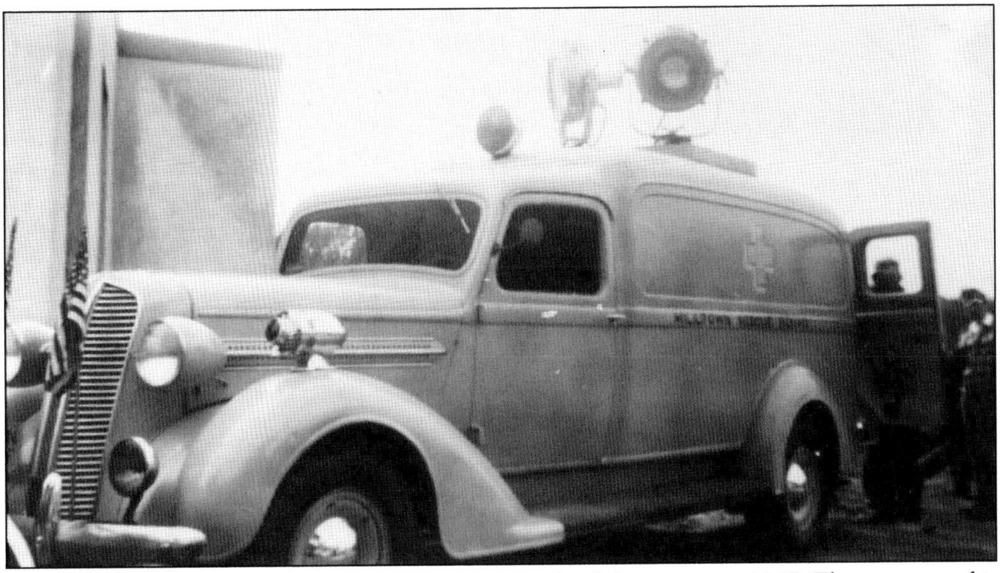

The Milltown Rescue Squad purchased this 1937 Dodge delivery van in 1947. They converted it into Milltown's first "crash wagon," with a gas generator to power the portable lights. (Courtesy of Rita Carina.)

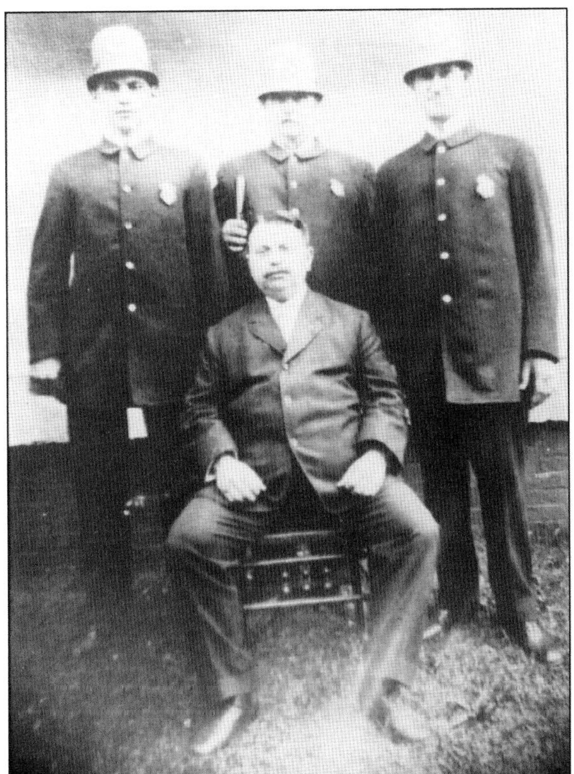

The Milltown Police Department, c. 1912. Pictured here are, from left to right, Charles Foerter, Joseph Rupprecht, Mayor Conrad Richter (seated), and George Lins.

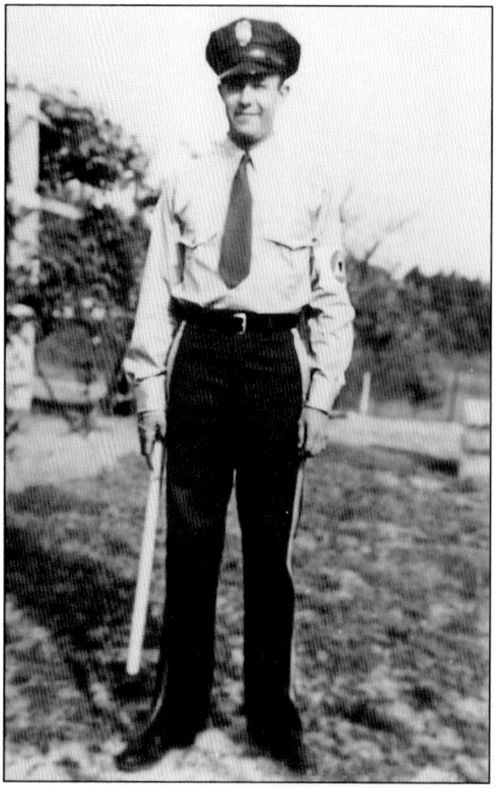

Ray Thompson, a police reserve officer, pictured in the 1940s. He is wearing a Civil Defense armband. (Courtesy of George H. Stilwell Jr.)

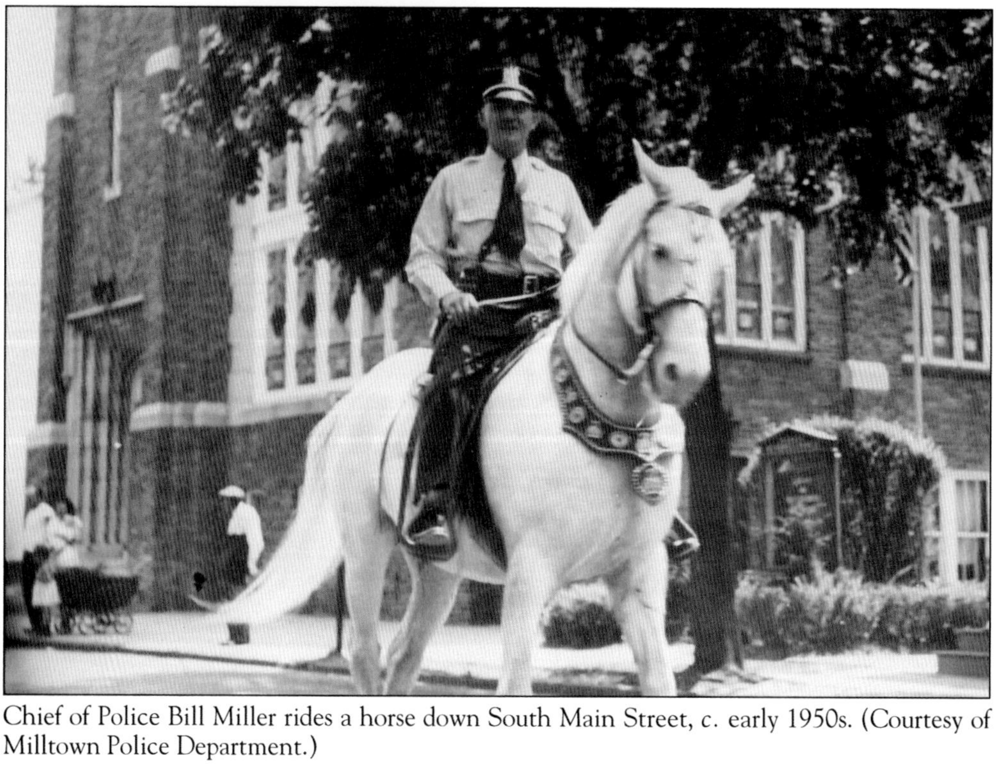

Chief of Police Bill Miller rides a horse down South Main Street, *c.* early 1950s. (Courtesy of Milltown Police Department.)

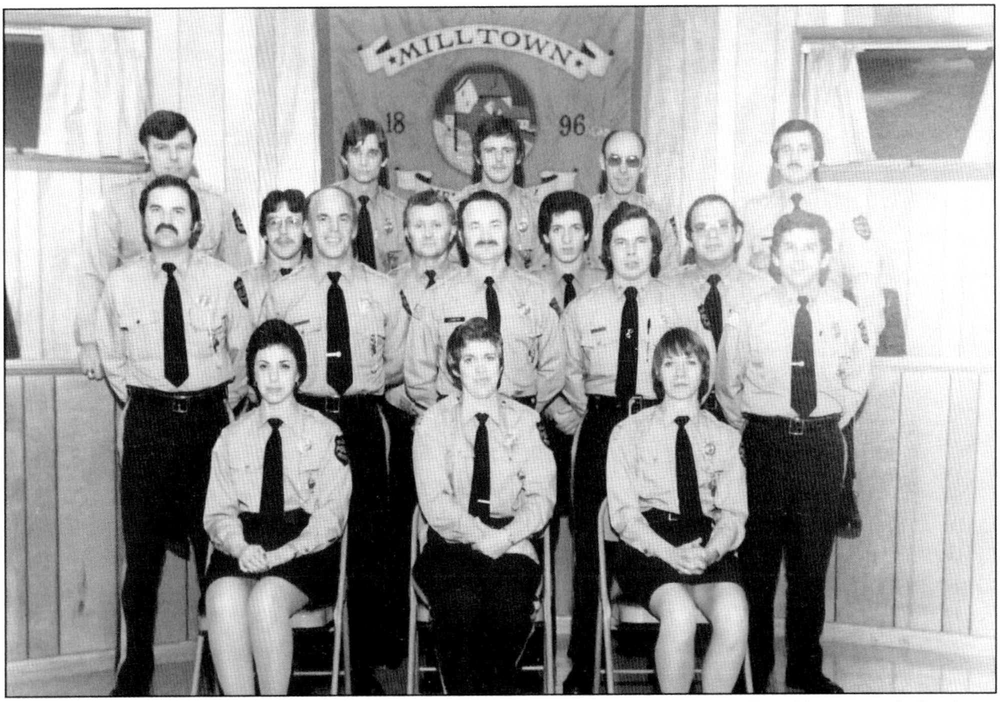

The Milltown Police Reserves, 1976. Posing here are, from left to right: (front row) Barbara Weiss, Bonnie Gartner, and Carol Mecca; (second row) Don Latourette, Steve Burke Sr., Steve Vargas, Don Devine, and Mike Weiss; (third row) Ron Gillespie, Otto Polgardi Sr., Howard Susan, and Roy Manfredi (president); (back row) Lou Lesko, Fred Thompson, Steve Burke Jr., George Gartner, and Joe Kish. (Courtesy of Milltown Police Department.)

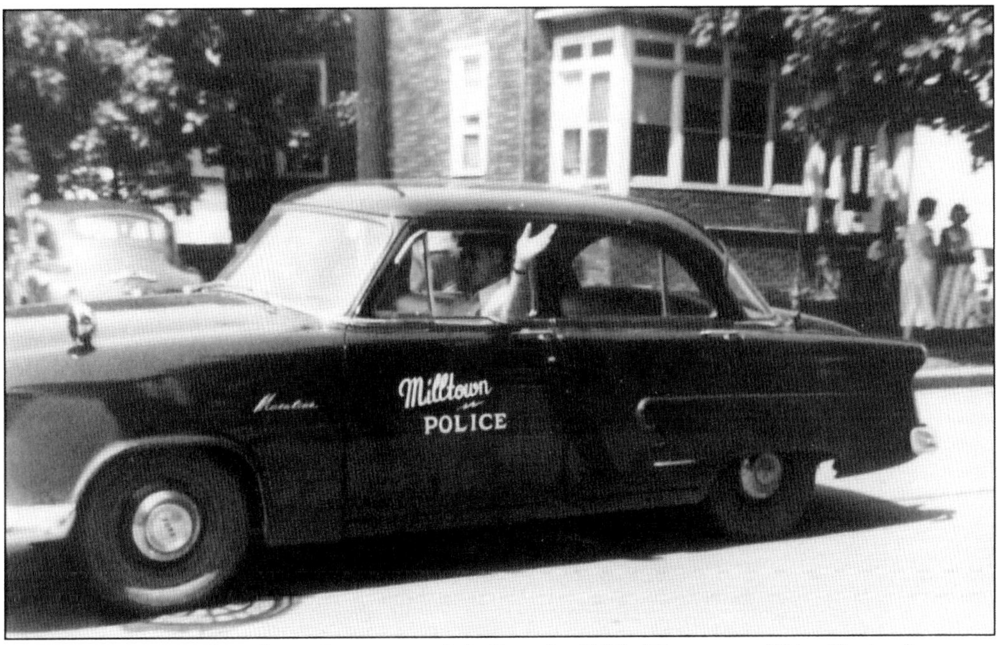

Hylan Petry waves from his police car, on July Fourth, 1953. (Courtesy of Rita Carina.)

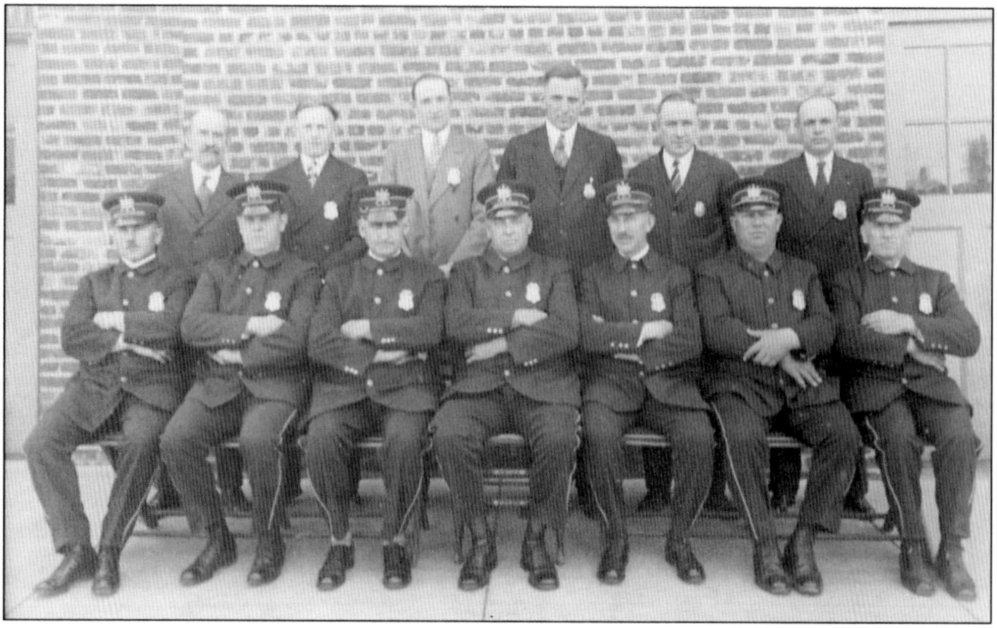

The Milltown Fire Department, outside the Cottage Avenue Firehouse, 1925. Posing here are, from left to right: (front row) Mike Nikola, Ed Beecher, Ed Acker, Gilburt Pander, Nick Young, Casper Graulich, and George Buhl; (back row) Judge Jacob Morris, Fred Lins, Gus Janicker, Councilman John Lins, Councilman Conrad Ochs, and William Butler. (Courtesy of Eureka Fire Museum.)

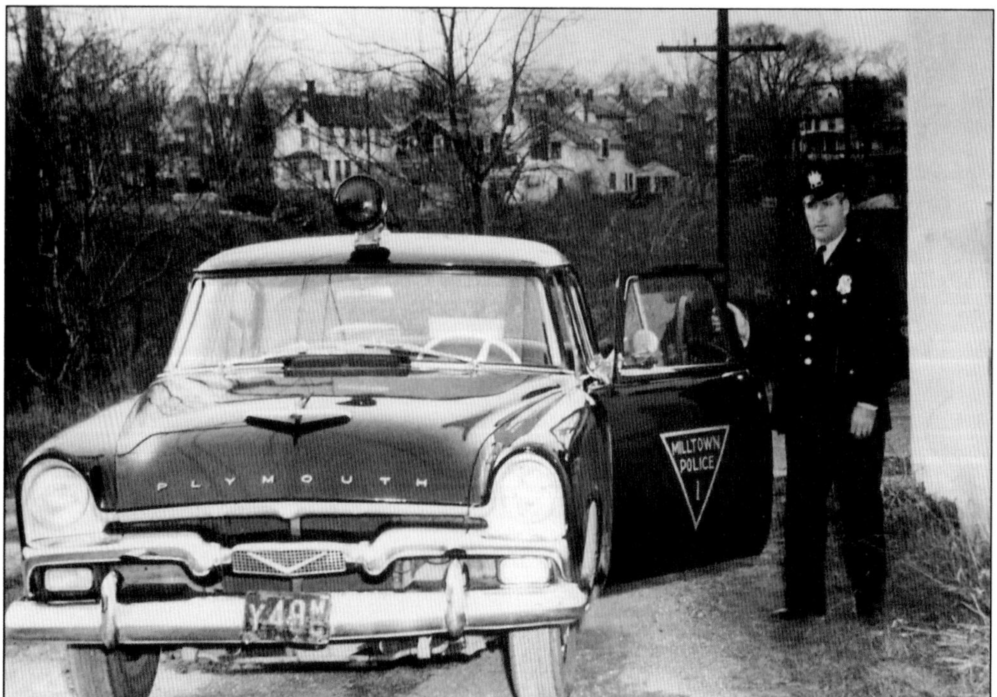

Officer Hylan Petry and the Milltown patrol car, late 1950s. (Courtesy of Milltown Police Department.)

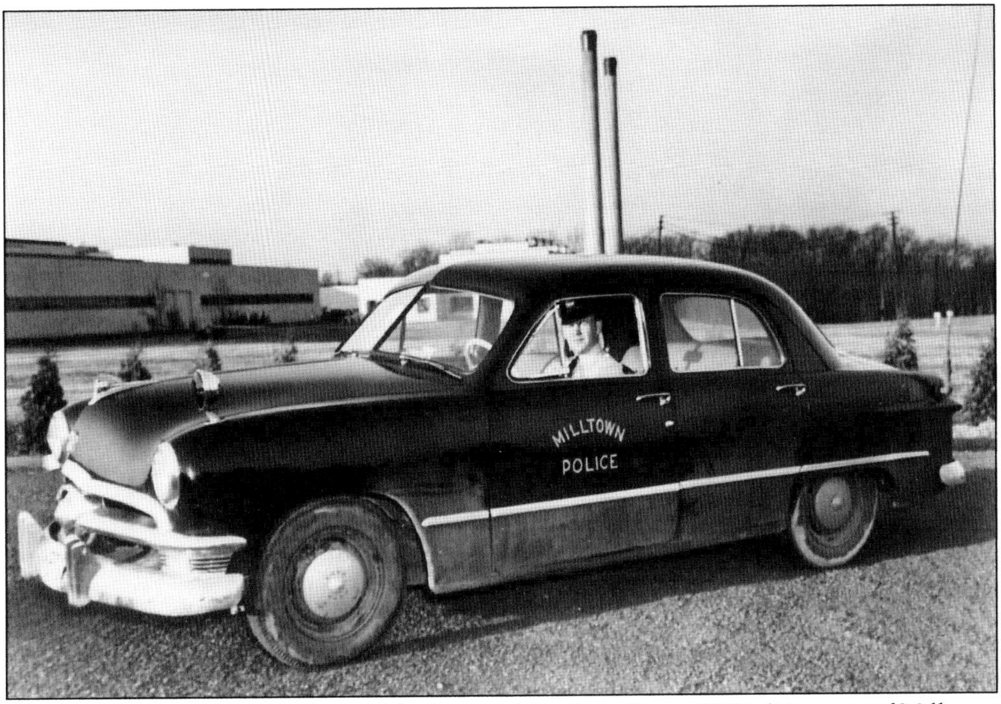

Officer Walter Spratford, in front of the Personal Products Plant, 1950. (Courtesy of Milltown Police Department.)

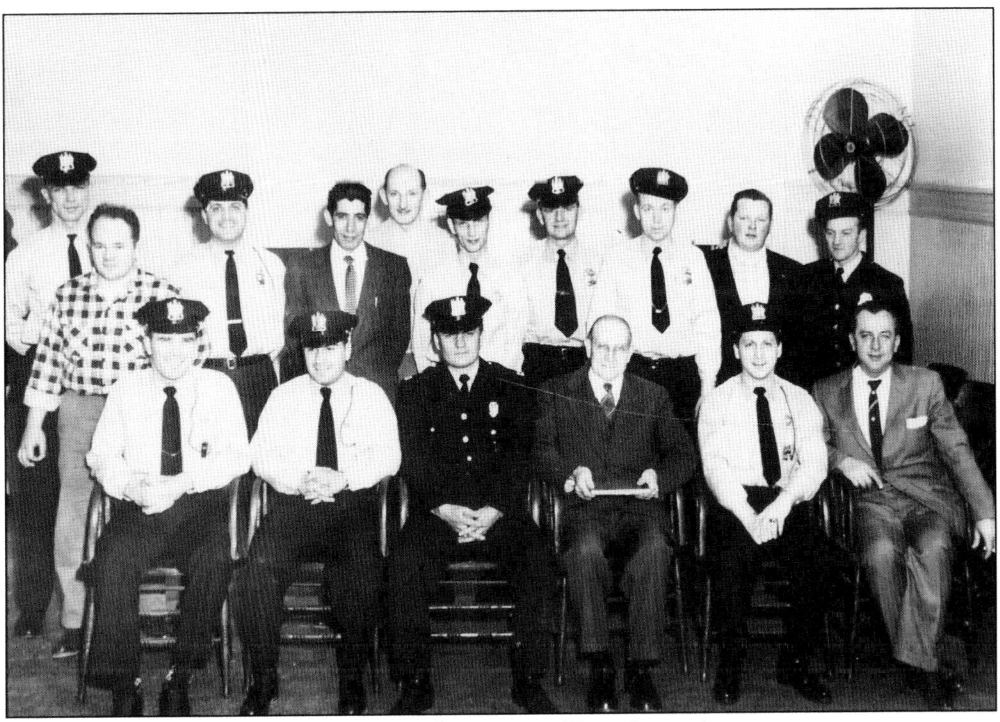

The Milltown Police Reserves, c. 1950s. (Courtesy of Rita Carina.)

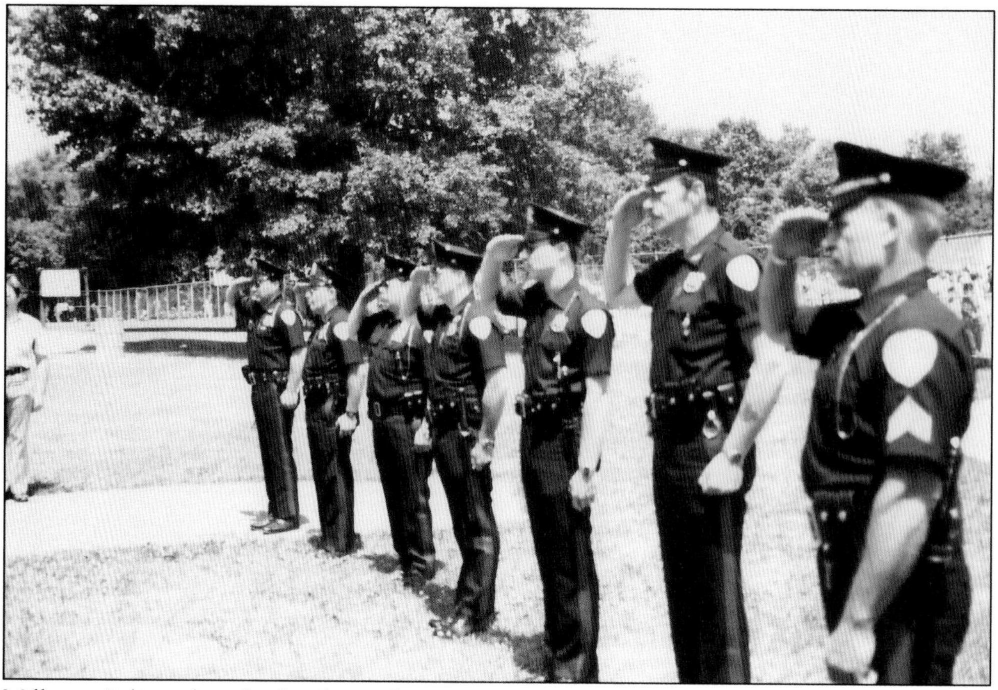

Milltown Police salute the flag during flag-raising ceremonies on July 4, 1985. Seen here are, from left to right: Patrolmen John "Skip" Schuck, Roy Manfredi, Clifford Kumpf, Raymond Geipel, Steve Biro, John Krajceck, and Sergeant Larry Mecca. (Courtesy of Joan Herbert Whitman.)

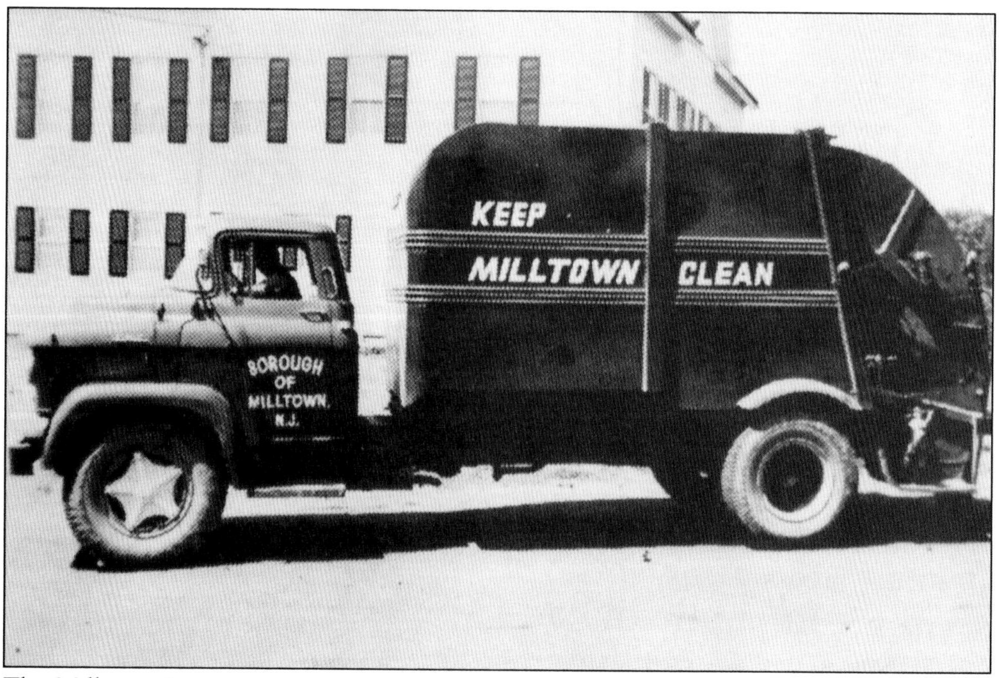

The Milltown Department of Public Works' 1950 garbage truck, as photographed in 1965. (Courtesy of Rita Carina.)

Ten

North Side, South Side, All Around the Town

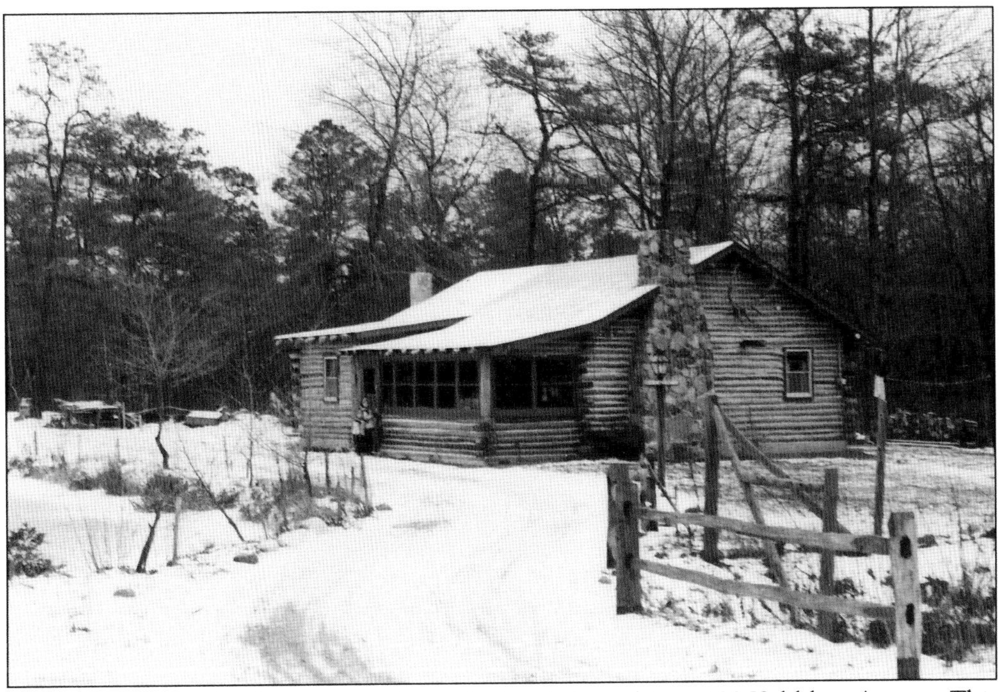

In 1958, Arthur and Lillian Schwendeman built this log cabin at 120 Kuhlthau Avenue. This picture was taken in December 1958. (Courtesy of the Schwendeman family.)

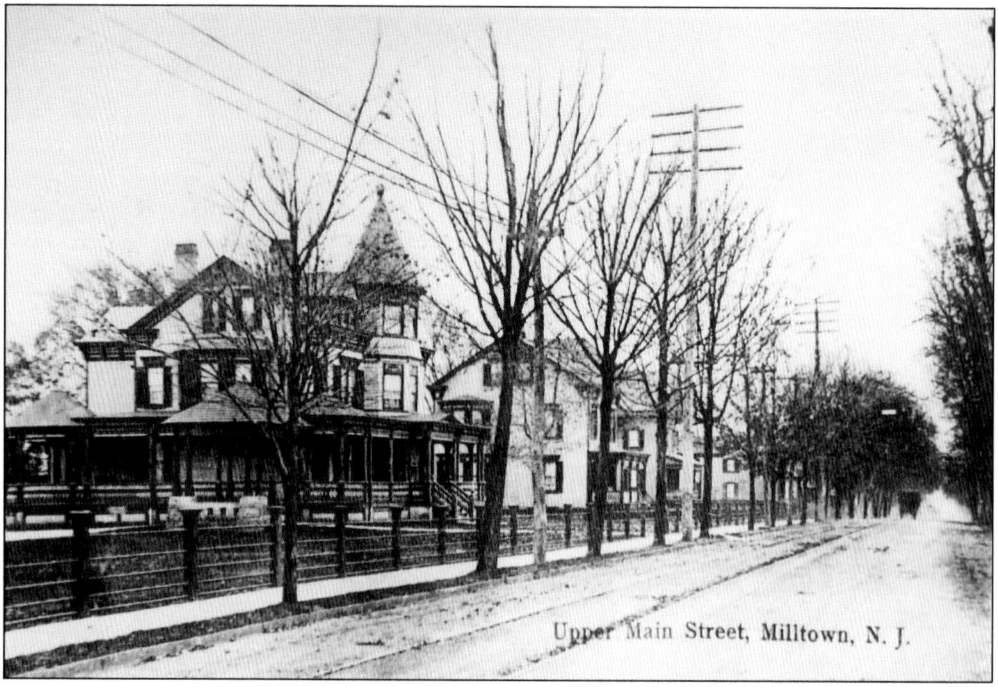

John C. Evans was Milltown's first mayor, serving from 1889 to 1901. He resided at this Victorian home at 97 North Main Street, now a bank and parking lot. (Courtesy of Brian Harto.)

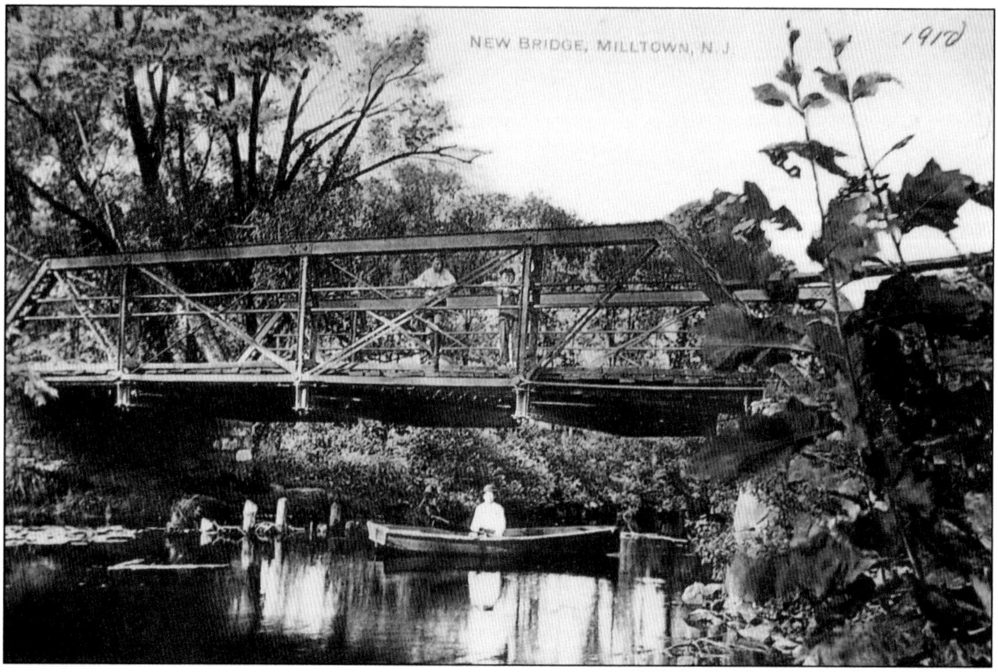

The Riva Avenue Bridge, as seen from the Sucker Brook, 1910. Riva Avenue was also known as the "New" road, or the road to Davidson's Mill. (Courtesy of Rita Carina.)

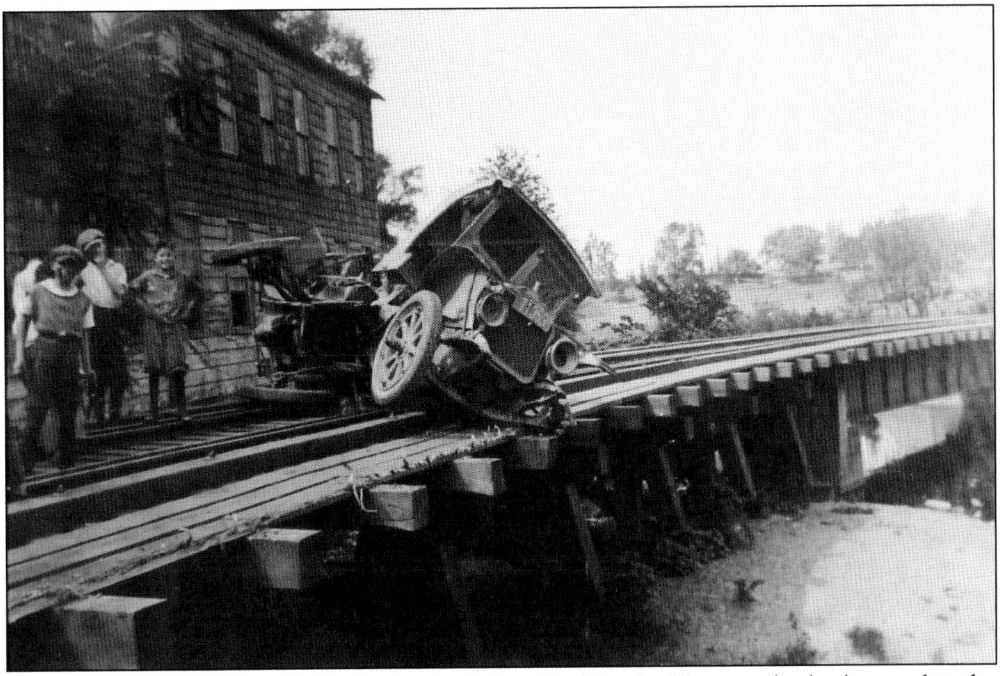

A truck hit by a train on Main Street, in the 1920s. The building in the background is the Rinky Dink. (Courtesy of Gertrude Bailey.)

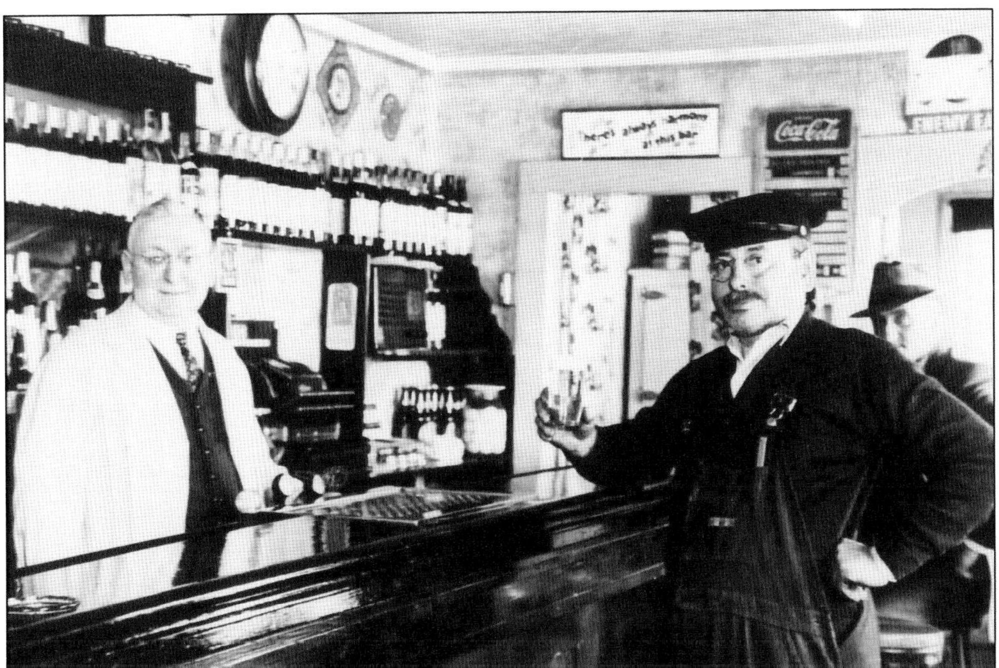

Martin Pulyer serves Joe Carina a drink at Pulyer's Tavern at 20 Cottage Avenue, c. 1940s. (Courtesy of Richard Pulyer.)

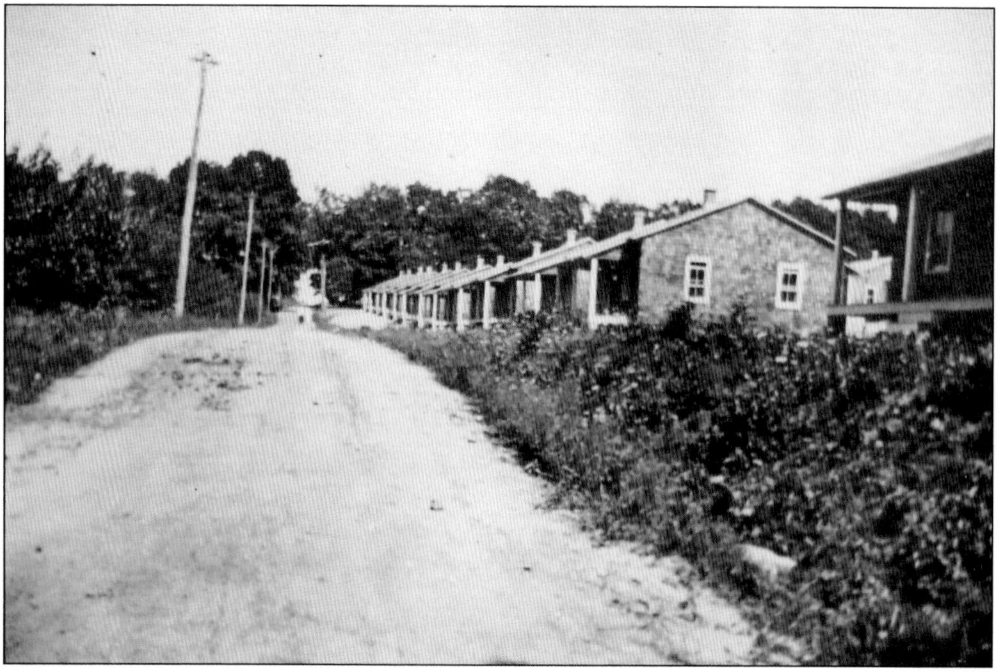

Riva Avenue, looking toward North Main Street, *c.* 1920. The Michelin Tire Company built these bungalows for their employees. The large gap between the houses is now Scott Avenue. (Courtesy of Edward Mierau.)

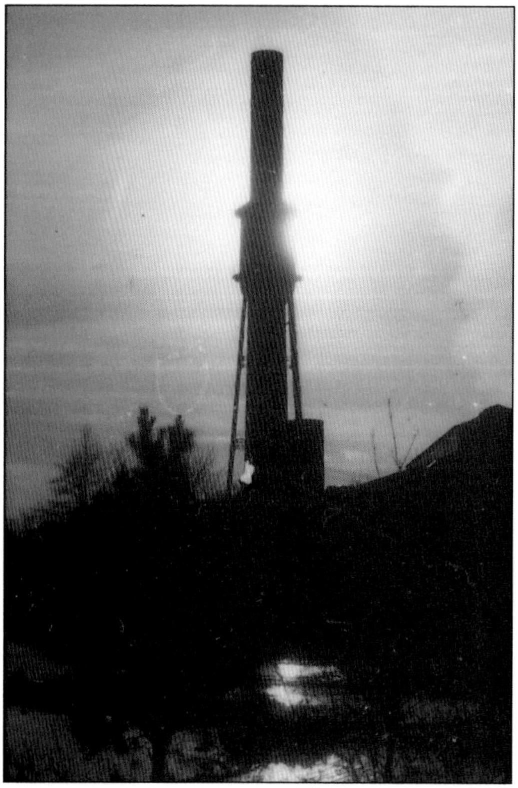

The sun sets over Milltown. (Courtesy of Jane Herman)